CALVINISM IN EUROPE

1540–1610

A collection of documents

selected, translated and edited by
Alastair Duke, Gillian Lewis
and Andrew Pettegree

MANCHESTER UNIVERSITY PRESS
Manchester and New York

distributed exclusively in the USA
and Canada by St. Martin's Press

Published by Manchester University Press
Oxford Road, Manchester M13 9PL, UK
and Room 400, 175 Fifth Avenue, New York, NY 10010, USA

Distributed exclusively in the USA and Canada
by St. Martin's Press, Inc., 175 Fifth Avenue, New York, NY 10010, USA

British Library Cataloguing-in-Publication Data
A catalogue record for this book is available from the British Library

Library of Congress Cataloging-in-Publication Data
    Calvinism in Europe, 1540-1610 : a collection of documents / selected,
        translated and edited by Alastair Duke, Gillian Lewis, and Andrew
        Pettegree.
            p.   cm.
        Includes index.
        ISBN 0-7190-3551-1 (cloth). — ISBN 0-7190-3552-X (paper)
        1. Calvinism—Europe—History—Sources. 2. Europe—History—Sources.
    I. Duke, A.C. II. Lewis, Gillian. III. Pettegree, Andrew
    BX9422.5.C35   1992
    284'.24'09031—dc20   92-8973

ISBN 0 7190 3551 1 hardback
    0 7190 3552 X paperback

Typeset in Stone Serif and Sans
by Koinonia Ltd, Manchester
Printed in Great Britain
by Bell & Bain Limited, Glasgow

Contents

[v]

CONTENTS

Section 2 FRANCE

(a) The beginnings of French Calvinism

(b) The Geneva mission and the crisis of the French monarchy

(c) The organisation of French Calvinism, 1562-71

(d) Weathering the storm. From the massacre of St Bartholomew to the Edict of Nantes

CONTENTS

Section 3 THE NETHERLANDS

(a) Beginnings of Dutch Calvinism

(b) The Wonderyear

(c) The establishment of the Reformed churches

(d) Church and State

(e) Retrenchment and consolidation

CONTENTS

Section 4   INTERNATIONAL CALVINISM

(a) Doctrinal solidarity. Solidarity of confessions

(b) Fast-days, collections and donations

(c) Pastors and professors. Printing, intellectual contacts and Calvinist higher education

(d) Politics in adversity. Calvinist solidarity in diplomacy and war

Acknowledgements

A work of collaboration inevitably involves many debts of gratitude, both mutual and to other friends and colleagues who have assisted with suggestions and generous sharing of their particular expertise. For help in proposing and searching out documents, and on occasions with translation, we wish to thank Ernest Blake in Southampton, Robin Briggs in Oxford, Jane Dawson, Bill Naphy and Karin Maag in St Andrews, Johan Decavele in Ghent and Guido Marnef in Antwerp. Julian Crowe of the St Andrews Computer Laboratory provided invaluable assistance in rendering our computer discs into a compatible form. We also wish to acknowledge the part played by Jane Carpenter of Manchester University Press, first in encouraging us to proceed with this project and then in carrying it so swiftly through to publication.

The extracts from the Edict of Nantes (document 31) are published with the kind permission of Faber and Faber.

Introduction

A generation after Luther's protest had first ignited the Reformation in Germany, it must have seemed to many contemporaries as if the evangelical movement had reached the natural limits of its potential growth. After two decades of apparently effortless expansion in Germany and central Europe, the years around Luther's death (1546) saw an equally serious contraction. This decade brought a whole series of damaging reverses for evangelicals, particularly in England, France and the Netherlands: in these last two countries, persistent persecution all but eliminated traces of an organised evangelical movement. With reform sentiment also in retreat in Italy, and even in Germany itself, harassed evangelicals had no doubts as to the extent of the problems they faced in bringing back to the movement for church reform something of its early fervour. The Reformation badly needed a second wind.

This it found with the emergence from the second half of the century of the new force of Calvinism. From a secure base in Reformed Switzerland, Calvinism from the mid-century progressively transformed Europe's religious and political landscape. The rapid growth of Calvinist churches in France was the first sign of the movement's explosive potential, but within a few years the new confession had also secured many adherents in the Netherlands, Scotland, and large parts of Germany and Eastern Europe. Even without calling in aid the more ambiguous phenomenon of Anglican England (Calvinist in doctrine, if not church organisation), then there could be little doubt that Calvinism was the most dynamic - and disruptive - element in the consolidation of the Reformation's early gains during this period.

Explanations of Calvinism's phenomenal success have varied. Some writers, particularly those with a background in church history, have stressed the importance of Calvin's writing in developing a coherent system of belief, of the sort that could inspire an individual layman to independent action: in this scheme Calvin's *Institutes* takes on an almost canonical importance. Others who come at these questions from a more secular perspective have laid stress on either the vulnerability of the states in question at this particular juncture, or the particular suitability of

[1]

Calvinist organisational structure to take advantage of this weakness. Whichever explanation is preferred there can be little doubt that Calvin's movement gained much of its strength and potency from its ability to make headway in countries where the State remained hostile; it was this that made the Huguenot movement (in contrast to the early French evangelical movement) so threatening to the French monarchy and gave the early stages of the Dutch Revolt such explosive force. And in spreading across national borders Calvinism also contributed something unique to the international political scene: a profound if at times frustratingly elusive sense of solidarity of purpose which could move congregations, ministers and even on occasions princes to see that the common interest lay squarely in the preservation of the faith against the threat posed by rival confessions and visions of society.

The documents collected in this volume represent an attempt to bring home something of the explosive impact of Calvinism as a creed and political force in the context of sixteenth-century society; the unique character of the Calvinist system, and not least its extraordinary disruptive force. Ranging over a broad geographical frame, it treats first the origins of Calvinism as a system in Geneva, then its impact on the two great religious conflicts of the age, in France and the Netherlands. The final section is devoted to different aspects of the confessional solidarity across national borders generally described as 'International Calvinism'. These introductory remarks will serve to introduce the sources exploited in compiling this collection, indicating something of what has governed the principles of selection, and what materials are available elsewhere in print. Inevitably in the case of a movement which has spawned churches throughout the western world, Calvinism has been the object of a great deal of scholarly attention: the problem from the point of view of the modern student is that coverage has been very uneven. While there is no shortage of volumes intended to illustrate the history of the churches, or burnish the memory of the great figures of the founding years, even for countries as central to the movement as France and the Netherlands there is often a critical shortage of usable materials in English. These following remarks will indicate what is at present available in printed sources and other collections, and therefore what is newly made available here. For the most part thereafter the documents will be left to tell their own story.

Calvin and Geneva

As befits a figure of Calvin's stature, access to his voluminous works is the least serious problem for a serious student of Calvin's movement. The volumes of the *Calvini Opera* in the *Corpus Reformatorum* [C1], mostly published in the nineteenth century, contain most of his writings then known in their original languages along with much valuable supporting material. These are now enhanced by important new materials, such as his sermons, published in the ongoing *Supplementa Calviniana* [C2]. At the time of writing a new critical edition of the works is also planned. English versions of many of Calvin's major writings are also available: firstly in the volumes of the nineteenth-century edition of Calvin's theological works, dated but still highly usable [C3]. There are also modern critical editions of the *Institutes* in both the 1536 and 1559 versions [C4, C5], and a number of smaller tracts [C7, C8].

Geneva is also reasonably well served. All of the formal documents of the Geneva Reformation are available in print, including the Confession of Faith and Ecclesiastical Ordinances [G1]. The excellent edition of the Register of the Company of Pastors, the chief organ of ecclesiastical organisation for the Genevan church and its wider activities, has now progressed from its inception into the early years of the seventeenth century [G2]. There exists also a useful volume of extracts in English translation, though now sadly out of print [G3]. The Geneva Academy, founded in 1559, also possesses important records: here invaluable material is to be found in the published list of matriculations, published by Susanne Stelling-Michaud along with biographical notes on all the students [G4].

For all that, there remain major lacunae. Astonishingly, the records of the Geneva consistory, an institution central to the understanding of the Calvinist system and Calvin's role in Geneva, remain in manuscript, and virtually unused: most published work on the consistory is in fact based largely on nineteenth-century transcripts which abstracted about 10 per cent of the cases dealt with (and inevitably, usually the most colourful).[1] The distorting effect of this selection can easily be imagined. All students of Calvin's system must welcome the project proceeding under the supervision of Robert Kingdon, aimed at making available to scholars a complete version of the Geneva consistory minutes. In the meantime impressions of day-to-day life in Geneva continue to rely on highly partial sources: the Register of the Company (which inevitably reflects the ministers' view), and not least, Calvin's own correspondence [C8]. Major sources which could provide a different perspective on Genevan affairs, such as the minutes of meetings of the city council, criminal records and notarial records (useful in identifying connections and allies in Genevan politics), remain in manuscript in Genevan archives. The value of such

[1] See E. William Monter, 'The Consistory of Geneva, 1559-1569', *Bibliothèque d'Humanisme et Renaissance*, 38 (1976), pp. 467-84.

[3]

records in providing a corrective to the often idealistic determinations of church orders and disciplines is indicated in this collection by the advice of a Genevan country pastor to his successor: a document which makes eloquently clear how far reality could diverge from the ministers' recommended best practice.[2] Such informal sources deserve more weight in our perceptions of life in Calvin's Geneva.

France

For a movement of such importance and size, French Calvinism is remarkably poorly documented. This may partly be attributed to the unkindness of history: put bluntly, the French Huguenots were on the losing side, and the gradual erosion of church numbers during the later sixteenth and seventeenth centuries took a heavy toll on the records of church life. If one adds to this the wholesale deliberate destruction of church records at the time of Louis XIV's Revocation of the Edict of Nantes (1685) then the surviving documents of individual communities are remarkably sparse: the consistory records and church registers we possess elsewhere hardly survive for French churches,[3] and there are no surviving records for the lower levels of the national church organisation, the *classis* or *colloque*.

In these circumstances one must be grateful that those records that do survive are of such high quality. The deliberations of the French National Synod exist in a continuous sequence from the first synod of 1559 to modern times. These are available both in French and in an English translation: by a quirk of fate the English version edited by John Quick [F1] is generally reckoned to be more accurate than the subsequent French edition of Aymon [F2]. There is also an excellent edition of the *Histoire Ecclésiastique* [F3], the compendium of events surrounding the early years of the French churches compiled under the supervision of Geneva. Although this serves an obvious polemical purpose, it presents an atmospheric view of the early years of church-forming. A similar purpose, though with a different focus, lies behind the martyrology of Jean Crespin.[F4] A more sober view of the progress of the new religion is provided by the succession of Edicts of Pacification which punctuated the French wars. These are accessible as an appendix to E. and E. Haag's

[2] Section 1, document 12.
[3] A small number of records survive in manuscript, including a good series for the important church of Nîmes, and a less full run for Coutras. See Raymond Mentzer, 'Disciplina nervus ecclesiae: the Calvinist Reform of Morals at Nîmes', *Sixteenth Century Journal*, 18 (1987), pp. 89-115; A. Soman and E. Labrousse, 'Le registre consistorial de Coutras, 1582-1584', *Bulletin de la Société du Protestantisme Française*, 126 (1980), pp. 193-228.

biographical dictionary, *La France Protestante* [F5].

Apart from this, the student of the French Calvinist movement is heavily reliant on what survives in archives abroad. A search of the the the archives of Grenoble at the turn of the century led to the discovery of transcripts of proceedings of a number of provincial synods from the early 1560s; these were subsequently published [F6]. The archives of Geneva also contain enormous bodies of material relevant to French churches, much of it now published in either the Register of the Company of Pastors [G3] or the correspondence of Calvin and particularly Théodore de Bèze; this latter project has now progressed as far as 1574 [F7]. The problem here is that such sources inevitably overstate the degree of external control over the French movement, and particularly the influence of Geneva: we possess very little information regarding ministers with no connections with the churches abroad (these must of course, have been the large majority). The lists of 'vagrant and deposed ministers' published by each national synod provide a glimpse of the sort of men who intruded themselves into the ministry.[4] A further and radically different perspective is provided by hostile witnesses such as Florimond de Raemond and Blaise de Monluc [F8, F9]. Both committed supporters of the old Church, the two chroniclers give a clear sense of how very threatening the growth of Calvinism must have seemed to many contemporaries unwittingly caught up in these turbulent events.

The Netherlands

Students of Dutch Calvinism enjoy, in contrast, a comparatively luxurious level of surviving documentation; reflecting the fact that while the French Huguenots were ultimately destined for the status of a small minority, the Dutch Reformed would enjoy a central and privileged position in the new Dutch State. The early congregations are inevitably the least well documented: no consistory records or registers survive for any congregation before 1572. For what is known about these churches we are dependent on three sources: contacts maintained with the exile churches abroad, reflected particularly in the voluminous correspondence of these congregations [D1, D2, D3]; the interrogations of arrested sectaries, preserved in official town records (and published in a particularly full sequence in the case of Antwerp) [D4]; and martyrs' testimonies, recorded (no doubt with a degree of licence) in the work of Adriaen van Haemstede, the Dutch Crespin [D5]. There is also an excellent compilation of documents, drawing on a variety of official sources, illustrative of early evangelical activity

[4] See section 2, document 23.

in the strategic area of West Flanders [D6]. The explosion of activity in 1566 produced a new wave of church-building, and, following its failure, a systematic and extremely well-documented repression. The most graphic account of the events of 1566 is in Brandt's history of the Reformation, written in the mid-seventeenth century but based on many contemporary documents [D9]. This is also available in a relatively accurate English version. An important contemporary witness is the account provided by the journal of the Ghent patrician Marcus van Vaernewijck [D10]. The repression that followed the failure of the first revolt is copiously documented in the records of the Council of Troubles, preserved in the Royal National Archive in Brussels. These have been systematically exploited to produce the list of victims published by Verheyden [D7], and for partial publication in a number of regional sources, notably for Holland in the volume edited by Jacob Marcus [D8].

It is only with the successful establishment of churches in Holland after 1572 that congregational records have survived in any numbers. Most of these remain unpublished, though available for consultation in local offices as well as in the archive of the Nederlandse Hervormde Kerk.[5] The early consistory records of the Dordrecht community provide an insight into the first years of one of the most important churches [D11]. Of the greatest importance is an ongoing project aimed at publishing the records of the all-important *classis*: two volumes for the *classis* of Dordrecht have now appeared [D12]. Also long available are the records of the provincial synods [D13] and the national synods [D14], together with a selection of synodal gatherings of the churches abroad [D15]. Taken together, they make possible a fairly comprehensive reconstruction of church organisation in the emerging independent State. Needless to say, virtually none of this material is available in English: the selections used here make clear how essential these sources are for an understanding of the individuality of Dutch Calvinism.

Scotland, Germany, and International Calvinism

Scottish Calvinism is again reasonably well documented. There are splendid modern editions of both the *First* (1559) and *Second* (1578) *Books of Discipline* [S1, S2]. Otherwise the modern researcher is mainly indebted to publications of the nineteenth-century record societies, which have put into print a large range of important material: these include the minutes of the St Andrews Kirk Session, a splendid run of consistory material from

[5] Listed in *De Archieven van de Nederlandse Hervormde Kerk* (2 vols., Leiden, 1960-74).

the first foundations of the church [S3]; the records of the Scottish General Assembly (the national synod) [S4]; and the works of John Knox [S5]. John Knox's history of the Reformation also provides a first-hand, if inevitably partisan account of the first years of the new Church [S6]. Also useful is the slightly later work of David Calderwood, which though compiled in the early seventeenth century, like Brandt for the Dutch draws heavily on contemporary material [S7].

German Calvinism remains, in contrast, a relatively untilled field, though the object of increasing interest in recent years. Scholarly work has traditionally concentrated largely on Heidelberg and the Palatinate: good editions exist of the Heidelberg catechism and church orders [Gy1, Gy2, Gy5], and the matriculation lists of Heidelberg University, an important centre of Calvinist learning in these years, have also been published [Gy3]. The letters of the elector Frederick III and of his son John Casimir provide many insights into the policy of a princely reformer who observed events in the Reformed lands of western Europe with particular attention, and the military initiatives which followed after the emergence of the Palatinate as a force in international politics [Gy4, Gy5]. Elsewhere important sources, though copious enough, remain largely in manuscript, with the exception of the outstanding series of published church orders, compiled and edited under the supervision of E. Sehling [Gy6]. In a rather separate category are the records of the congregations established in the north German exile towns, which though located in Germany were essentially part of the wider international movement [Gy7, Gy8, Gy9]. These records provide many useful insights into Calvinism as an international movement; otherwise this theme can be illustrated from a wide variety of sources drawn from all of the above categories. The sheer variety of materials used to compile the extracts collected in the fourth section of this volume bears eloquent testimony to the fact that whether concerned primarily with doctrine, church organisation or the political struggle, church leaders never forgot they were part of an international movement; and it was this which gave International Calvinism so much of its strength and resilience.

Select bibliography
of printed sources

[C1]   *Joannis Calvini Opera quae supersunt omnia*, ed. W. Baum, E. Cunitz
       and E. Reuss (59 vols., Brunswick, 1863-80). Vols. 29-87 of the
       Corpus Reformatorum.

[C2]   *Supplementa Calviniana: sermons inédits*, ed. E. Mülhaupt *et al.* (7
       vols., Neukirchen, 1961-81).

[C3]   Published (under separate titles) by the Calvin Translation Society,
       Edinburgh, 1843-53.

[C4]   *Institutes of the Christian Religion. 1536 Edition*, ed. F. L. Battles (rep.
       ed., Grand Rapids, 1986).

[C5]   *Institutes of the Christian Religion*, ed. J.T. McNeill (Library of the
       Christian Classics, 20, 21, 1960).

[C6]   *Letters of John Calvin*, ed. Jules Bonnet (4 vols., Edinburgh and
       Philadelphia, 1855-58).

[C7]   *John Calvin and Jacobo Sadoleto. A Reformation Debate*, ed. John C.
       Olin (rep. ed., Grand Rapids, 1990).

[C8]   *Jean Calvin. Three French Treatises*, ed. Francis M. Higman (London,
       1970).

[G1]   *John Calvin. Theological treatises*, ed. J. K. S. Reid (Library of the
       Christian Classics, 22, 1954). The Ecclesiastical Ordinances also in
       G3, below.

[G2]   *Registre de la Compagnie des Pasteurs de Genève*, ed. J.-F. Bergier, *et
       al.* (Geneva, 1964-).

[G3]   *Register of the Company of Pastors of Geneva in the time of Calvin*,
       ed. P. E. Hughes (Grand Rapids, 1966).

[G4]   *Le livre du recteur de l'Académie de Genève, 1559-1878*, ed. Susanne
       Stelling-Michaud (6 vols., Geneva, 1964-80).

[F1]   *Synodicon in Gallia Reformata*, ed. John Quick (2 vols., London,
       1692).

[F2]   *Tous les Synodes Nationaux des Eglises réformées de France*, ed. J.
       Aymon (2 vols., The Hague, 1710).

[F3]   *Histoire ecclésiastique des Eglises réformées au royaume de France* (3
       vols., Paris, 1883-89).

[F4]   Jean Crespin, *Histoire des Martyrs persecutez et mis a mort pour la verité de l'Evangile depuis le temps des apostres iusques à present*, ed. Daniel Benoit (3 vols., Toulouse, 1885-89).

[F5] *La France Protestante: Pièces Justificatives*, ed. Eugene and Emile Haag (rep. ed., Geneva, 1966).

[F6] *Documents protestants inédits de XVIe siècle*, ed. E. Arnaud (Paris, 1872).

[F7] *Correspondance de Théodore de Bèze*, ed. Hippolyte Aubert *et al.* (Geneva, 1960–).

[F8] Florimond de Raemond, *L'Histoire de la naissance, progrez et decadence de l'heresie de ce siècle* (2 vols., Rouen, 1628-29).

[F9] *Commentaires de Blaise de Monluc* in J.-F. Michaud and J. J. F. Poujoulat, *Nouvelle Collection de Mémoires pour servir à l'histoire de France* (32 vols., Paris, 1839-54).

[D1] *Ecclesiae Londino-Batavae Archivum*, ed. J. H. Hessels (3 vols. in 4, Cambridge, 1887-97). Letters from the archive of the Dutch church, London.

[D2] E. Meiners, *Oostvrieschlandts kerkelyke Geschiedenisse* (2 vols., Groningen, 1738-39). Letters from the Emden church archive.

[D3] *Brieven uit onderscheidene kerkelijke Archieven*, ed. H. Q. Janssen and J. J. van Toorenenbergen (Werken der Marnix Vereeninging, ser. 3, part 2, 1878). Further letters from the Emden archive.

[D4] Pierre Génard, 'Personen te Antwerpen in de XVIe eeuw voor het feit van religie gerechtelijk vervolgd', *Antwerpsch Archievenblad*, vols. 7-14 (n.d.).

[D5] *Historie des Martelaren die om de getuigenis der evangelische waarheid hun bloed gestort hebben* (rep. ed., Utrecht, 1980).

[D6] *Troubles religieux du XVIe siécle dans la Flandre maritime, 1560-1570*, ed. E. de Coussemaker (4 vols., Bruges, 1876).

[D7] A. L. E. Verheyden, *Le Conseil des Troubles. Liste des condamnés (1567-1573)* (Brussels, 1961).

[D8] J. Marcus, *Sententien en indagingen van den Hertog van Alba* (Amsterdam, 1735).

[D9] G. Brandt, *Historie der Reformatie en andere kerkelyke geschiedenissen in en omtrent de Nederlanden* (4 vols., Amsterdam, 1671-1704); *The History of the Reformation and other Ecclesiastical Transactions in the Low Countries* (4 vols., London, 1720-23).

[D10] Marcus van Vaernewijck, *Van die beroerlicke tijden in die Nederlanden en voornamelijk in Ghendt, 1566-1568*, ed. F. Vanderhaegen (5 vols., Ghent, 1872-81).

[D11] *Uw Rijk Kome. Acta van de Kerkeraad van de Nederduits Gereformeerde Gemeente te Dordrecht, 1573-1579*, ed. Th. W. Jensma (Dordrecht, 1981).

[9]

[D12] *Classsicale Acta 1573-1620. Particuliere synode Zuid-Holland. I: Classis Dordrecht, 1573-1600*, ed. J. P. van Dooren (The Hague, 1980). *II: Classis Dordrecht, 1601-1620. Classis Breda, 1616-1620*, ed. J. Roelevink (The Hague, 1991).

[D13] *Acta der Provinciale en Particuliere Synoden, gehouden in de Noordelijke Nederlanden gedurende de jaren 1572-1620*, ed. J. Reitsma and S.D. Van Veen (8 vols., Arnhem, 1892-99).

[D14] *Acta van de Nederlandsche Synoden der zestiende eeuw*, ed. F. L. Rutgers (Werken der Marnix Vereeniging, ser. 2, part 3, 1889).

[D15] *Acten van Classicale en Synodale Vergaderingen van ... Cleef, Keulen, Aken, 1571-1589*, ed. H .Q. Janssen and J. J. van Toorenenbergen (Werken der Marnix Vereeniging, ser. 2, part 2, 1882).

[S1] *The First Book of Discipline*, ed. J. K. Cameron (Edinburgh, 1972)

[S2] *The Second Book of Discipline*, ed. James Kirk (Edinburgh, 1980).

[S3] *Register of the Minister, Elders and Deacons of the Christian Congregation of St Andrews, 1559-1600*, ed. David Hay Fleming (2 vols., Edinburgh, 1890).

[S4] *The Booke of the Universall Kirk. Acts and Proceedings of the General Assemblies of the Kirk of Scotland, 1560-1618* (3 vols., Edinburgh, 1839-45).

[S5] *The Works of John Knox*, ed. D. Laing (6 vols., Edinburgh, 1846).

[S6] John Knox, *History of the Reformation in Scotland*, ed. W. C. Dickinson (Edinburgh, 1949).

[S7] David Calderwood, *The History of the Kirk of Scotland*, ed. Thomas Thomson (8 vols., Edinburgh, 1842).

[Gy1] *Quellen zur Geschichte der kirchlichen Unterrichts in die evangelische Kirche Deutschlands zwischen 1530 und 1600*, ed. J.M. Reu (Gütersloh, 1904).

[Gy2] A. C. Cochrane, *Reformed Confessions of the Sixteenth Century* (London, 1966).

[Gy3] *Die Matrikel der Universität Heidelberg von 1386 bis 1662*, ed. G. Toepke (3 vols., Heidelberg, 1884-93).

[Gy4] *Briefe Friedrichs des Frommen*, ed. A. Kluckhohn (2 vols., Brunswick, 1868-72).

[Gy5] *Briefe des Pfalzgrafen Johann Casimir mit verwandten Schriftstücken*, ed. F. von Bezold (3 vols., Munich, 1882-1903).

[Gy6] *Die evangelische Kirchenordnungen des 16. Jahrhunderts*, ed. E. Sehling (15 vols., Leipzig and Tübingen, 1902-77).

[Gy7] *Die Kirchenratsprotokolle der Reformierten Gemeinde Emden, 1557-1620*, ed. Heinz Schilling and Klaus-Dieter Schreiber (2 vols., Cologne and Vienna, 1989-92).

[Gy8] *Das Protokollbuch der Niederländischen Reformierten Gemeinde zu*

Frankfurt am Main, 1570-1581, ed. Hermann Meinert and Wolfram Dahmer (Frankfurt, 1977).

[Gy9] *Kölnische Konsistorial-Beschlüsse ... 1572-1596*, ed. E. Simons (Bonn, 1905).

Section 1
CALVIN AND GENEVA

Calvin's association with Geneva was wholly accidental. He was born in Noyon in Picardy, a region of northern France with few real links with the territories of the French-speaking south-west, where Geneva was then a regionally important but relatively small trading town.[1] The story of how Calvin, after years studying in Paris, came to leave France and settle in Geneva, is well known, not least from Calvin's own brief autobiographical reminiscence published twenty years subsequently as a preface to his *Commentary on the Psalms*.[2] Forced with other Parisian intellectuals to leave France in the the wake of the Affair of the Placards (1534), Calvin settled first in Basle, where he devoted himself to finishing the first version of the *Institutes* (1536), the work which established his reputation as an intellectual force in the international evangelical movement. It was this work which had so impressed Guillaume Farel that he was moved to detain Calvin as he passed through Geneva *en route* to Strasburg, persuading the reluctant young scholar that he could play a part in Farel's work in evangelising the newly Reformed city. Calvin's inital baptism in the world of ecclesiastical politics was not a happy one. Geneva in 1536 was a city in transition. In the recent upheavals the citizenry had succeeded in throwing off the government of their ruler, the Bishop (and therefore also the Catholic Church). But these events still left the small independent territory vulnerable both to larger predatory neighbours (principally Savoy and their ally in the struggle for liberation, the Swiss canton of Berne), and to the play of faction within the city. Within a year Farel and Calvin had fallen foul of their former allies among the city elite, and early in 1538 they were stripped of their offices and expelled from the city.

Calvin settled in Strasburg, where he spent the next three years, years which he was later to remember as the happiest of his life. It was also a period important to his development as a reformer, since he was able both to practice the art of church leadership within the less demanding theatre of the city's small French refugee congregation, and to observe

[1] The best introduction is still E. W. Monter, *Calvin's Geneva* (New York, 1967).
[2] *John Calvin. Commentary on the Book of Psalms* (Calvin Translation Society, 1845), pp. xxxv-xliv.

the ecclesiastical politics of the Empire from this strategic imperial city. It was only with the greatest reluctance that he was persuaded, following new convulsions in the city elite, that his duty lay in a return to Geneva. Returning in October 1541, he quickly set about moulding the institutions of a church settlement, but his position was still far from secure. Although the Council's eagerness to secure his return placed him initially in a position of some strength (the speedy enactment of the Ecclesiastical Ordinances was in this respect a condition of his return), they were far from wishing to submit themselves to a new clerical government, and the problems Calvin faced during the next decade in implementing his vision of a godly society went some way to justifying his initial grave misgivings. It would be fifteen years before Calvin would feel fully secure in Geneva, and only in the last years of his life was he prepared to formalise his relationship with the city by taking out Genevan citizenship.

The problems Calvin faced in Geneva fell essentially into three categories. First, and initially most pressing, were the difficulties posed by his lack of confidence in his ministerial colleagues. Farel remained only for a few months after Calvin's return, and thereafter Calvin was forced to rely on colleagues who had forfeited his trust by remaining in Geneva after his expulsion, and whom he suspected of plotting to undermine his new ecclesiastical settlement [**document 2**]. It would be five years before Calvin had succeeded in weeding out the weaker links, and replacing them with reliable supporters. Thereafter Calvin's principal difficulties lay in his relations with the civic hierarchy and his growing band of theological critics. By 1546 opponents of Calvin's vision of a godly society were beginning to show their face: this was the year in which his uncompromising demand for the imposition of an impartial social discipline earned him the emnity of several of Geneva's leading families, and particularly of Ami Perrin, captain-general and formerly a strong supporter of the Reformation [**document 3**]. The ten years that followed were a period of almost permanent crisis, marked by incessant bickering, frequent riots, and occasional challenges to Calvin's theological views. It was only in 1555 that the ebb and flow of factional advantage would turn decisively in Calvin's favour, when the anti-ministerial forces were manoevred into precipitating the ill-prepared coup whose failure sealed their destruction [**document 8**].

Through these difficult and turbulent times Calvin was sustained by two vital advantages: his growing reputation as a reformer of international stature, and the committed support of the increasing population of French refugees. It was a factor of no small significance in the domestic squabbles of these years that Calvin, through his preaching, controlled the one organ of regular public communication. Calvin was an assiduous and popular preacher: he preached a regular cycle of sermons, at least five times a fortnight, and though generally devoted to a methodical scheme of biblical exegesis was not afraid to extemporise harsh and partisan reflections on the domestic political issues of the day [**document 4**]. The fame of these orations is captured in the wry and sceptical observations of Florimond de Raemond, a hostile witness who nevertheless makes clear that even Catholic travellers were lured by Calvin's celebrity to a visit to Geneva [**document 6**]. This renown, combined with Calvin's increasingly authoritative interventions in international ecclesiastical politics [**document 7**], and with his repeated victories over domestic theological critics [**document 1**], made it increasingly difficult for opponents in the city elite to impose their will, particularly since to dispense with Calvin would almost certainly this time have brought the resignation of the entire ministerial body, now composed entirely of scholars and clergy of French extraction loyal to Calvin's view of ecclesiastical polity. But in the last resort it may well have been structural changes in the Genevan population which did most to consolidate Calvin's position. Since 1546 Geneva had experienced an enormous immigration, almost entirely of French refugees attracted by Calvin's presence in the city [**document 6**]. The newcomers strained the resources of the small city, increasing ethnic tensions, but also introducing a massive injection of new resources. It was new enrolments of French immigrants as citizens (thus threatening the delicate electoral balance) which in both 1546 and 1555 sparked the most acute tensions with Calvin's opponents, and in the end precipitated the final confrontation with Perrin. Although Calvin in his letter to Bullinger presents the issue largely in terms of discipline, his account also contains a hint of the ethnic element in the dispute which may indeed have been more basic to the struggle than the issue highlighted by Calvin's inevitably partisan appraisal of his 'libertine'[3] opponents.

Be that as it may, Calvin's emphatic rout of his opponents in 1555 (confirmed by a second remodelling of the Council in 1557 to remove the last doubters) ushered in a decade when the minister's authority was limited only by his own increasing ill-health and preoccupation with events abroad. These years saw the development of the mature Calvinist regime, based on close co-operation between the ministers, gathered in the Company of Pastors, and a sympathetic city government [**documents 9, 10**]. These years also witnessed the most concerted attempts to bring the whole population under a rigorous discipline [**document 11**], efforts

[3] A term not generally used by contemporaries, who saw the factional struggles much more in terms of traditional allegiances dating from the liberation struggle with the Bishop and foreign policy issues connected with relations with Berne and Savoy.

which attracted the enthusiastic admiration of contemporaries such as John Knox, but have been less generously judged by historians. Three points should however be made before accepting too readily the stereotype picture of Geneva as a repressive theocratic regime. Firstly, even in this era, the ministers in the consistory restricted their concern to religious and moral issues: there was no attempt to usurp the authority of the city's lay authorities over crime. It was this identity of interest, and the close co-operation between the two organs in this period which gave Geneva its sense of being governed to a particularly strict morality; a level of co-operation which Calvinist ministers elsewhere generally struggled in vain to replicate.[4] Secondly, there remained a good distance between the theoretical provisions of the *Ecclesiastical Ordinances* and the reality on the ground; this was most evidently the case for the city's rural parishes, which remained bastions of ignorance and misconduct despite the efforts of an unusually capable rural ministeriat, some of whom at least had the sense and humanity to adapt their expectations to the capacities of their humble flock [**document 12**]. Thirdly, this period of Geneva's existence as a beacon of Reformed practice was in fact remarkably short-lived. By the 1570s visitors to the Genevan Academy (founded 1559) were recording their disappointment at its offerings, and at the end of the century a major international relief effort was required to beat off the threat of a revived Savoy [**documents 64, 68**]. By this point Geneva's importance was mainly symbolic; other mature Reformed regimes had emerged, building on the church structures worked out by Calvin during the first tumultuous years of his ministry, to carry his vision of a godly society into the new century.

(a) Geneva and the establishment of the Reformation

1 Théodore de Bèze, *Life and Death of John Calvin*

Calvin's teachings and his combats against error

Now as concerning his doctrine, whereof I will first speak, the multitude which have spoken against him are unable to render it suspect with ... men of good judgement ... . None hath at any time stood against it, but he hath well felt that he hath addressed himself not against a man, but against a very true servant of God ... . The *Anabaptists* can bear witness, who shortly after the beginning of his Ministry in this Church, to wit the year 1536, that he could so well

[4] See below, section 3c.

and happily behave himself in open disputation without the help of the Magistrate that immediately the race of them was utterly destroyed in this Church: which is the more to be wondered at, because that the greatest number of the Churches of Germany are yet at this day greatly hindered by them: and if there be any that is free from them, it hath been rather by rigour of Justice than otherwise.

He had another combat to fight against an Apostate named *Caroli*, upon certain calumnies and false reports: who being also overthrown as well by writing as by word, and cast out of the Church of God, died miserably at Rome in an hospital, as an example to those which do revolt from Jesus Christ, to follow a Master which doth so well recompense his servants, both in this world and in the other.

And another time, to wit the year of our Lord 1553 *Michel Servet* a Spaniard of cursed memory, happened to come, who was not a man, but rather, an horrible Monster, compounded of the ancient and new heresies, and above all an execrable blasphemer against the Trinity, and namely against the Eternity of the Son of God: This same being come to this town, and apprehended by the Magistrate because of his blasphemies, he was here so substantially encountered that he had no defence but a certain untamed obstinacy, by reason whereof by the just judgement of God and man, he ended by the punishment of fire, his wicked life and blasphemies which he had vomited, both by mouth and writing by the space of thirty years and more.

About two years before there came a certain deceitful Friar, a Carmelite, suddenly become a divine, a Physician, named *Hierosme Bolsec* of Paris, who ... began in open congregation to condemn the doctrine of the eternal providence and predestination, as though we made God the author of sin, and culpable in the condemnation of the wicked: Calvin ... did so answer him by word both openly and privately, and afterward also by writing that the adversary had no truth of his side remaining, but a certain Monkish shamelessness which made him and doth make him at this daye filthy and stinking to every man that hath any good understanding ... .

As for the ... enemies [who] have assailed him from afar off ... he hath touched them more nigh than they would willingly: his learned works against the Anabaptists and Libertines can make sufficient declaration. Who did shut up the mouth of the glorious Cardinal Sadolet, but only he? Who hath more boldly and more aptly made answer to the wicked *Interim*[1] which hath so troubled Germany? Who

[1] The Augsburg *Interim* of 1548, imposed by Charles V on the German Lutheran states after their defeat in the Schmalkaldic War. Melanchthon's willingness to accept the *Interim* was much criticised by other leading German reformers.

hath more constantly defended the purity of the doctrine against the most dangerous kind of enemies, to wit those which under the colour of peace and union do endeavour themselves to corrupt the purity of the same?

And as touching the miserable contention that was moved about the matter of the Supper, seeing the fire so greatly kindled, his whole desire was to quench it by clear exposition of the matter: without naming of any man: the which he hath so well and so aptly done, that he that shall well consider his writings, must confess that next after God, it is to him, that the honour of the resolution is due, which since hath been followed by all men of good judgement.

This notwithstanding, Satan enforced himself by all means possible, to have set division between him and the Church of Zurich in this dissension; which among others he has always esteemed and honoured. But it was in vain, for on the contrary when they had in presence conferred together, they continued thoroughly of one accord: and then was the consent of all the Churches of Switzerland and of the Swiss, framed and imprinted in many tongues, to the great edification of the people of God.[2]

That did much displease certain obstinate men, among whom there was one named *Joachim Westphal*, another *Tileman Heshusius*, which were the most earnest and fervent enemies of the truth and concord. He was then forced to enter into combat, whereby he did so maintain the truth, and overthrow and suppress the ignorance and shamelessness of such personages, that he won great commendation, and the above named great shame: yea even among those of their sect and nation, and the Church of God hath been the more confirmed in the true and wholesome doctrine.

In conclusion, I think there is no heresy ancient, nor renewed, nor newly forged in our time, which he hath not destroyed to the very foundations. For among all his other excellent Graces there were two that did shine in him: to wit, a singular sharpness of spirit to discover where the difficulty of matters did lie, and then also a marvellous dexterity and aptness to make his answers without the losing of any one word, as all they will confess, yea, the very enemies of the Gospel, which would attentively read his works.

I have also omitted one Monster which he likewise did defeat, albeit that in that behalf I fought on his side: it is one named *Sebastian Castellio*, who because he had some knowledge in the tongues, and

---

[2] The *Consensus Tigurinus* of 1549. It was not in fact published until 1551 by John à Lasco in London. Its appearance set off the Sacramentarian controversy with Westphal (Lutheran minister in Hamburg) and Heshusius, to which Beza refers.

had also a certain aptness in the Latin tongue, he was here received to govern the school. But this spirit being so naturally inclined to please himself, did so dive him in his vanity that in the end he drowned himself therein, because we could never win so much of him, as to cause him to take the pains to read the Commentaries and other works to resolve him. That was the cause why he did openly condemn the song called *Canticum Canticorum*, in Latin, as a filthy and wanton Book: which when it was laid to his charge, he vomited out openly a thousand injuries against the pastors of this Church: whereupon being commanded by the Magistrate to avouch his sayings, and being of manifest malice and evil speaking, by justice he was appointed to depart the town after he had acknowledged his fault: being in the end retired to Basle ....

As touching the rest, in this discourse I think I have entreated of the greatest part of his life: for what was his life other than a continual doctrine, as well by word as by writing, and by all his manners and order of life? ... which ... will do very well to be declared ... to the end that every man may understand the marvels of God in the person of this excellent man.

He was born in Noyon, an ancient and famous town of Picardy, the year 1509, the tenth of July, of an honest house and of a reasonable wealth, his father was named Gerard Calvin, a man of good understanding and counsel, and therefore greatly desired in the houses of noble men dwelling in those parts: by reason whereof his said son was the better and more liberally brought up, at his father's charges notwithstanding, in company with the children of the house of Montmor, with whom he was also in company at the school in Paris.

He was always a singular good wit and above all other things of a very good conscience, enemy to vices, and greatly given to the service of God as men did then call it: in such sort as his mind was wholly to divinity, which was also an occasion that he was provided of a benefice in the Cathedral Church of Noyon.

Yet was his father always minded that he should study the Laws, and he also on his part having already (by the mean of a cousin and friend of his, named Master Pierre Robert, otherwise Olivetanus, who afterwards turned the Bible out of Hebrew into French and imprinted it at Neuchâtel) tasted something of the pure Religion, began to withdraw himself from the popish superstitions: which was the cause that beside the singular reverence that he had towards his father, he did agree to go to Orléans to the same end, where there did then read an excellent man named Pierre de l'Estoile, who was afterwards President of the Court of the *Parlement* in Paris, under whom he did so profit in short space, that he was not accounted a scholar, but as an ordinary Doctor, as often times he was rather a teacher than a hearer, and he was offered to proceed Doctor without paying anything, which thing also he did refuse.

[Calvin studied briefly in Bourges.] Among other with whom he did frequent and company then at Bourges there was ... an excellent personage, a professor of the Greek tongue, named Melchior Wolmar .... This good man seeing Calvin not to be well instructed in the Greek tongue, caused him to study the same, wherein he did greatly help him, as he himself hath witnessed, dedicating to him his Commentaries upon the Second Epistle of St Paul to the Corinthians, and did him the honour to call him his Master and instructor.

In the meantime his father died, which was the cause that he left the study of the Laws and returned to Noyon, and then to Paris: where notwithstanding his youth, he was not long unknown nor without honour, by all such as had any feeling of the truth: he of his part did then resolve to dedicate himself wholly to God, and did travail with great profit in such sort, that being in Paris at the time of the Rector named Monsieur Cop, there happened a sedition ... . In the end seeing the miserable estate of the realm of France, he determined to absent himself and to be where he might live more quietly and according to his conscience.

He departed out of France in the year 1534 and in the same year he caused to imprint at Basle his first instruction, as an Apology, dedicated to Francis the first French king of that name, in the behalf of the poor faithful that were persecuted, whom they did most falsely name Anabaptists, to excuse them toward the Protestant Princes, of the persecutions that they then used against them.[3] He passed also into Italy where he saw my Lady the Duchess of Ferrara, yet at this day living, thanks be to God, who when she had seen and heard him, forthwith judged of him as he was, and ever after until his death, did love and honour him as an excellent organ of the Lord.

In his return from Italy the which he had but seen, he passed (in a happy time) through this town of Geneva, which not long before had received the Gospel by the preaching of M. Guillaume Farel, and did mean nothing less than to tarry there, but to pass through it and go to Basle, or else to Strasburg. But the Lord ... did put in the heart of the said Farel to stay him; which thing was very hard for him to do, in such sort that after many requests and desires he was fain to use adjurations. Then he was contented to stay, not to preach, but to read

[3] The first edition of the *Institutes* (in fact Basle, 1536). The dedicatory epistle to Francis I is also printed in subsequent editions.

Divinity, and this came to pass in the year 1536 in the beginning of September. When he was in this sort declared Doctor in this Church by lawful election and authority, he then formed a brief form of Confession and Discipline to give some shape to this new erected Church. He made also a Catechism which may be well called one of his excellent works, and hath yielded marvellous fruit, being so well framed, that it was afterwards turned out of French into Hebrew to win the Jews, into Greek and Latin for the schools, also into Italian, Dutch, English, Scottish and Flemish, and also Spanish, for all these nations.

These prosperous beginnings did greatly mislike Satan and his, who failed not (as it was an easy matter to do in the first change of the estate of Religion) to set himself against the proceeding of the Gospel. ... Master Calvin ... withstood firmly and constantly with Master Farel the seditious persons ..., it was ordained (the greater part of the Council not being the best) that the forenamed should depart the town within twenty-four hours, because they would not minister the Supper of the Lord in a city that was so troubled and stirred. When this was declared to the said Calvin, his answer was that if he had served men, he should have been ill recompensed, but he served him, who instead of evil recompensing his servants, did always give them more than they deserved. And he might justly so say: for he had followed the example of St Paul, in serving of the Church upon his own charge and cost.

He then departed, to the great grief of all the good, first to Basle and then to Strasburg, where being received as a treasure, by those excellent men Masters Martin Bucer, Capito, Hedio, and others, who at the present did shine as precious pearls in the Church of God, he there created a French Church, and therein did establish ecclesiastical discipline in such sort, as the Germans could never yet attain unto, for their Church, even to this very day; he did also read Divinity with great admiration of every man, and then he began to write upon St Paul, dedicating his Commentary upon the Epistle to the Romans to Master Simon Grynaeus, who was accounted to be the best learned of the German nation, and was his great friend; he had also this grace among others that he brought to the faith a great number of Anabaptists which were sent unto him out of all parts, and among others one named John Stordeur of Liège, who within short time after dying of the plague at Strasburg, he took his widow to wife, whose name was Idelette de Bure, a very grave and honest woman, with whom he lived afterwards very quietly, until our Lord took her away to himself, the year 1548 without having had any child.

At the same very time there were held in Germany certain imperial assemblies or Diets for the matter of Religion, at Worms and at Ratisbon,[4] in the which Calvin was chosen for one of the chief by the advice of all the Divines of Germany, where he did so behave himself that his renown became great even among the very enemies, and Philip Melancthon among others, did even then receive him into singular friendship which did always last afterwards, and did then ordinarily call him the Divine, in token of singular honour.

In the meantime the Lord did execute his judgements at Geneva, punishing certain who holding the office of Syndic in 1538 were the cause of the banishment of Calvin and Farel, in such sort as one of them being guilty of a sedition, and thinking to save himself through a window did all burst himself, another of them having committed a murder, was by order of justice beheaded, the other twain being convinced of certain untruth against the state of the town, fled away and were condemned in their absence.

When the town was purged of this froth, they began then to bewail Calvin, and he was desired thither again by sundry embassies from Geneva, and by the intercession of the lords of Zurich to the lords of Strasburg, who made great difficulty. On the other side, Calvin seeing how he profited in Strasburg would in no wise consent thereunto, albeit to declare the good-will that he bore to the town, the year 1539, a whole year after his banishment, he maintained the cause thereof, or rather of the truth of God, against the Cardinal Sadolet, in a large and learned Epistle which is printed among the rest of his works. In the end he was threatened with the judgements of God if he did not obey to that vocation, in such sort that to the great sorrow of the lords of Strasburg, and especially of Master Bucer and his companions, he was licensed to be at Geneva for a certain time. But when he came thither and was received of singular affection by those poor people which acknowledged their fault, and having a great desire to hear their faithful Pastor, they held him there continually: whereunto in the end the Lords of Strasburg consented, upon condition that he should be always a Burgess of their town. They would also that he should have had always the revenue of a prebend that was appointed unto him for his stipend of his reading. But as he was a man clearly void of all greediness of the goods of this world, so could they never bring to pass that he would receive so much as the value of one denier thereof.

And in this sort he was again established at Geneva, the year 1541

---

[4] Now Regensburg. The Colloquy of Regensburg (1541) represented the last realistic opportunity to reunite the Catholic and Protestant confessions in Germany. It foundered on a failure to agree a satisfactory formula on eucharistic doctrine and the question of church authority.

the 13 of September, where forthwith he framed an order of Ecclesiastical discipline, which hath always since continued there firmly, albeit Satan and his adherents have employed all their forces to abolish it.

... If we shall speak of integrity he is yet unborn, that hath seen him commit any fault in his office, or to yield, be it never so little, for any man living, or to have varied in doctrine or life, nor never misreported man. If we shall speak of labour and pain, I believe that his like is not to be found, beside that he preached continually every day in the week, and most commonly and as often as he was able, he preached twice every Sunday; he did read divinity three times in a week; he made declaration in the Consistory or as it were a whole lesson every Friday, in conference of the scripture which we call Congregation, and did continue this order thoroughly without interruption until his death, and indeed never did fail so much as once, except it were by extreme sickness ... .

The only multitude and number of his books and writings are sufficient to astonish any man that shall see them: but much more those that shall read them. And that which makes his labours more wonderful, is that he had a body so weak of nature, and so low brought with watchings and overmuch sobriety, yea and being subjected to so many diseases, that all men that had seen him would have thought that he could not have lived at all. And notwithstanding this, he never left off day nor night his travail in the works of the Lord: and he could not endure to hear the requests and exhortations of his friends which they daily made unto him, to the end that he should take some rest. The year 1559 being assailed and marvellously grieved with a fever quartan, he did notwithstanding, in the chiefest of his sickness, set forth the last edition of his Christian Institution, and did translate it throughout out into French. Likewise in his last sicknesses ... he did himself translate wholly that great volume of his Commentaries upon the four last Books of Moses: examined the translations of the first: made this book upon Joshua, and did peruse the greatest part of the translation and annotations of the New Testament, in sort that he never ceased from writing but only eight days before his death, his voice beginning to fail him.

Beside his innumerable pains and his charges, in all the mischiefs and perils wherein this poor City hath been assailed within by many mutinous and desperate Citizens, tormented without a hundred thousand ways, threatened by the greatest Kings and Princes of Christendom, because it was always a refuge and defence for all the poor children of God afflicted in France, Italy, Spain, England and elsewhere ... .

And it was not without cause that every man had his refuge to him:

for God had adorned him with so wise and good counsel, that never man repented him of the following of it, but I have known many fall into great and extreme inconveniences which would not believe him. This has been found so by many experiences and proofs, namely in the seditions which happened in the years 1548, 1554 and 1555 to break and disorder the discipline of the Church, where he thrust himself naked in among the swords drawn, and with his presence and words he so frayed the most desperate mutinies of them, that they were enforced to praise God. The like was in the Catiline conspiracy, which was the very year 1555 to have murdered all the French by the Captain of the town named Ami Perrin and his conspirators, which conjuration carrying with it a marvellous number of dangers and travails, in the end, the Lord of his great grace, by the wisdom of his servant, brought it to that pass that it is now at: to wit, to the greatest quietness and felicity that ever this City did know ... .

I will not answer those that do call him heretic and worse than heretic (whereupon they have forged a name of Calvinists), for his doctrine maketh answer on the contrary more than sufficiently. Some have charged him with ambition, but if they be able in any point to prove it, I am content to be condemned. Is there any man that hath followed greater simplicity in the exposition of the Scriptures, and hath more wherewith to set himself forth if he would have profaned the Scriptures with subtle and vain ostentations?

He would rule all, say they. O villain and false shamelessness: what pre-eminence did he ever seek? And if he had sought it, who could have kept him from it? With whom did he ever strive for the first or the second place, when men have not given unto him that which the gifts and graces that God had given him did require? When hath it been seen that ever he did abuse his charge and his authority towards the simplest in the world? To be short, what difference was there ever between him and us, but that he did excel us all in all humility among other virtues, and also in that he took more pain than all we did? Was there any man more simply apparelled or more modest in all respects? Was there any house considering the estate of the man, I do not say less sumptuous, but more slenderly furnished with movables? ...

There have been others which have named him to be irreconcilable, cruel and also bloody, which some of them would moderate, naming him only too severe. The defence is soon made, God be praised, and it should not be necessary, were it not that it shall do well to rebuke some of them for their perversity, and to advertise the others of their ingratitude towards God. I said in the beginning that which I do now say, which is that he never had enemies but such as

[23]

did not know him, or else such as made open war against God ... . He never pursued any man in any court nor attempted the law against any, no, he never sought any revenge ... . I confess that he has always showed the Magistrates how detestable the excepting of persons is in the sight of God, that they must hold the Balance aright: and that God abhorreth not only those which do condemn the innocent but also those which pardon the offender.

But, say they, he was over rigorous against adulterers and heretics. I may well answer that which is true, as all the town doth know, that he never judged any man, for it was not his office, and he never thought to do it; and if they have demanded his advice, not to confound the estates which God hath divided, but to be governed according to the Word of the Lord.

As concerning heretics, where is, I pray you, that great rigour? Where is it that this bloody man hath showed one iota of a bloody nature? There are few towns of Switzerland and of Germany where they have not put Anabaptists to death, and lawfully: they have been contented here with banishment. Bolsec hath here blasphemed against the providence of God. Sebastian Castellio hath here spoken evil of of the very books of the Holy Scripture. Valentino hath here blasphemed against the essence of God: None of them have here been put to death, two of them were only banished, the other was set free by an honourable amends towards God and the Seignory. Where is this cruelty? Only one, Servetus, was put to the fire. And who was ever more worthy than that wicked one having for the space of thirty years in so many sundry sorts blasphemed against the Eternity of the Son of God, giving the name of Cerberus to the Trinity of the three persons in one only Divine essence, making the baptism of young children of no value, having gathered and heaped together all the filthy stinks Satan did vomit out against the truth of God, having seduced an infinite number of persons, and for the chief and principal of all his wickednesses, would never neither repent in giving place to the truth, whereby he had been so often times convinced, nor show any token of conversion. And if we should come to the judgement of the Churches, who would not rather allow that which all the Churches of Germany, and namely Philip Melancthon, a man greatly renowned for his meekness, hath not only spoken but also published by writing, the praise of so just an execution? ... [Calvin] did but the office of a faithful Pastor, putting the Magistrate in mind of his duty, endeavouring him by all means to bring such a wicked man to some amendment, and in the end, not forgetting any thing that might let that such a pestilence should not infect his flock.

There are others which have reported him to be very choleric. I will not make of a man an angel, yet notwithstanding, because I do know how marvellously God hath been served by that same very vehemency, I ought not to keep silent that which is true, and that I do know. Beside his own natural inclination to choler, his wit being marvellous prompt, the folly of many, the multitude and infinite variety of the affairs for the Church of God, and toward the latter end of his life, his great and continual diseases, had made him unquiet and froward: but sure he was far off from any delight therein ... . Such as have seen and known with what kind of men he hath most commonly had to do, the things that God hath declared and done by him, the circumstances of times and places, they indeed may judge whereto such a vehemency, I say a vehemency indeed Prophetical, did serve and shall serve to all posterity ... . And that which made him more marvellous, was that the most obstinate and perverse were constrained to bend under the great power of God, which did compass about his faithful servant. They which shall read his writings, and shall rightly seek the glory of God, shall there see this majesty (whereof I speak) to shine ... .

Source: Théodore de Bèze, *Life and Death of John Calvin* in an anonymous sixteenth-century English translation (spelling and punctuation modernised). See also Daniel Ménager, 'La *Vie et Mort de Jean Calvin* de Théodore de Bèze,' *Bibliothèque d'Humanisme et Renaissance* xlv (1983), pp. 231-55.

2 Establishing the new regime. Calvin to Myconius, 14 March 1542

On my first arrival here I could not, as you had requested, write to you with certainty as to the state of this church, because I had not then myself sufficiently ascertained its condition. Since that time also I have not ventured to say anything for certain, while matters were not very settled, that I might not shortly have occasion to repent having praised it so soon ... . The present state of our affairs I can give you in few words. For the first month after resuming my ministry, I had so much to attend to and so many annoyances, that I was almost worn out: such a work of labour and difficulty had it been to build up once more the fallen edifice. Although certainly Viret had already begun successfully to restore, yet, nevertheless, because he had deferred the complete form of order and discipline until my arrival, it had, as it were, to be commenced anew. When, having overcome this labour, I believed that a breathing space would be allowed me, new cares presented themselves, and those of a kind not much lighter than before. This however somewhat consoles and refreshes me, that we do not labour altogether in vain, without some fruit appearing; which although it is not so plentiful as we could wish, yet neither is it so scanty that there does not appear some change for the better. There appears a brighter prospect for the future if Viret can be left here with me: on which account I am the more desirous to express to you my most thankful acknowledgement, because you share with me in my anxiety that the Bernese may not call him away; and I earnestly beseech, for the sake of Christ, that you will do your utmost to bring that about. For whenever the thought of his going away presents itself, I faint and lose courage entirely ... .

Our other colleagues are rather a hindrance than a help to us: they are rude and self-conceited, have no zeal, and less learning. But what is worst of all, I cannot trust them, even though I very much wish that I could; for by many evidences they show their estrangement from us, and give scarcely any indication of a sincere and trustworthy disposition. I bear with them, however, or rather I humour them, with the utmost lenity: a course from which I shall not be induced to depart, even by their bad conduct. But if, in the long run, the sore need a severer remedy, I shall do my utmost and shall see to it by every method I can think of to avoid disturbing the peace of the Church with our quarrels; for I dread the factions which must necessarily arise from the dissensions of ministers. On my first arrival I might have driven them away had I wished to do so, and that is even now in my power. I shall never, however, repent the degree of moderation which I have observed, since no one can justly complain that I have been too severe. These things I mention to you in a cursory way, that you may perceive more clearly how wretched I shall be if Viret is taken away from me. What you observe, from the example of your church, of the great injury which is inflicted by the noisome plague of discord among the ministry, I can confirm from my own experience to the fullest extent, in the calamity that has befallen this church. No persons could be on closer terms of intimacy than we were here with one another. But when Satan had stirred up the deplorable misunderstanding between these brethren and ourselves, you know yourself what followed thereupon. My determination was therefore made at once, that unless with the evidence of an entire reconciliation, I would never undertake this charge, because I despaired of any benefit from my ministry here, unless they held out a helping hand to me. Meanwhile, many in their assembly are not over friendly, others are openly hostile to me. But this I carefully provide against, that the spirit of contention may not arise among us. We have an intestine seed of discord in the city, as I have already mentioned; but we take special care, by our patient and mild deportment, that the Church may not suffer any inconvenience from that circumstance, and that nothing of that kind may reach the common people. They all know very well by experience the pleasant and humane disposition of Viret. I am in no way more harsh, at least in this matter. Perhaps you will scarcely believe this; it is not the less true, however. Indeed I value the public peace and cordial agreement among ourselves too highly, that I lay restraint upon myself: those who are opposed to us are themselves compelled to award this praise to me. The feeling prevails to such an extent that from day to day those who were once open enemies have become friends; others I conciliate by courtesy, and I feel that I have been in some measure successful, although not everywhere and on all occasions.

On my arrival it was in my power to have disconcerted our enemies most triumphantly, entering with full sail among the whole of that tribe who had done the mischief. I have abstained; if I had liked, I could daily, not merely with impunity, but with the approval of very many, have used sharp reproof. I forbear; even with the most scrupulous care I avoid everything of the kind, lest even by some slight word I should appear to persecute any individual, much less all of them at once. May the Lord confirm me in this disposition of mind. It happens, however, sometimes, that it is necessary to withstand our colleagues; but we never do so unless they either compel us by their unseasonable importunity, or some weightier consideration demands our interference. I will relate an instance to you, which the complaint you make in your letter, owing to the similarity of the case in point, brought very forcibly to my recollection. When we were considering about the introduction of ecclesiastical censure, and the Senate had given us a commission to that effect, these worthy persons appeared in public to assent; doubtless because they were ashamed to offer direct opposition in a matter that was so plain and evident. Afterwards, however, they were to be seen going about secretly, dealing separately with each of the senators, exhorting them not to lay at our feet the power which was in their hands (as they said), not to abdicate the authority which God had entrusted them, and not to give occasion to sedition, with many other arguments of a like nature. We dared not close our eyes to such perfidious conduct. We endeavoured, however, to arrange the matter in such a way as not to stir up strife among us.

We at length possess a presbyterial court, such as it is, and a form of discipline, such as these disjointed times permit. Do not, however, allow yourself to suppose that we obtained so much without the most vigorous exertion. And besides, those troops of unclean spirits break forth in all directions, who in order that they may escape from healthy discipline, which they can in no way submit to, seek every sort of pretext for slipping away from the authority of the Church. The world, moreover, holds this laxity to be an established custom, which, for the sake of its lust, must reign paramount, because it cannot endure to resign the dominion of the sensual appetites to Christ. But however impostors of this kind may plead the plausible case of the world and the flesh, the Lord will consume them with the breath of his mouth, provided we go forward to the assault with a united courage and resolution, and fight manfully, with a stout heart and unwearied zeal, for that sacred authority over the members of the Church which ought ever to be held inviolable. For indeed, the truth of God shines more brightly of itself in this evangelical order of discipline, than to allow of it being easily overlaid with such lying devices. They adduce Moses and David as examples, as if these two rulers had exercised no other charge over the people than to rule them in the ordinance of civil government. Let those insane pleaders for the authority of the magistrate give us such men for magistrates as were Moses and David, that is excelling in the singular spirit of prophecy, and sustaining both characters, not at their own mere will and pleasure, but by the calling and commission of God, we shall then willingly concede to such persons that authority which they demand. I have no doubt that Moses himself discharged the functions of priesthood before the consecration of Aaron to the office: afterwards he prescribes, by the command of God, what was to be done. David also did not proceed to take order in settling the administration of the Church, before he was invested with that power by the permission of God. Other pious godly kings defended and protected the established order by their authority, as became them; they let the Church alone, however, in the exercise of her peculiar jurisdiction in spirituals, and left to the priests the charge assigned to them by the Lord ... .

Source: Calvini Opera [C1], xi. 376-8 (no. 389); *Letters of Calvin* [C6], ii. 288-9 (no. 83), lightly modernised.

3 Disputes. Calvin to Farel, April 1546

After your departure the dances caused us more trouble than I had supposed. All those who were present being summoned to the Consistory, with the two exceptions of Corne and Perrin, shamelessly lied to God and us. I was incensed, as the vileness of the thing demanded, and I strongly inveighed against the contempt of God, in that they thought nothing of making a mockery of the sacred obtestations we had used. They persisted in their contumacy. When I was fully informed of the state of the case, I could do nothing but call God to witness that they would pay the penalty of such perfidy; I, at the same time however, announced my resolution of revealing the truth, even though it should be at the cost of my own life, lest they should imagine that any profit was to come of lying. Francisca also, the wife of Perrin, grossly abused us, because we were so opposed to the Favres. I replied as seemed proper, and as she deserved. I inquired whether their house was inviolably sacred, whether it owed no subjection to the laws? We already detained her father in prison, being convicted of one act of adultery, the proof of a second was close at hand; there was a strong report of a third; her brother had openly contemned and derided the Senate and us. Finally I added that a new city must be built for them, in which they might live apart, unless they were willing to be restrained by us here under the yoke of Christ; that so long as they were in Geneva, they would strive in vain to cast off obedience to the laws; for were there as many diadems in the house of Favre as frenzied heads, that would be no barrier to the Lord being superior. Her husband meanwhile had gone to Lyons, hoping that the matter would be silently buried. I thought that they should be forced to a confession of the truth by an oath. Corne warned them that he would by no means suffer them to perjure themselves. They not only confessed what we wished, but that they on that day danced at the house of the widow of Balthazar. They were all cast into prison. The Syndic was an illustrious example of moderation; for he publicly spoke against himself and the whole herd so severely that it was unnecessary to say much to him. He was, however, severely admonished in the Consistory, being deposed from his office until he gave proof of repentance. They say that Perrin has returned from Lyons; whatever he may do he will not escape punishment.

Henri was stripped of his office with our consent ... . Much was said, backwards and forwards, but the result was that he departed loaded with the reproach and odium of all.[1] Being deprived of his

[1] Henri de la Mare, whom Calvin regarded as the most unreliable of his

ministry he was at the same time thrust into prison, whence however he was liberated in three days. There he was a strenuous patron of the dances, that he might embitter as far as was in his power the hatred towards me of those who were already more than sufficiently alienated from me. But whatever Satan may essay by the like of him, he will afford a striking example. For two things are already matter of public talk, that there is no hope of impunity since even the first people of the city are not spared, and that I show no more favour to friends than to those opposed to me. Perrin with his wife rages in prison; the widow is absolutely furious; the others are silent from confusion and shame.

Source: *Calvini Opera* [C1], xii. 333-7 (no. 791); *Letters of Calvin* [C6], ii. 38-41 (no. 163), lightly modernised.

(b) The appeal of the new teachings. Natives and exiles

4 Calvin the preacher. Extracts from Calvin's *Sermons on Micah*

When a city becomes renowned for having received the Word of God, the world will reckon that the city ought to be, as a result, so much better governed, that such order will there prevail as to accord right and justice to one and all. Therefore, if things turn out to be no better than anywhere else, or worse than this, as if the truth of God were not to be found there at all, what is one to say? Will we not appear to be the worst people in the world? Listen to the papists talking! 'Oh the Genevans! They claim to be better than everybody else, because they want to reform the entire world; anyone would think they were angels themselves. But just look at the way they actually behave! If you go to Geneva you will find just as many tricks and petty frauds as ever in their shops. You will be robbed and fleeced, not only in business dealings but in everything else as well. You cannot have dealings with anyone at all in that city, even about the most trivial matter, without their getting around you and deceiving you. If you go to Molard[1] to stock up with merchandise you are bound to encounter deception and malice even worse than the kind of thing you might

---

ministerial colleagues, and whom he subjected to a remorseless persecution. Exiled to a country parish, his plaintive complaints concerning the inadequacy of his income and difficulties of his charge were frequently aired in the Company of Pastors.

[1] The Geneva market-place.

have expected had they never heard speak of God. And afterwards, if you take your case to law, you will notice, if you watch closely what is happening, that the man who is most highly regarded by his peers is the one who has the most ruses and dirty tricks up his sleeve.'

Let us take heed, therefore, of the teaching of the prophet Micah, when he says, 'The defenceless passer-by has been robbed, his coat and raiment stripped from his back.' It is to us that his words should speak.

These words should make it plain to us that when God has called us to this state of grace, it is our duty even more than before to refrain from all sharp practice, for we will be expected to be open and friendly and trustworthy to deal with. I say that once we have made a profession of faith like ours, we are more severely to be condemned if we do not deal equitably and fairly with our neighbours, or if we indulge in any violence, force, crookery or deception. When the Lord through the mouth of the prophet declares, 'My people arose and robbed the unwary traveller of his clothes' it is beyond doubt that these words also are pronounced against us. What is more, we should notice that the prophet is not referring to petty larceny of the kind which is easily dealt with, or to thefts by small-time crooks who end up on the gallows because they were no good at thieving; justice reigns there well enough. No, he has in mind the kind of thief who is altogether more subtle and, as a result, more cruel, and who is so canny that it is impossible to bring him to justice; such men are the true highway-robbers who slit the throats of poor men, and strip them right down to their bones. It is difficult to legislate against things like that. Our Lord in his understanding knows well that human judgement is powerless against such robbers, that it can offer no redress against the way they stealthily cut the throats of ordinary people, and that it cannot even reckon up how much has been stolen from them; he makes it plain, therefore, that although robbers of this variety are more or less immune from retribution at the hands of human justice, this by no means implies that they will also be exempt from having to give account of themselves before him.

Thus one can see that those who argue that the Word of God should not be taken further than human judgement can reach, are taking up a position which is completely wrong-headed. One sees it in those pig-headed fools who say 'it is obvious, really, that all a man has to do is to pay his debts, and take a bit of trouble to behave as decently as he can, without preachifying or making a great song and dance about it'. Obvious, indeed! As I have already said, such people just do not see that it really is necessary that the Word of God should extend much further than the ordinary comprehension of human beings. Let us imagine a situation which never in fact happens in practice, where a magistracy is putting all its efforts into maintaining the honour of God, as well as into upholding equity and right between men: in such a situation there would need to be rules and regulations about everything, as I have already pointed out. How otherwise would punishment be imposed upon the thievery, the pilfering and the taking of cuts which abound in the world of commerce? Once such law and order was introduced, even bigger crooks than the ones who nowadays commit their robberies on the quiet would find it impossible to avoid disclosure before the Lord as the thieves they are. For what hope is there of mere earthly justice having efficacy against the examples of rapine and usury, fraud, perjury, cruelty, extortion and robbery which occur daily among tradesmen? They are none the less detestable to God, and must, therefore, be identified and condemned out of his Word ... .

It is sometimes asked, 'Is it fair of God to punish his own people who are not in any way guilty?' The answer is plain: we are never so guiltless in the eyes of God that he does not have good reason to punish us. For when God treats his people with gentleness, it is in order to support and protect them. Were God to reward the most holy and innocent being in the world, not with any special strictness, but precisely in accordance with his true deserts, that being would find himself totally confounded and cast into the abyss. Since this is so, no one can complain that God is treating him with over-much severity, when good men finding themselves among the wicked, refuse to put up with the abuses prevalent in their local community. When nothing is to be found but impurity, when there is evidence of contempt of God and of his Word, when scandals go unchecked, and when adultery, drunkenness, dissolute behaviour and every other sort of wickedness are tolerated, then we can do no other than declare that it seems to us that all is lost and ruined. True, not everyone is as disorderly as this, and many people do their best to resist such temptations as well as they can; but not enough are of sufficient zeal to prevent the cry, 'How can it be that God makes such sport of us that we cannot trust his Word? Why is it that we, who confess and declare ourselves to be God's people, are allowed to suffer such misfortunes?' Each one of us should think carefully about such an attitude and resist it as strongly as possible. It is tragic to behold how cold we are in our faith and how heedless we are. This is true not only of the prominent members of society in general, but in particular of those in power. The very men who should be upholding order remain silent about the iniquities committed by the wicked, either because their indifference to these crimes is as cold as ice, or because they are dozing off and turning a blind eye to what is going on every day, so that they will not have to take things in hand and do something about the situation. All this makes it only too clear that in the sight of God we are all guilty, from the smallest to the greatest of us, and that when God chastises his own people, he is giving them no more and no less than their due. In the light of this, then, we may anticipate the evil, as I have already indicated. If we see that the wicked are getting out of hand, let us try to lead them away from their bad way of life by our example. When we see that evil is beginning to triumph and that we can do nothing to stop it, let us submit ourselves to God, and await the correction which we know we must expect, preparing ourselves in patience; and at all costs let us not lose our trust in him, given the certainty with which we have been assured that he will turn evil to good, and that out of our afflictions only good effects will proceed; for in the midst of these afflictions he never ceases to work for and to advance the cause of our salvation ... .

How sad it is that nowadays there is among us more unbelief and impiety than has ever been seen before, and that this is so plain to be observed. In truth the Lord makes his Grace available to us in as much abundance as one could ask, but we trample it underfoot. We have such malicious impiety in us that it looks as though we have decided deliberately and on purpose to despise God. Everywhere around, there is nothing to be seen but blasphemies, scandals and ruin; the world is so disorderly that the impiety I can see in Geneva today is of such enormity that it is like seeing down a chasm into the very mouth of hell. Certainly, there are many people who fancy the name of Christian, and who put up some sort of a fine show, but when one sounds them out one sees that it is merely hypocrisy, and that it is all a sham. I don't know whether one would find as many as one in twenty truly resolved and assured that it is indeed God who is speaking to us. Certainly, it is true that in the past they were stupid, intoxicated with their foolish superstitions and with their mass, but now they are even more so, for the Word of God should be like a sharp two-edged blade penetrating right to the heart, and pricking into wakefulness those who slumber in unawareness of their own vices. But just the opposite has happened: once more they have frozen up in such a way that you would think they had never even heard of the Word of God. It is noticeable, also, that they are all out for themselves; fair play and straight dealing are nowhere to be found. It is tragic to see how disorderly everything has become; sexual irregularity is regarded with such easy-going tolerance that you would think there was nothing wrong with it at all; and even those people who should be restoring order, who should be chastising such behaviour and penalising such offences are perfectly happy to tolerate them in their vicinity, so that the grubbiness of it all rubs off on to them as well. In the same way they readily pass edicts forbidding the singing of obscene songs, but then they allow it to be asserted that disgusting and disreputable songs about illicit love do not fall into this category, and can therefore quite licitly be sung. See how these people want to make adultery respectable. If that's what pleases them, let them have it, but don't let them bring their dirty rubbish in here, carrying their infection into the Church of God, let them get on with their business in their dens and caves, not that they would care where they were, brazen prostitutes as they are. By 'prostitutes', I mean all those – the men as well as the women – who mock in this way the name of God. Because by that act they show clearly that there was never anything in them except hypocrisy, especially when they show such derision and hatred towards the Word of God, and towards all sermons and prophetic words of warning.

Source: Jean Calvin. Sermons sur le livre de Michée, ed. J.D. Benoît (Supplementa Calviniana [C2], 5, Neukirchen, 1964), v. 63-4, 151, 163.

5 Calvin's prayer before work.

Our dear God, Father and Saviour, since it has pleased thee to command us to work in order to supply our needs, so bless our labour by thy grace that we ourselves are covered by thy benediction, without which nothing goes well or can prosper; and grant us this favour as testimony of thy good-will and assistance, so that we may recognise the paternal care in which you hold us.

And, Lord, may it please thee to assist us with thy Holy Spirit so that we may faithfully exercise our estate and calling without any fraud or deception, and so that we shall have regard more to follow thy ordinances than to satisfy our appetite to make ourselves rich; that if nonetheless it pleaseth thee to make our labour prosper, that thou wilt give us also the courage to support those who are indigent, according to the ability that thou hast given us, reining us in in all humility so that we shall not in any way raise ourselves higher than those who have not received so great an outpouring of thy liberality.

If it is thy wish to subject us to greater poverty or need than our flesh would desire, may it please thee to give us grace to have faith in thy promises, so that we fall not into mistrust, but may rest certain that in thy goodness thou wilt always provide for us. May we wait patiently in the expectation that thou wilt furnish us not only with thy temporal graces but with thy spiritual ones, so that we will always have occasion to render thanks unto thee and to rest with entire assurance in thy pure goodness. Hear us, Father of all mercy, through Jesus Christ thy son Our Lord. Amen.

From the Geneva Catechism (edition of 1562).

Source: Calvini Opera [C1], vi. col. 137, n. 3.

6 Converts and immigrants. Extracts from Florimond de Raemond

Large numbers of people from all over the place flocked to Geneva to see Calvin, just as in antiquity people used to flock to Corinth to see the no less notorious and celebrated Laïs. Many entire families went into voluntary exile from France in order to go and live in that dead-end of Savoy where he was to be found, in a town which they liked to call 'Hieropolis', the Holy City. This is what Etienne le Roy calls it in his little *Book of Martyrs*.

The first to fall easy victims were, especially, painters, clock-makers, draughtsmen, jewellers, booksellers, printers - all those whose crafts demand a certain degree of superior discernment. For just as the whitest of fabrics stains most readily, dark colour taking more of a hold there, and showing up more clearly, so fancy ideas catch on more readily in minds which are already alert and lively than in those which are coarser and more sluggish. Craftsmen of this kind, behaving as they do as if they were a law unto themselves just as the products of their trades are uncontrolled, making their own decisions, mixing their own colours, keeping their own half-crazy records, muddle up their heads with many fantasies and grotesque ideas. All those genteel Poets with their cultivated sensibility, those refined intellects which penetrate the secrets of the Heavens, readily joined their number. The wise Emperor Marcus Aurelius once said that the frequenters of brothels often turn out to be the most beautiful women in a population, as well as the most handsome and bold of its men, and that the bravest men become bandits, the most cunning become thieves, while those with the liveliest minds go mad. We can certainly confirm that in the early days of the birth of the Heresy, those men who had the keenest intelligence (unless they were also armed with

[35]

the shield of Faith) were the ones *par excellence* who became its lovers and its courtesans; in their efforts to sink the Church they sank themselves; they used the gifts God had given them as a maniac uses a knife, striking out indiscriminately and slashing and wounding themselves as well as those around them.

Medical men, it is said, were the first intellectuals who became reluctant to believe anything without good evidence. After they had dissected and explored all the different parts of the science of nature, without having been able to pin down the efficient cause, or the mysterious secrets of the Christian religion (which, being above nature, are by definition inaccessible to all Naturalists), they came to regard most things as matters indifferent, and the rest as impossible, because their best techniques had not been sufficient to penetrate to the heart of the matter. Suddenly waking up to the fact that their religious faith was as insecurely grounded as their science was full of doubt, they threw themselves on the mercy of the sick Heretics, rather than into the arms of the Catholics, who are healthy and sound. Just as the snail prefers to smear its trail over dung than over roses, so they make up their spiritual medicines higgledy-piggledy from any ingredients that come to hand, concocting from fragments of all kinds of other religion, a concoction which is no religion at all ... .

This story was told to me by one of the most trustworthy witnesses in Guyenne: One day when he was a student, he and some friends of his were strolling about under the arcades of the Schools in Toulouse, when all of a sudden the Holy Ghost descended upon them. It was not in the form of a dove, or of tongues of flame, but was a new and invisible spirit which kept the name of Calvin and of Geneva humming and singing perpetually in their ears. 'I don't know whether it was a white spirit or a black one, like Zwingli's,' he told me, 'but whatever it was, it affected five or six students simultaneously.' All of them were carried away by the same emotion, they abandoned their studies, packed their bags and set off for Geneva, travelling day and night. Their longing to see the holy man lent wings to their feet. From what my informant told me, the gratification they experienced on seeing the sacrosanct city-walls of Geneva was hardly less than the joy of that devout and pious knight Godfrey de Bouillon when his eyes beheld the long-desired walls of Jerusalem.

On their arrival, hearing that the 'exhortation' (as preaching was called there) was in progress, they made their way all out of breath to see Calvin in the pulpit. They were surprised how unattractive and disagreeable he seemed. However, at the end of the service they followed him to his house, and introduced themselves to him. There was a crowd of people pressing about him. Calvin said to them, 'My brothers, it is one of the wonders wrought by the Lord, that he has called you to labour in his vineyard.'

After my informant (and some of the others) had stayed in Geneva for three or four months, and when he had hardly grasped even the first rudiments of Theology, Calvin awarded him the designation of Minister: but although this young man was of a fine intelligence and well-educated in good letters, he felt that he was incapable of fulfilling this charge, and excused himself from taking it on; but Calvin reminded him that the Apostles, ignorant men, had been chosen to confound the knowledge of the world, and pressed him to obey. Théodore de Bèze, Calvin's creature, who will appear in several of the scenes of this Tragedy, was present when he made this refusal, and added his own persuasions, saying that Titus and Amos had taught in the Church when they were much younger than he. 'My brother,' he said - taking a tag from Virgil as if it was a text from Holy Scripture - 'If the Fates call you, grasp it with your hand, for everything will follow easily thereafter.'

At last he was beaten: Calvin held out his hand to him as a sign of association, he became a Minister, although he was still wet behind the ears, and within a few days they had packed him off to Lorraine, having designated him Founder of a Church there. Unfortunately, however, this young hopeful created a scandal in the Church of the Lord. He seduced (or, in fact was seduced by) the daughter of the gentleman in whose house he lodged, or so he tells me. Before he left Geneva Calvin had made him drop his family name and take the pseudonym 'Villeroche', but he got rid of this as soon as he deserted Calvinism. He died a Catholic. In my *History of the Heresy of this Century* I have quite often relied upon his testimony in my account of various secret matters and other particulars about this wretched schism, because he was an active man of business, prominent and engaged, just at the time that the newly-named Huguenotage was coming into being in France.

... A gentleman of Languedoc, called the Sieur de Clairé, returning from his garrison, when the territory of Piedmont was given back to the Duke of Savoy, took it into his head that he would like to see Geneva. He went there accompanied by a lord from Saintonge and a certain gentleman from Guyenne called the Sieur de Laval, who is still alive, all of them impelled thither by the same curiosity.

On their arrival in Geneva, they went to hear Calvin, Catholics though they all were. The Sieur de Clairé, letting his eye run over the troop of women sitting close to the pulpit, suddenly spotted his own wife. He was astonished; was he dreaming? Did his eyes deceive him? But the more he looked the more he became certain that it was indeed his wife, and his daughter, who must have fled here from their home. He contained his impatience until the end of the sermon, and when the whole troop got up he made his way through it towards his wife. When she saw him coming she shrieked, and ran after Calvin, who was just going out of the church, crying, 'Oh sir, save me!' Calvin stopped, saw this gentleman, who by this time had got his daughter by the hand, and asked what was going on. 'It is Monsieur my Papist husband,' she said, 'who has come to get me. Oh, my God, help me!' Calvin, seeing the crowd which had gathered and which was pressing round wanting to see the outcome of this farce, drew the gentleman, his wife and daughter aside, and took them to his house to hear what they had to say. But the gentleman was not allowed to speak to his wife without permission. Later the same day Calvin heard them all, and the next day the matter was remitted to the Consistory. He claimed the right to take back his wife and daughter, but they pressed him to follow her example, and to embrace the Gospel. They urged that he should leave everything for love of Christ. He was privately advised that since he would get nothing more out of them, and since there might be worse to fear, he had better make his escape secretly and without delay. This he did, leaving his wife and daughter at Calvin's mercy, where they both remained ever afterwards.

Source: Florimond de Raemond, *Histoire* [F8], livre VII, chap. XIX, section 4, pp. 1393-7; livre VIII, chap.xiii, section 6, p. 1534.

7 International activity. Calvin to Bullinger, 28 April 1554

Your last letter was delivered to me by our brother, Thomas Lever. I chanced to be away from home at that moment, so that he could not avail himself of my services in procuring a comfortable lodging. Nevertheless things turned out well in my absence, for the Lord directed them to a better host than any that we could at random have selected. He indeed and his companion loudly proclaimed that they have been provided for to their hearts' content. And certainly, such is their merit, that all good men should strive to assist them with advice, and console them with sympathy during their exile. One of them will shortly set out for Strasburg on private business, but with the intention of returning shortly to us; Thomas will remain quietly here, as he has found that this repose contributes to afford him a little relief from his distress.

In my little treatise, I have been under a constant apprehension lest my brevity should occasion some obscurity. This, however, I have not been able to guard against, nay with deliberate intention and induced by other reasons, I have not even sought to guard against it. For what I had not only principally but I may say singly proposed to myself, was to make manifest the detestable impiety of Servetus. But an eloquent treatise on the matters in question would have seemed a feat of cunning, and by the pomp of its style, not well suited to refute tenets so impious. In my style, I do not perceive that stateliness which you speak of; on the contrary, I made it my constant endeavour, so far as it was possible, to give, even to the unlettered reader, a clear notion of the perplexing sophisms of Servetus, without any troublesome deduction or laboured explication. However, it does not escape me that though I am concise in all my writings, in this one I have been more than usually succinct. But let it only appear that with sincere faith and upright zeal, I have been the advocate of sound doctrine, and this single consideration will have more weight with me than that I should repent of the work I have undertaken. You yourself, from your affection towards me, and the natural candour and equity of your temper, judge with indulgence. Others animadvert on me with greater harshness, even that I am a master of cruelty and atrocity – that I now mangle with my pen the dead man who perished by my hands. There are also some not malevolently disposed, who could wish that I had never touched on the question of the punishment of heretics. For they say that all the others, in order to avoid odium, have expressly held their tongues. But it is well that I have you for the partner of my fault, if fault indeed there is, since you were my prompter and exhorter. Look then that you get yourself ready for the contest. You have been informed in one of my letters, that your book on justifying grace was received by me some time ago. Moreover, that labour which I trust will be useful to the Church, cannot but be grateful to me. I wish that the aptness of your readers may correspond to your diligence. Your preface reminded me that I ought to think of what was to be done by us, of which I had previously written to you. For though anything more foolish than the book of the good Westphal can barely be conceived, yet because you see that the minds of the princes are corrupted by such calumnies, of which we have one sad example in the recent conduct of the King of Denmark, it seems to be our duty to obviate such an occurrence, by all the lawful means in our power.[1] Besides a refutation coming from the pen of any private individual would carry with it less weight. On the other hand I see how difficult it will be to obtain the assent of all the churches. Do you then reflect in your wisdom, if any method of which we should not have to repent can be found.

Most willingly I looked over the answer which you gave to the Scotsman. He had talked over these matters with me before he came among you.[2] As I had freely exposed to him in familiar conversation my opinion, he did not press the subject any further, and not even after his return did he ask me to communicate to him my ideas in writing. The substance of what I had expressed orally, moreover, tallied with what you had written. For respecting hereditary succession in monarchies I had taken nearly the same view as yourself. On the second head, whether it is lawful for us to uphold the Gospel by force of arms, there was not the least discrepancy between our ideas. About the government of women I expressed myself thus: since it is utterly at variance with the legitimate order of nature, it ought to be counted among the judgements with which God visits us; and even in this matter, his extraordinary grace is sometimes very conspicuous, because to reproach men for their sluggishness he raises up women endowed not only with a manly but a heroic spirit, as in the case of Deborah we have an illustrious example. But though a government of this kind seems to me nothing else than a mere abuse, yet I gave it as my solemn opinion that private persons have no right to do anything but deplore it. For a gynaecocracy or female rule badly organised is like a tyranny, and is to be tolerated until God sees fit to overthrow it. If any tumult shall arise for the sake of religion, I pronounced that to me it seems the better and the safer course to remain quiet until some peculiar call for interference should clearly appear; that it is our duty rather to ask God for a spirit of moderation and prudence, to stand us in aid at the critical moment, than to agitate idle enquiries.

The state of our church still continues to be wavering, but I am obliged to break off, because since the time that I found fitting messengers to whom I might venture to entrust my letter, I have been prevented by the pressure of other business from continuing it, as I should have wished, any further. Farewell then, most accomplished

[1] A reference to the expulsion from Lutheran Denmark of the refugee London stranger church, the incident which prompted Calvin to take up the cudgels against Westphal in the second Sacramentarian controversy.

[2] John Knox. Calvin's comments to Bullinger are significant, given his later protestations to an outraged Elizabeth of England of his innocence of any involvement in Knox's publication in Geneva of his notorious tract *Against the Monstrous Regiment of Women*.

sir, and to me highly esteemed brother in the Lord. Do not fail to salute in my name M. Gualter, Pellican, and the other pastors. In their turn my colleagues, the Marquis of Vico, and many other friends salute you. May the Lord continually protect and bless you and your family.

Source: Calvini Opera [C1], xv. 123-6 (no. 1947); *Letters of Calvin* [C6], iii. 35-8 (no. 348), lightly modernised.

8 Victory over internal opponents. Calvin to Bullinger, 15 June 1555

With the request contained in your last letter that I should give you a distinct and detailed account of our recent riot, I comply the more willingly, because it is very much our own interest that the affair should be put in a proper light among you and your neighbours. For it is perfectly well known that unfavourable reports are spread about concerning us, and that too by the the artifices of those who for their own advantage wish to render us everywhere an object of detestation. You will therefore do us a very acceptable service, if you will take the trouble to have read over to your illustrious senate the substance of what I am about to write to you. Besides, if it is not taxing your patience too much, I should wish a part of my letter to be copied and sent to our brethren the ministers of Schaffhausen, that they too may acquit our city of the defamatory charges brought against it. Here is an exact statement of the whole affair. There were in the senate two unprincipled men and audacious to the highest pitch of impudence, both also in the most abject poverty. The one was named Perrin, the other Vandel. The former being Captain of the city, had attached to his person a rabble of profligate fellows, by holding out to them the prospect of impunity for their crimes. For whatever knavish, riotous or dissolute act was committed throughout the city, to screen the offender from the punishment of the laws, he was ever ready to undertake his defence. The other was his trusty abetter in all these enterprises. A part of the senate, whom they gained in their flatteries, was at their disposal. They forced, through their fears, certain mean creatures to obsequiousness – creatures who were unable to maintain their rank, if not countenanced by these men. Their kinsmen bound to them by the tie of relationship chimed in with them. By all these means their power had been so firmly established in the lesser council, that scarcely anyone dared resist their humour. Certainly all judicial proceedings had for several years been directed at their pleasure, and this sale of justice was a secret to nobody. Not only the city saw this, but even among our neighbours and foreigners, through their fault, we were very ill-spoken of. And loud were the complaints of a great many, because they were frequently molested by the most atrocious acts of villainy ... . And when formerly if the lesser council had committed any fault, the Two Hundred were accustomed to afford some remedy for its errors and defects, now they have obtruded on the latter body many of the dregs of the population, partly noisy and turbulent young men, partly individuals of flagitious and disssolute lives. And lest they should fail in having a majority, without paying any attention to the established numbers, they have thrust into the crowd whosoever they think will be the most fit for their purposes. In a word, their license was so disorderly, that certain broke forcibly into the council who were not even elected by themselves. That was the faction which, seeing the judgement of the Church alone opposed a barrier to them and checked the unlimited impunity granted to all kinds of vice, in order that every vestige of discipline should disappear, stirred up a contest with us about the right of excommunication, nor ceased to turn everything upside down, until after much contention we obtained that they should at least consult the churches of Switzerland. But as your answer defeated the hopes and wishes of those profligate men, we afterwards enjoyed a little more tranquillity; not however, that after that time, ever on the watch for an opportunity, and shaking off all sense of shame, they did not attempt to break through every restraint. Moreover, tired of being kept in continual agitation, at length we plucked up courage to attack them in our turn, and so force them to take some decisive step. And here in a wonderful manner God disappointed their expectations. For in that promiscuous rabble, we gained the majority of votes.

Soon after followed the elections for the syndics in which an unexpected revolution showed itself. Here indeed these depraved men began to vent their fury openly, because they saw themselves forcibly reduced to order. They began then insolently to attempt many things in order to undermine the existing order. Our party always held it sufficient to quash, without any disturbance, or at least to impair their attempts. But because it was perfectly evident that they were gaping after innovations, the council resolved to oppose an excellent remedy to their license. Of the French sojourners who have long lived here, and whose probity was well known, some were adopted into the rank of citizens, to the number of fifty perhaps. The worthless felt how much more secure the party of the good would be rendered by this succour. They therefore thought that they should leave no stone unturned in order to defeat this design. The affair was discussed among them everywhere in the cross-ways, about the taverns, and clandestinely in private houses. When they had drawn over certain persons to their project, they began to make head against us, not only with murmurings but open threats. The prefect of the city was suborned who, accompanied by a numerous but vile and disreputable crew, going up to the town house, signified to the council the danger of its persisting in its scheme ... . The council replied with dignity that they were introducing no new precedents, but such as had been sanctioned by the immemorial practice of the city; that it was shameful indeed that now both an ancient usage of the city should be abrogated, and those expelled from the rank of citizens who had been so long and so honourably settled in the city ... . The prefect was sharply reprimanded for having lent his aid to insolent men, in so unjust a cause. At the same time, a decree was voted for convoking the Two Hundred, and when the affair was carried before them, the decision of the lesser council was ratified, and permission granted them, that henceforth at their good pleasure they might select from the French sojourners those on whom they wished to confer the rights of citizenship.

But before the Two Hundred had passed this last decree, the fury of those suddenly broke out more violently, who as is generally the case in desperate situations, had determined to hazard the most perilous extremities. For from a nocturnal riot the state was brought almost to the brink of ruin. The day preceding this event, a dinner scot-free had been given to a number of scoundrels. The ringleaders feasted elsewhere, of whom one whom I have named Vandel took on himself the expenses of the dinner, Perrin those of the supper ... . Now it is the custom, when the sentries for the night have been stationed at the gates, for the captain of the watch to go his rounds and inspect the posts. This duty each of the senators takes in his turn. When the sentries of that night are posted in the middle of the city, they hear a shout at no great distance. For in the quarter situated behind the booths of the market-place, an individual hit by a stone cried out that he was killed. The guards in the discharge of their functions run up to him. Against them rush out two brothers, boon companions of Perrin and Vandel, men indeed of the lowest class, confectioners by trade, but who supped gratis at the same table ... . One of those brothers with drawn sword rushes against the syndic. The syndic, relying on the badge of his authority, lays hands upon him, that he may be led away to prison. Several of the faction fly to the aid of their confederate. The lights are put out in the scuffle, and they declare that they will not suffer an excellent comrade to be dragged to prison. Immediately Perrin presents himself, and at first, feigning a desire for pacification, wrenches away the syndic's rod, whispering in his ear, 'It is mine, not yours.' The syndic, though a man of diminutive stature, was not however inclined to yield it, and struggled manfully and stoutly against this violence. In the meantime a cry was everywhere raised along the streets and spread about almost in a moment, that the Frenchmen were in arms, and the city betrayed by treachery; the house of the senator who was captain of the watch that night was crowded with armed men. Emissaries shouted out tumultuously for those whom they knew to be favourable to their party. Perrin, when he was fully persuaded that his band was sufficiently strong, began to vociferate, 'we are in possession of the syndic's rod, for it is in my hands'. To this cry no mark of approbation was returned, and nevertheless he was surrounded by conspirators, so that it was very evident that they were held back by some mysterious suggestion from God. Then troubled by shame and at the same time terrified, he gave ground a little. But falling in with the other syndic, a relation of his, he wrested from him by force and with great violence his rod of office. The latter called out for help - that his person was assaulted, that the rights of the city were violated. But as the profligate party was much superior in force of arms, on the complaint of the syndic, no one moved a foot to come to his aid. But again a kind of religious scruple held back some of the very worst from chiming in with Perrin. Thus compelled by fear, he privately gave back the rod of office.

There was now in arms a numerous body of villains. One cry was heard everywhere: the Frenchmen must be massacred, the city has been betrayed by them. But the Lord in a wonderful manner, watching over his wretched exiles, partly threw them into so deep a sleep that, during these horrid outcries, they were tranquilly reposing in their beds; partly strengthened their hearts so that they were not dismayed by the threats nor fear of danger. What is certain none of them stirred out of the house. And by this signal miraculous interference of God, the rage of the ungodly was defeated because no one presented himself to the conflict. For they had resolved, as was afterwards discovered, if any should essay to defend themselves, after having dispatched a few, they should fall on the others, as if the sedition had originated with us. Nor were the sojourners alone threatened, but some cried out that their protectors should be put to death, and punishment inflicted on the senate ... .

Nevertheless, contrary to our expectations, through divine interposition this tempest gradually blew over. Two days after, it was decreed that an enquiry should be set on foot respecting this public outrage. The council having spent three days in summoning witnesses, that no one might say that he was crushed under false pretences, call together the Two Hundred. While the evidence is being taken, among the other judges were seated even those who had conspired. According as any of these appeared chargeable with guilt, or violently suspected of doubtful conduct, they were ordered to leave the court, as it was impossible they could be sufficiently impartial to pronounce a proper sentence. But Perrin, seeing his crime detected made his escape with three others... . All disturbances have been appeased since their departure. The mist which they had spread over affairs has been dissipated; the laws have recovered their vigour; tranquillity has been restored to the city.

Source: Calvini Opera [C1], xv. 676-85 (no. 1947); *Letters of Calvin* [C6], iii. 192-202 (no. 405).

(c) The Mature Calvinist regime

9 The ministry. Extract from the register of the Company of Pastors, 1559

January 1559. On 13 January it was unanimously resolved by the brethren that their Lordships be requested to write to Master Pierre Viret at Lausanne, saying that they do not want to leave him unthanked for the use God has made of him from the earliest days in planting the Gospel here; and that for this reason they would regard it as a great benefit if he would take refuge in their city, now that he is to be expelled from Lausanne. This they have now done, making the declaration in a long letter to this brother, after this was begged and requested of them.

M. Viret elected minister of this church. On the 23rd of the said month, the brethren all being assembled after prayers had been said, all with one voice elected our brother the aforesaid Master Pierre Viret to be with them a minister of the Word of God in this church.

February 1559. Death of M. Jacques Bernard. On the 3rd of February our brother Master Jacques Bernard, minister of the Word of God at Peissy, passed away at about four hours in the morning.

Death of M. du Pont. In the same month, died also our brother Master Claude du Pont at Saint Gervais, constant to the end in the faith he had preached, his death being to the great regret of all the brethren, on account of the learning and piety found in him.

March 1559. M. de Bèze confirmed as minister. On the 27th March, the day of our censures, M. Théodore de Bèze was elected minister of the Holy Gospel, to replace our late brother M. Claude du Pont.

M. Merlin elected minister. Further, on the same day Master Jehan Merlin, minister, was also elected to be in Peissy in place of our late brother master Jacques Bernard.

1559. M. Antoine Chevalier, professor of Hebrew. Further, by the same brethren and at the same time Master Antoine Chevalier was elected to be professor of Hebrew literature.

M. François Berauld, professor of Greek. Further, Master François Berauld to be public professor of Greek literature, in place of M. de Bèze.

M. Tagaut, professor of mathematics. Further, Master Jehan Tagaut, to be professor of mathematics.

M. J. Randon, first regent. Further, Master Jehan Randon to be first regent in the College.

Source: Registre de la Compagnie des Pasteurs [G2], ii. 84-86.

10 Modification to the Ordinances. Extract from the Council minutes, 1560

Tuesday 30 January 1560. Calvin and Viret, ministers, knowing that the election of the Lords Syndic takes place today, and that this is the moment for representations and petitions to be made, urge that it would be wise to choose god-fearing men in this time of great troubles: and that it should be resolved that in the matter of the said elections all should be done in accordance with the Word of God.

Next they point out that there are some people of good standing who would like those areas of ecclesiastical policing which are the concern of the Consistory to be more clearly separated from temporal jurisdiction, as they were in the time of the early Church, and as they were also in the early days after the Reformation, when there was no intention to have things as they are now, nor was it in the Edicts. If we are to conform as precisely as we can to Christianity, we must follow as closely as possible the footprints of the Word. Under such a rule, temporal jurisdiction would not be entrusted to the citizens in general but election would be made from among those who belonged to the Church, except in posts which required expertise in enquiry and in legal practice. Again, there is one matter contained in the Edicts which is not observed, namely that all the ministers should be called and consulted, whereas nowadays it is Calvin alone who is called every time, as if he himself represented all the ministers ... .

Similarly it would be good if those who are forbidden to attend the Lord's Supper, instead of being banished from the town, were compelled to make reparation in the church after they had proved rebellious, and that they should be presented in the church with the aim of getting them received back into the fold.

Item: since it is difficult to recognise all those who might profane the sacrament, it would be good idea to make some lead tokens, and on the day of the Communion everyone should come provided with a lead token for each instructed member of his household. Any foreign guest who could make satisfactory testimony as to his faith should also be admitted, but not those who could not do so.

The above-named ministers pray that the Lords Syndic will deliberate and legislate in such a way that God may be glorified and that we may be governed in all things according to his Spirit.

It was decided to ask for these representations in writing, this week if possible, so that the matter could be more fully deliberated.

Edicts for reformation of the Consistory

Thursday 1 February. Assent is here given to the proposition and request recently made by the ministers touching the reformation of the Consistory and of ecclesiastical jurisdiction.

On the first point of their request, namely that in elections to the Consistory one should have liberty to elect anyone who is a member of the Council of Two Hundred, without distinction between citizens and burgesses [*bourgeois* and *citoyens*]: for when one is endeavouring to follow the Word of God one needs freedom to choose the most suitable candidates from among the entire people.

It was decided also that such a reading also demands that the elders be selected from the entire Council of Two Hundred without distinction between citizens and burgesses, although this is not specifically contained in the Edicts.

For that matter it was also requested that it be laid down that the Lord Syndic's role in the Consistory shall be such that the temporal jurisdiction is kept quite separate from the spiritual: for the Edicts do not state that he should preside or possess any jurisdiction there; the practice should be that a Syndic who is present will not carry his staff of office, but shall merely take his place there among the other elders ... .

Sunday 4 February. After opening the meeting of the general Council of the city with a prayer to God, the Honourable Master John Calvin, minister of the Word of God and burgess of this city, made a speech of Christian exhortation and admonition concerning the election of the Lords Syndic and the Treasurer which must take place during the session of this Council: in particular he drew attention to the very present dangers, threats and troubles which beset us on all sides. In the past it had always been necessary to entrust high office only to those who had the knowledge and the capacity as well as the readiness to respond to so heavy a calling; nowadays it was incumbent upon us also to think carefully and to take God as our president and governor in our elections, and to make our choice with a pure conscience without regard to anything except the honour and glory of God in the security and defence of this republic: he also adduced the example of the boy-king Jehosaphat who reminded the judges of Judaea that they must take account of themselves, for in presiding over justice they sat in the place of God.

Source: Calvini Opera [C1], xxi. 726-7.

11 Common offences dealt with by the consistory

The matters and cases which come most commonly before the consistories are cases of idolatry and other kinds of superstition, disrespect towards God, heresy, defiance of father and mother, or of the magistrate, sedition, mutiny, assault, adultery, fornication, larceny, avarice, abduction, rape, fraud, perjury, false witness, tavern-going, gambling, disorderly feasting, dancing and other scandalous vices: and because the magistrate usually does not favour such gatherings, the consistory will use the ordinary reprimands, namely, brotherly admonition, as sharp and as vehement as the case demands, suspension from the Lord's Supper, deprivation of the Lord's Supper for a stated period of time; and persistent offenders shall be publicly named, so that people will know who they are.

Source: [Pierre Viret], La Forme de dresser un Consistoire; Arnaud, Documents protestants inédits [F6], pp. 72-8.

12 Managing a country parish. A country pastor's advice to his successor

I must not forget, at the beginning of this memoir, to beg all those who read it, and especially those of my brethren who succeed me in this charge, to take it all in good part, to regard what I have to say with tolerance ... and to adopt (at their discretion), anything in it which may help in the edification of the flock ... . I would not wish it to be thought that I want to constrain anyone to follow my judgement, which is not founded on as much experience as I would have liked. Each person has to make out as best he can, and this is as it should be, provided that no innovations or changes are introduced without good reason. For my part, I learned a lot from my predecessors ... indeed I am indebted to them for most of what follows here. ... Charles Perrot.[1]

Concerning the order of the Sermon

Every Sunday morning between the September celebration of the Lord's Supper and Easter, the Minister enters the temple as soon as the tolling of the church bell has stopped, which will probably be at about eight o'clock. He waits for a little while until the people have finished arriving, especially those who can help with the singing. If there is a wedding or a christening, the custom is that the master and mistress of every family must be present, together with their servants and those of their children who take communion. In practice one is often obliged to let them off, provided that they do not miss the catechising which comes afterwards; one has also to let off nursing mothers, provided they do not turn this into a prescriptive right, and provided that they at least make an effort to come to the catechism class.

At the sermon the following psalms are sung: 1, 3, 15, 24, 42, 119, Aleph et Beth, 129, 130, 128, and sometimes the Ten Commandments. Each psalm is divided into two halves, one for the beginning and one for the end of the service. At the Lord's Supper the whole of Psalm 23 is sung at the beginning, and the whole of Simeon's canticle[2] at the end, before the closing prayers and the Grace. In the prayers, we never

---

[1] Charles Perrot, a French immigrant to Geneva, was a prominent member of the Geneva Company of Pastors for more than fifty years; when he wrote the above memoir he was still a young man and had just finished serving his ministerial apprenticeship as pastor to three rural parishes under the control of the Geneva Church. In later years Perrot taught theology in the Geneva Academy.

[2] The Nunc Dimittis.

[49]

use the paraphrase of the Lord's Prayer.

I decided that I would not sing at those services where there wasn't another man present to help in the singing, but I did sing with another man even if there were no women or girls to join in. Some people know the psalms very imperfectly, or can just about repeat after the others, which usually means only Pierre Chapusi, Godmar, Jeanne from Monet's house, the Defosses woman and the Gervaise woman's daughter, together with anyone who happens to have come over from Geneva. It was my practice to time the service to last until the last grain of sand had trickled into the bottom of the hour-glass, but then to bring it to an end as rapidly as I could, because people watched out for this, and were irritated if it was done otherwise.

What one should do on Sundays after the service

1. After the service the minister remains behind a little with the two elders to make a note of any absences, sick people to visit, or scandalous ones to call to account. Those who have failed to attend the Sermon, or who have committed some other fault, are then called upon and warned by the Minister in the presence of the elders in a manner appropriate to the particular case and to the persons involved. If you think it will be good for the offender, you may refer the matter to the Consistory in Geneva, which will then summon the offender to appear there. Also, if there is a really clear allegation of blasphemy, drunkenness, adultery, and if the charge, as far as you can judge, is well-founded and the offence proven, you should refer it to the Consistory in the city, because it is there that the safeguard on the Lord's Supper is upheld, not in the village. It is also the duty of the minister to seek out those who have already been forbidden to attend the Supper to take heed of their position, and to predispose them to go back to the said Consistory to apply for reinstatement. It is not permissible for the minister to take it upon himself to readmit them, as I have discovered by personal experience.[3] If there was any quarrel

[3] As Perrot indicates, a country pastor did enjoy a certain amount of discretion about disciplinary matters. This did not rule out the possibility, however, that he might from time to time be sharply called to order. Rural ministers were expected to ride into Geneva as often as they could to attend the regular meetings of the Venerable Company of Pastors, and were by no means exempt from the watchfulness and 'fraternal correction' practised by that body. As this extract reveals, the Geneva consistory jealously guarded its right to debar 'scandalous' individuals from outlying areas as well as from town parishes from attending communion.

or bad feeling which those involved were willing to make up in front of the minister, I used not to send the matter to the city, provided the matter was entirely clear and no great harm had been done.

Preaching services during the week

At the end of a catechism class, people can be called to respond, and also at sermons preached on weekdays. My practice was to preach on Thursdays, at least from the first Thursday in October to the last Thursday in March, or thereabouts. For the people simply have to work in the fields most of the time. Such sermons (prayers included) should not run beyond the hour-glass, if at all possible. They should be attended at the very least by one leading member of each household in the village of Moin, that is to say by the husband or the wife.

When I had some announcement to make to the parishioners I used to make it at the end of the prayers, in order to catch the masters of households, because after the Benediction they made their escape so quickly. I could not abide the way they hung around in the graveyard after the service making a noise, but since this was the time they chose for settling their business deals, I kept quiet about it, at least when they behaved decorously enough.

I would advise the minister not to take his text from those parts of the Scriptures which are difficult to understand out of context because they are all connected with other passages, as is the case with the Epistles of St Paul, for the people here rarely carry over anything they have learned from one sermon to the next; I think they profit more from the catechising.

Concerning the order to be observed in catechising

I used to run these classes for about one hour and a half after the Sermon. I used to set about it, every Sunday, by singing through the Ten Commandments with the men, and the women or girls, one table of the law at the beginning and the other at the end. Except during the extreme cold of winter I used to take each of the two tables separately, concluding with a brief general confession and a prayer .... Afterwards I would read out the Creed, and the Lord's Prayer, but I have never yet entered into any teaching on the sacraments with the people here. What is more, I used to explain everything in as brief and simple a way as I could, over three or four consecutive Sundays, for

[51]

there are questions and doctrines in the catechism which one cannot readily teach people, for fear of confusing them. This being so, in order to do as little harm as possible, my practice used to be to take each article word-for-word as it is in the catechism, paraphrase the content in a couple of lines at most, and then to get all the boys and girls, the menservants and the maidservants, one after another, to recite it twice, out loud. It was above all the children and the servants who were supposed to attend the catechising. After I had asked them to do this, we came to the final prayer, and those children at whom I pointed had to recite 'Our Father...' or 'I believe...' or 'Hear, O Israel ...' just as it is done in Geneva. I made sure that they got it more or less right, allowing them to get away with a good deal of inaccuracy provided that the substance was not corrupted - but one had to watch out. After that we sang the Commandments, either the whole lot, or (if we had sung the first table earlier) the second table only, and finished with the Blessing, just as they do at the weekday services in the city. In summer, when the catechising was done after dinner, I used to take the little children, at the bottom end of the church, or sitting outside it in the open air and try to get them to say nicely the words of 'Our Father ...' and 'I believe ...' and to teach them something about the commandments.

Concerning the interrogations which should take place before Easter Communion

During the four or five Sundays before Easter I used to announce that everyone should turn up at the temple at the catechism hour, and that instead of holding a catechism class I would question people individually, asking them to think carefully about the state of their faith, without using any set form of words of prayer, although occasionally I would use a short prayer when they came in and when they left. I used to call them together in this place and at the catechism hour because in the village of Moin it proved impossible conveniently to get them to assemble, house by house, during the week. In Magny however I was able to get people together once or twice, on a weekday, in the house of Tombeti the tailor. I used to begin by getting the one or more individuals from the row of men to recite the Lord's Prayer, the Creed or the Commandments, choosing especially those who seemed the most likely to be ignorant. And I would counsel all those who did not have too poor a memory to learn the Commandments by heart, and I would try to help them to do so before they came to the Lord's Supper. At the very least I would try to get them to recite the Summary, and I used to give some of them a bit of a fright, in order to gain at least something. The women came next, after the men. And if the whole session lasted an hour and a half, that was enough for one occasion, for there was still to come the catechism class which the interrogations had displaced, and which could not last more than another three-quarters of an hour. As for the form of the interrogation, I used to follow rather freely the one in the catechism, or indeed to use a form of questioning I had worked out specially. Those who answered reasonably well were received at Communion, and those who genuinely had good intentions were tolerated also. Those to whom all of this meant nothing at all were warned that they must not present themselves in so ignorant a state. However, the minister should not refuse to admit to Communion anyone who presents himself, except those he has earlier decided to report to the Consistory in the city.

It is also to be noted that in order to get people to answer properly (in the interrogations) you have to put the questions to them several times over, and also to take care not to vary the wording from one year to the next, if you can. It is the duty of the elders to get the people assembled.

Baptisms

At baptisms I used to see that the father and the godfather were both standing side by side and that these two (and only these two) were involved when it came to making the promise to do their Christian duty. Because from time to time the women will push in if you don't watch out. I always refused to confer names which were too outlandish, and sometimes instead of 'Vincende', for example, I would say 'Suzanne', using liberty for the sake of edification.[4] I wrote the godfather's name down, and I recorded the day of the baptism. I did not readily agree to the postponement of baptism on the pretext that godparents were being sought, and I used to warn that there was danger in thus undervaluing the role of the parents. When they invited me to the christening party, I used sometimes to go, out of friendliness, or for some other good reason, but usually I did not attend.

[4] This practice of discouraging the use of certain Christian names was also followed by the Genevan ministers, and caused considerable controversy. Particularly unpopular was their attempt to ban the use of 'Claude' because of its idolatrous association with the local patron saint.

Marriages

At a wedding – and I performed only one – one must not tolerate the appearance of a bride with an insufficiently modest head-dress. The banns must be read on the three Sundays before the wedding, just before the main sermon. If the announcement concerned a wedding in another parish, I used to record in Latin as is customary: 'Proclamatum Tridominico nomine intercedente Car. Perrottus.' If it was for my parish, one of the parties being from another parish, a similar attestation, signed by the representative of the civil power, had to be provided by the minister there. If the parties had slept together before marriage, and this matter had come before the Consistory, one had to get them to acknowledge this before one married them, or one wrote a litle note to this effect on the copy of the banns one sent to the minister of the other parish to alert him to the fact that he had to secure this admission from them, so that no one should remain under the shadow of scandal or be encouraged to act as they had done.

Visitation of the sick

When I visited the sick, I used either to cheer them up with exhortation or to offer them consolation, whichever I judged to be the more appropriate in the light of their condition, and then I would pray, and try to get them to pray also, and to make them (in true repentance and faith) embrace the remission of their sins in the death and passion of our Lord Jesus Christ. I would question them on a number of points, as far as their condition permitted, and I would exhort them that if by chance any rancour or ill-feeling existed between themselves and anyone else, they should put it aside in a spirit of reconciliation.

Do not wait to be summoned to the bedside, especially in Genthod or in Malagny. And be sure to mention the sick in your prayers during church services, as they do in Geneva.

Catechism class at Genthod

When I took the catechism class at Genthod, I would come down from the pulpit, the little children all being there, and I would sit down on a bench and start to get each of them to recite in turn 'Our help cometh from the Lord who has made heaven and earth ...' and then I would teach them how to pray. All the little ones would recite 'Our Father' – one should correct their pronunciation. Then in the same way I would ask those who knew it to recite the Creed, or the Ten Commandments. Once that was done, I would go on to explain to them what the Lord's Prayer and the Creed and the Commandments were all about, but I would do so in a much simpler and more straightforward way than at Moin. But just as in Moin, here too the older boys and girls were expected to be able to answer questions. So far, I have not managed to go any further than this with instruction. I have also tried to teach the older ones, a line at a time, to recite 'Lift up your hearts.' All this can go on for about half an hour or more. I used to conclude with a brief prayer.

Form of interrogation before Communion[5]

Q.What is necessary if one is to be properly prepared for coming to the Supper?
A. It is necessary to have true faith and repentance.
Q. What is repentance?
A. Repentance is renouncing our own desires so that the spirit of God can dwell in us.
Q. What is faith?
A. Faith is a firm assurance that God, for love of his son Jesus Christ, extends his grace towards us.
Q. How can we have that assurance?
A. Through the power of the Holy Spirit, in the preaching of the Gospel.
Q. What is the Gospel?
A. Good news.
Q. What does it contain?
A. The letter of the grace of God in Jesus Christ his son, of which baptism and the Lord's Supper are the two seals.
Q. What does the word 'baptism' mean?
A. Washing.

[5] Perrot's reaction to his unschooled flock was to cut down to basics the teaching offered to them and the requirements made of them. His interrogatory formulae omit much which the Geneva formulae considered indispensable: baptism, for example, is not spoken of as entry into the Christian community, nor as a renewal of life, but simply as the washing away of sin through the blood of Jesus Christ. No attempt is made by Perrot to explain the significance of the bread and the wine or to indicate what occurs during the communion rite.

C

Q. What does the word 'Supper' mean?
A. A meal.
Q. What does baptism signify to us?
A. That we are washed in the blood of Jesus Christ through the power of the Holy Spirit.
Q. What does the Supper signify to us?
A. That our souls are nourished by the body and blood of our Lord Jesus through the power of the Holy Spirit, in hope of everlasting life.

Source: Archives d'Etat de Genève, Archives Communales, *Etat Civil*, Genthod, 1. See also Louis Dufour, 'Les notes d'un pasteur de campagne,' *Etrennes religieuses* 41 (1890), pp.144-65.

Section 2
FRANCE

Calvin's works were known in France from at least the early 1540s. The *Institutes* seems to have been in circulation among French intellectuals within a short time of publication of the first French edition in 1541, and the following year the book was specifically singled out for condemnation in a proclamation against heretical works. The first comprehensive Index of forbidden books was largely made up of Genevan imprints, including no fewer than nine of Calvin's writings. That, these prohibitions notwithstanding, his works continued to be read is evident from the Edict of Châteaubriand, Henry II's persecuting edict which rationalised and systematised previous legislation against evangelicals [**document 13**]. The edict repeatedly singled out Geneva as a notorious centre of heresy, and forbade any contact with it. Calvin's remarkably accurate recitation of its terms in his letter to Bullinger [**document 14**] is a further indication of how closely he was able to keep in touch with French events.

Nevertheless it was only in the next decade that these informal groups of evangelicals, sustained by Calvin's writings, gave way to formally planted Calvinist churches. The extract from the *Histoire ecclésiastique* [**document 15**] suggests that these first churches were largely the result of local initiatives, though the church at Geneva did everything in its power to respond to insistent requests for ministers for the new congregations [**document 16**]. Inevitably, in a period of rapid growth, many of those who proposed themselves for the ministry were less than ideal; Geneva-trained men were at a premium, and many of those employed fell far short of Calvin's ideal. It was a problem that would continue to plague the French churches until well into the next decade [**document 23**]. Nevertheless by 1559 church-building had progressed sufficiently far for the French churches to attempt to develop a skeletal national organisation. The first national synod in Paris in this year was in fact attended by representatives of only eleven churches, but through its drafting of a church discipline and adoption of a common Confession of Faith it would prove an important milestone in the formation of a coherent national church [**document 17**].

The year 1559 in fact signalled the beginnings of a period of expansive growth for the movement following the unexpected death in this year of the persecuting King, Henry II. That the accession of the young Francis II would assist the further growth of heresy was not immediately apparent, since power in the first instance devolved on the young King's uncle, the fiercely orthodox Duke of Guise. But since the domination of Guise excluded other leading nobles such as Anthony of Navarre and Henry of Condé, both now flirting with Calvinism, the religious and political crises soon became closely connected. When in 1560 a group of the more impetuous opposition nobility attempted to free the King from Guise domination by an armed attack on the royal palace of Amboise, Huguenot nobles were heavily involved. Nor was Calvin as innocent of knowledge of the plot as he later claimed. Although Calvin continued to stress the need for obedience to the civil power in his letters to French churches, his pronouncements on the French situation laid ever greater emphasis on the legitimate rights of the Princes of the Blood (principally Anthony of Navarre) to intervene to right injustice. In the inflamed atmosphere of the time these hints were all too easily misinterpreted, as his embarrassed denials in the wake of the Conspiracy's failure bear witness [**document 18**].

The French Calvinist leadership was saved from greater disaster in the wake of this fiasco by the death of Francis II in December 1560. This second providential death – and Calvin's letter to Sturm leaves little doubt that he saw a higher power at work [**document 19**] – resulted in a new palace coup, which saw Catherine of Medici seizing power in the name of the new King Charles IX, a boy of nine. With the Guise ascendancy broken the policy of persecution was relaxed; the Huguenot congregations sensed imminent victory. The anonymous report from a Norman minister [**document 20**] catches very well the sense of excitement and sheer unpredictability which gripped the movement during these months. With churches springing up throughout France it should be little surprise that Catherine's well-meaning attempts to promote compromise between the rival confessions at the Colloquy of Poissy (1561) should have ended in failure. Despite the presence of Théodore de Bèze, the aggression and confidence of French Calvinism in this period is much more marked than the disposition to make concessions. The evidence from the provinces, as here from the commentaries of Blaise de Monluc [**document 21**], suggests that a confrontation was inevitable some months before the massacre of Vassy ignited the first conflict (April 1562).

In retrospect the end of the first war may be seen as a decisive moment for the French Calvinist movement. Although the Peace of Amboise [**document 22**] which brought an end to the fighting provided the Huguenots with apparently generous provisions for their worship, it arguably also broke the apparently unstoppable momentum of the previous two years. The Huguenot churches now entered a period of consolidation rather than growth. The fact that Condé had accepted terms which were weighted so heavily towards the nobility and gentry also had a major distorting effect on the movement. None of this was immediately clear as the churches set about consolidating their organisational structures in the wake of the first war [document 23]. The synodal acts evoke very tellingly the problems of church-building; the French churches were grateful to be able to continue to look for advice to Geneva during these years, and particularly following Calvin's death in 1564 to the increasingly authoritative figure of Théodore de Bèze [documents 23, 25]. But the French churches were very far from unquestioning obedience to Genevan precepts, as the long drawn-out controversy surrounding the writings of Jean Morély would demonstrate. Morély was a free-thinking French nobleman whose speculations on church government were anathema to de Bèze and Geneva loyalists in the French church (Morély proposed a degree of congregational involvement in both the election of ministers and church government no longer contemplated in the more hierarchical Calvinist church structure). The remorseless manner in which Morély was pursued reveals how seriously this challenge was taken, and also perhaps a measure of residual animus from the time of Morély's involvement in the Conspiracy of Amboise [documents 18, 24].

Ironically it was only the massacre of St Bartholomew's Day which finally laid this controversy to rest, by removing from the scene many of the main protagonists. In all other respects this notorious act was a calamity for the French church. De Bèze's letter to Hardenheim captures very clearly the sense of bewilderment and despair which temporarily gripped the Calvinist leadership, and prompted many French Calvinists to abandon their church faced with so clear a manifestation of God's disfavour [document 26]. Consequently the losses to the movement were much more serious than the 20,000 slaughtered in Paris and the wave of subsequent provincial massacres. That the movement survived at all was as much a consequence of the failure of the French Crown to press home its advantage as a tribute to its residual strengths. These however were considerable: in the years after 1572 the Huguenot movement was able to consolidate its hold on a solid block of territory in the south and west, where Calvinism became the dominant political creed. The price was an inevitably greater reliance on the Huguenot grandees to whom the churches increasingly looked for political leverage and and leadership. The care with which the national synod dealt with the La Rochelle church's dispute with Condé in 1578 tellingly evokes this changed balance of power [document 28]. The French Church was thus destined for minority status long before Henry IV brought the wars to an end with his edict of pacification, the Edict of Nantes (1598) [document 31]. Although the churches were sufficiently numerous and powerful to continue to command respect [document 32], both the provisions of the edict (which imposed many restrictions on the apparent freedom of worship) and the evidence of its implementation (heavily slanted towards the Catholics) [document 33] seem to foreshadow the gradual erosion which was to be the fate of French Calvinism in the succeeding century.

(a) The beginnings of French Calvinism

13 The edict of Châteaubriand, 1551

Henry, etc. One and all have seen and acknowledge the good, laudable and entire devotion to duty shown constantly during his life by the King, our most honoured lord and father (whom God absolve) as a most Christian and most Catholic prince in his endeavour to smoke out the errors and false doctrines which were swarming against our holy faith and the Christian religion, so that they would no longer find a home in this kingdom; this he did by issuing on the subject many ordinances and edicts adapted to the variety and exigencies of the times and of the incidents as they occurred. As early as the year 1534 on the 29th of January he issued a certain very express edict against those who protected and sheltered heretics and sectaries and against those who encouraged them, imposing great and grievous penalties on them ... . [Yet despite this and subsequent measures] whatever trouble our said lord and father took in the matter, whatever diligence and watchfulness he showed, employing every device open to him, the said errors continued to grow, secretly and covertly, being transformed into a universal malady, a plague so contagious that it infected and contaminated many leading cities and other places and areas of our kingdom, and a majority of the inhabitants, men and women of all ranks, even little children who had been weaned upon and forcibly fed with this poison, to our great regret and displeasure. Therefore, very shortly after our accession to the throne, being alerted to the fact that the foundation upon which was built this edifice of error and false doctrine, lay in part in books, which were printed, published and exposed for sale far too freely in our kingdom, without having first been examined, we issued an edict in December 1549 against the booksellers and printers of the said books, expressly forbidding them, on pain of loss of life and of property, to continue to print or to sell them, unless beforehand communication had been made with the Faculty of Theology of Paris, and the books had been seen and inspected by representatives of that Faculty. ... but the said delinquents and favourers of heretics abused the law as they still do all the time: and as we do not see any amendment or hope of being able to remedy the situation except by extreme care and diligence and with all the rigorous procedures which one must use in order to deal forcefully with the damaging effect and persistence of so pernicious a sect and to purge and cleanse our kingdom of it:

I. Let it be known that we, on the advice and deliberation of the members of our *Conseil privé* ... have by this our edict ... provided and declared, and in our most certain judgement, with our plenary power and by our royal authority declare, lay down and command our sovereign courts, the judges of our *présidial* courts and all those to whom, from this time forward, the duty will be referred, to undertake cognizance punishment and correction, which we commit and attribute to them, of all persons contravening the edicts and ordinances and declarations of the late King our lord and father and of ourselves, with regard to the Lutheran heresy and the other errors and false doctrines ... .

VI. By these present we have most expressly forbidden and forbid all persons, whether they are our subjects or any others to bring into our kingdom and into the territories of our obedience any books whatsoever, from Geneva and other notorious places separated from the union and obedience of the Church and of the Holy Apostolic See, on pain of confiscation of goods and of corporal punishment.

VII. In interpreting and setting in order the edict made by us at Fontainebleau in the year 1547 we have forbidden and hereby expressly forbid all printers and booksellers to print, sell, or have in their possession any prohibited books which have already been or in the future are reproved by the censure and judgement of the Faculty of Theology of Paris and which are put on the catalogue of reproved books made by the said faculty... .

VIII. Further it is also forbidden to all printers to carry on the trade and art of printing except in designated leading cities [*bonnes villes*] and in premises licensed and customarily used for the purpose, and not in secret places. And that it shall be under a master printer whose name, place of business and trademark shall appear in the books printed by him, together with the date of the said printing and the name of the author. The master printer shall be answerable for any mistakes and errors done and committed whether by himself or under his name or by his orders.

IX. And the said printers may not print any books except in their own names and in their own premises and workshops, as they are known, without assuming anyone else's name, on pain of confiscation of body and goods and of being declared to be forgers ... .

X. Similarly it is forbidden to the said printers to print or sell any books newly translated of the Old or New Testaments or any part of them and also of the doctors of the early Church unless these have first been approved by the aforesaid Faculty of Theology of Paris.

XI. It is forbidden to print or to sell any books, *scholia*, annotations, indices, epitomes, and summaries concerning the Holy Scriptures and the Christian religion written and composed during the last forty years, in Latin, Greek, Hebrew and other languages, even French, unless beforehand they have been seen and inspected, by the Faculty of Theology of Paris in the case of books printed in Paris, Lyons and other towns in the vicinity of Paris where there is no Faculty of Theology. In the case of towns where there is a Faculty of Theology the duty falls upon the doctors of that Faculty or others deputed by them.

XV. It is also forbidden to all book-dealers, printers and booksellers to open up any bales of books sent to them from outside, except in the presence of two good personages deputed by the Faculties of Theology in towns where there is a Faculty, and in the presence of the official and the judge of the *présidial* if there is such a court situated there ... .

XVII. And because our city of Lyons has many printers and ordinarily a great number of books from abroad come in there, even those greatly suspected of heresy, we order ... that three times a year there shall be a visitation of the offices and shops of the printers, book-dealers and booksellers of that town by two good personages, who shall be clergy, one appointed by the archbishop of Lyons or his vicars, the other by the Chapter of the church of the said place and with them the lieutenant of the seneschal of Lyons who may seize and put into our hand all the censured or suspect book s... .

XVIII. We forbid ... any persons whatsoever to portray or to have painted, to publish or to display on sale, to buy, to have, to hold or to keep any pictures, portraitures or figures against the honour and reverence of the Saints canonised by the Church and against ecclesiastical order and dignity, or maliciously to break, smash or deface images and portraitures which are and will be done in honour and remembrance of them.

XX. That all printers, book-dealers, merchants and sellers of books in whatever towns or places they are established, are ordered and obliged to keep a catalogue of all the books reproved by the Faculty of

Theology and to keep it in their shops stuck up in a place where it can be seen; also another catalogue of all the books they have had in their shops, these catalogues to be kept so that they can be shown to the aforesaid visitors whenever and as often as ever they are required. Anyone found to have in his shop any of the books on the lists shall be punished with whatever penalties the judges think appropriate, to serve as an example to others like themselves.

XXI. And because various offences have been committed by pedlars who under colour of selling some other sort of merchandise carry secretly books coming from Geneva and other places of ill fame, from now on it will not be permitted to the said pedlars to sell books, large or small, but if any of them carry them or expose them for sale, the books shall be seized, remitted into our hand and confiscated by us together with all other merchandise which they are carrying. In addition they shall be punished for contravention of this present article according to their quality and as the judges see fit.

XXXIII. Because assemblies and conventicles which are ordinarily held by the said heretics and sectaries are difficult to prove because of the lengths they go to in holding them with the greatest possible secrecy: it is our will command and pleasure that anyone who reveals the whereabouts of such assemblies and conventicles (even if he has been present at, taken part and consented to them) shall be and shall remain quit and absolute from any charge on that account, the present edict promising him immunity form any penalty he would otherwise be liable to from our justice … .

XXXIV. Because we have been made aware that through the fault and bad instruction given by their schoolmasters and family tutors many young children have fallen into error and heresy, as a result of the teaching they have received in these new doctrines, we ... provide that from now on no one shall be allowed to keep a school or to train children in their first letters without having first been duly approved by those to whom by right and custom the provision of suitably qualified schoolmasters belongs.

XXXVI. Because we have heard that it is now a widespread practice for all sorts of people with no knowledge or understanding of the Holy Scriptures to meddle indiscriminately therein, while they are at table, or even walking in the fields or otherwise when they are hidden away with one another in their secret conventicles, and that they speak, discuss and pronounce upon things concerning the faith, the Holy Sacrament of the altar and the constitutions of the Church, thinking up curious and fruitless questions which often lead them into great errors; to obviate this in the future we forbid all unlettered persons of any estate, quality and condition they may be, and all foreigners while they are in our kingdom, from having anything more to do from now on with such propositions, questions and disputes on the points of our faith, on the Holy Sacrament and on the constitutions and ceremonies of the Church, the holy councils and other things laid down by the Apostolic Holy See, under pain of being punished as infractors of our ordinances and prohibitions.

XXXVII. Similarly we expressly forbid all our said subjects to write, to send money or otherwise to favour those who have gone out of the kingdom to reside in Geneva or in other countries notoriously separated from the union of the Church and the obedience of the Apostolic Holy See, on pain of being declared favourers of heretics and as such disobedient persons, infractors and contravenors of the ordinances and edicts of ourselves and of the late King our father, to be punished exemplarily … .

XXXVIII. All carriers of letters coming from Geneva will be arrested and punished if it is found that the said letters are directed towards the end of diverting our subjects away from the truth and the observation of our faith and religion and into disobedience to the constitutions of the Church and will be proceeded against as true heretics and disturbers of public repose and peace.

XXXIX. It is our will and pleasure and we command … that all the goods whether movable or immovable of those who have retired to Geneva to live and reside, separating themselves from union with the Church, are declared confiscate to us. And if before they departed from our kingdom to go to Geneva they sold and alienated their said goods or portions of them, the which can be searched out and verified, these goods will be seized and taken into our hand until cognizance is taken by our judges as to whether the said sales and alienations was an act of criminal fraud, undertaken deliberately, committed in connection with their retreat to Geneva … .

Issued at Châteaubriand, 27 June, the year of grace 1551 and the fifth of our reign. Signed thus: by the King in his Council … .

Source: Haag, *La France Protestante: Pièces Justificatives* [F5], pp. 17-29 (no. 8).

14 Calvin's response to the edict. Calvin to Bullinger, 15 October 1551

My slowness in writing to you is owing to the want of messengers. For I do not care for sending a letter which may have lost its interest by being so long in reaching you. When Beza undertook to see my letter delivered to you without delay, I was unwilling to neglect a duty in which I must confess I am too remiss. I do not know how matters are moving in England. The matrimonial alliance with France does not, in my opinion, forebode so much good as many seem to think. Would, at least, that it might mitigate somewhat the fury of his father-in-law.[1] For in order to gain new modes of venting his rage against the people of God, he has been issuing atrocious edicts, by which the general prosperity of the kingdom is broken up. A right of appeal to the supreme courts has hitherto been, and still is, granted to persons guilty of poisoning, of forgery, and of robbery; yet this is denied to Christians: they are condemned by the ordinary judges to be dragged straight to the flames, without any liberty of appeal. It has been decreed that the friends of those whose lives are at stake must not dare to intercede for them, unless they wish to be charged with patronising heresy. The better to fan the flames, all informers are to receive the third part of the goods of the accused. Should any judge appear too remiss, he is liable to a penalty. The King's chancellor is to guard against admitting such to public offices, or any who may have, on any occasion, been open to the slightest suspicion. No one, besides, can hereafter occupy the place of a judge, unless he be hostile to Christ; and whoever would aspire to a public office, must furnish abundant evidence of being obsequious sons of the Church of Rome. Should anyone [gain office] by deception, a penalty attaches to those who recommend him. A penalty is imposed, besides, on all citizens who may, by their suffrages, have raised to the magistracy any individuals known to hold, or suspected of holding, the Lutheran doctrines. The Supreme Council is bound by law to compel any of their number who may seem to have a leaning to our doctrines to clear himself by oath. All are commanded, with more than usual earnestness, to adore the breaden God on bended knee. All parsons of parishes are commanded to read the Sorbonne articles every Sabbath for the benefit of the people, that a solemn abnegation of Christ may thus resound throughout the land. The goods of all who have migrated to us are to be confiscated, even though they should be sold or in any way disposed of previous to their departure, unless the authorities have been duly apprised of the sale before their departure was contemplated. Geneva is alluded to more than ten times in the edict, and

[1] This was a proposed marriage between the young King of England, Edward VI, and Elizabeth of Valois, daughter of Henry II. The treaty, agreed in July and ratified in December 1551, was never put into effect. Elizabeth would later marry Philip II.

always with a striking mark of reproach. But indeed every place of dissent from the see of Rome is referred to. This ferocity is necessary, in order that the direst confusion may follow. The flames are already kindled everywhere, and all highways are guarded lest any should seek an asylum here.

Source: *Calvini Opera* [C1], xiv. 186-8 (no. 1535). *Letters of Calvin* [C6], ii. 304-6 (no 283).

(b) The Geneva Mission and the Crisis of the French Monarchy

15 The establishment of Reformed Churches in France. Extracts from the *Histoire ecclésiastique*

1555. It would have been no surprise if Satan and his adherents had excelled themselves in cruelty, as was the case at this time in England. For he [Satan] began to be assailed and engaged in closer combat than ever before in France, where there was not yet in any part of the kingdom a properly established church; where the faithful being taught only by reading good books and as it pleased God to instruct them from time to time by particular exhortations, without their enjoying regular administration of the Word, or the sacraments, or having a properly established consistory. Rather they consoled each other as they might, assembling as opportunity presented itself for prayers, having no preachers other than the martyrs, save a small number, some of them monks, who preached less impurely than the rest. So that one might say that up to that time the Lord's field had merely been sown, and had borne fruit here and there, but that in this year the Lord's heritage began to be put wittingly in order.

The honour of this work belongs without doubt, after God, to a young man (a fact which renders this great work all the more amazing), named Jean le Maçon dit la Rivière. He was a native of Angers and the eldest son of the Sieur de Launay, the King's procurator in that place, a man of great wealth but a great enemy of those of the religion. This young man, being called by his father to the study of the law, wished before his return home to spend some time with the churches at Geneva and Lausanne. And certain of his friends, who knew his father's nature, tried to dissuade him from taking communion before his departure, fearing that he would be constrained by his father's commandment to pollute himself with the superstitions of the Roman Church. But he replied that for this reason he had all the more

[66]

need of good arms, because the combat would be greater. And, indeed, when his father suddenly realised his son's religion, he tried first to turn him by flattery and promises, holding out to him the goods which according to the custom of the land he would receive as his heir. He mentioned also the honourable estate he would soon inherit and then his marriage into some fine house, all of which would be his if he quit the so-called religion; while, on the contrary, if he persevered, not only would he lose all these benefits, he could also expect a miserable end. And this was accompanied by great lamentations, and repeating of these words: 'My son, do you want to kill me?' And truly, as La Rivière has subsequently admitted to his friends, all the measures which his father employed against him were as nothing compared to these parental tears, which he would scarcely have been able to resist without the supernatural power of the Lord, which forced the son's natural affection for his father to bend instead towards God. Having thus resisted these appeals for several days with his own humble prayer that his father might consider the truth of the doctrine to which he had been brought by the Word of God, the end was thus, that his father's love was changed, not only into hatred, but also into fury, so that he was on the point of delivering him up to justice; and he could scarcely have survived if some friends had not caused him to withdraw from there and go to Paris, in order to avoid his father's anger. But God used these means, wishing that La Rivière, who was twenty-two years old, should quit the earthly home of his carnal father, to build a spiritual home in Paris, and build there a church which has been one of the greatest and most flourishing, as will be revealed.

The occasion of the commencement of the church was by means of a gentleman of Maine, Le Sieur de la Ferrière, who had come to Paris with his family so as to be less bothered on account of his religion, and above all because his wife was pregnant and he did not wish the child that God had given him to be baptised with the superstitions and ceremonies customary in the Roman Church. After La Rivière and some others had assembled on a number of occasions at the house of this good gentleman, at the place called Le Pré aux Clercs, to pray and hear readings from Holy Scripture (as was then practised in many places in France), it happened that the lady being brought to bed, La Ferrière asked the assembly not to permit that the child that God had given him should be deprived of baptism, by which all Christian children ought to be consecrated to God, asking them to elect a minister who might perform this office. When the assembly showed some reluctance to do this, he remonstrated with them, saying that he could not in good conscience consent to the mish-mash and corruptions of the Roman baptism; also that it was impossible for him to go to Geneva for this purpose, and that if the child were to die without this mark, it would be extremely regrettable, and he would call them all before God if they would not agree to what he asked so reasonably in God's name. This then was the occasion of the first beginnings of the church in Paris, La Rivière being elected by the assembly after the fasting and prayers required in such a case, which was most scrupulously performed as it was such an innovation there. And they also established a small church order, according to what these small beginnings would allow, by establishing a consistory composed of some elders and deacons to watch over the church, all according to the example of the primitive Church of the time of the Apostles. This work must veritably have proceeded from God, especially if one considers the difficulties which might have removed any hope of being able to found a church in Paris. For besides the usual presence of the King, with all the greatest enemies of the religion ... whispering in his ear, the *chambre ardente* of the *Parlement* was like a furnace vomiting fire every day; the Sorbonne worked ceaselessly condemning books and persons; the monks and other preachers fanned the flames as much as possible; and any shop or house suspected, however slightly, was searched. The people themselves, being the most stupid in France, were enraged and hostile. Yet this notwithstanding, God gave grace to this little assembly, that they, remitting matters to God's providence, established the marks and signs of God's Church amongst them, according to the practice of the true Catholic and Apostolic Church, as the Apostles have laid down most explicitly in their sacred writings. And these small beginnings having been thus favoured by God, that with the King and his government totally preoccupied with their wars, the church in Paris was allowed, having commenced in September 1555, to grow in strength until 1557, as will be related in due course. ...

Jean le Maçon had no wish to forget his native land, which he encouraged, sometimes by letters and sometimes in person, as opportunity allowed, not without extreme danger to his person of being persecuted by his own father; so that here also a church was established, and a minister sent to them at their request by the ministers of Geneva, a learned man named Jean de Pleurs, who took the name 'D'Espoir'. And he continued his ministry very satisfactorily until the persecution which broke out in the following year, in 1556.

This same year, the plague having chased from Poitiers the most prominent enemies of the religion, the small assembly took courage and one by the name of Chrestien established an ordered church there, to the great benefit of the whole land; because soon after this church furnished ministers for many places, although it was soon after assailed by two miserable individuals, both natives of the place, one a disciple of Sebastian Castellion, the famous heretic, the other named Bienassis, a detestable apostate, who had lived a long time in Geneva but since returned to his vomit, in which he died, having defiled his own family by a detestable incest. ...

In 1556 the Lord marvellously increased his dominions by the establishment of a number of churches, amongst others at Bourges, where Simon Brossier, a man who in his time worked wonders in the Lord's work, having previously passed through frequently instructing numerous individuals, and who now established a church, causing elders and deacons to be elected. And his labour was so blessed by God that he had less than five months watching alone over this congregation, which was growing from day to day. And here one must not forget a remarkable incident. For, one day when he was with a large number of the faithful in a private house, performing his duties, a certain officer, one of the most fierce of their adversaries, having been alerted by spies, came in to the assembly and made as if to arrest the minister (for he was known throughout the town). But Brossier said, 'First listen to the prayer, then do as you wish', and upon that, after he had prayed most excellently for the conservation of the company, the sergeant was so touched that he left without saying a word. However, in order to avoid further difficulties, shortly after the church was provided with another minister, a man from the Basque country named Martin de Hargons dit de Rossehut, an excellent man experienced in preaching and in the exercise of the ecclesiastical discipline, and who, following the example of his predecessor, governed his flock with prudence and modesty ... .

The church at Tours was also established in this same year, not without great danger of being strangled at birth, as will now be related. The first to establish a church at Tours was a rich citizen of the place named La Bedoire, a man of great zeal, though presumptuous, who spared neither his goods nor his person in the cause; but who, as will shortly appear, was also the ruiner of what had been built by his effort. Simon Brossier, who has been mentioned above, also assisted at Tours, coming and going as he often did through France, never ceasing to exhort everyone to do his duty. In about 1556 one François de Beaupas dit Chasseboeuf also began to preach there, but more on the recommendation of La Bedoire alone than at the request of the whole assembly. This being recognised as a fault the faithful then, in order to prevent a schism, sent word to the ministers at Geneva, asking them to send two ministers, one a good and learned old man named Lancelot, and also a young man named Rouvière. These two arrived, and being received in the assembly began to preach, to general contentment. Except, that is, of La Bedoire and some few who had attached themselves to him, who simply stated that the newcomers were not to their liking. The division grew so great that little by little the ministers lost most of their auditors, and La Bedoire for his part brought one from Poitiers named Jacques L'Anglois, whom he made minister at Tours for him and his party. Lancelot and Rouvière did their duty and remonstrated with the schismatics, but in vain. Seeing this Lancelot, a mild and peaceable man, asked and received permission to depart, and went to Montoire, where he established a church (in this way the Lord caused good to come out of evil). Rouvière, however, remained, saying that as long as he had a flock he would continue as minister, or until he was dismissed with good cause. L'Anglois, meanwhile, seeing the opposition to his calling, did not wish to continue preaching. This moved La Bedoire to take him with him to Geneva, hoping they would take his side and reappoint him, or some other of his sort to succeed Lancelot. But the ministers of Geneva, having charged both of them with the faults they had committed against the proper order of the church, refused to take cognizance of the case, saying they had no authority over the churches of France. They sent La Bedoire away empty-handed, and retained L'Anglois at Geneva to continue his studies until he was legitimately called to the ministry. Some little time after this the congregation at Tours, or at least the better part, rallied to Rouvière, and having requested the ministers of Geneva to send them a minister, Charles Dalbiac dit du Plessis was sent to them. When he arrived and was received by the church, La Bedoire was called to the consistory, but it proved impossible to reconcile him and bring him back into the community. He was therefore excommunicated, of which he took little account and remained obstinate despite remonstrances made to him and certain afflictions that visited him and his household.

Source: Histoire ecclésiastique [F3], i, pp. 117-29.

16 Pastors from Geneva. Extracts from the register of the Company of Pastors, 1559

François de St Paul. At about that time M. François de St Paul was elected to go and preach the Gospel in Poitiers, in place of M. du Brueil.

Towards the end of May, Master Jacques Chappet was elected to go and preach the Word of God at ... [blank]

Further Master Jean Cousin for Caen.

Master Jean Voisinet for ... [blank]

Master Etienne Graignon for Surlac.

Master Bernard Seguin at Quiers.

Master Jacques Chapelli at Bergerac.

Master Elie Valtouchet.

Master Michel Mulot for Pons.

M. La Garde for Sancerre.

July 1559. On Friday 13 July the following brethren were elected to go into France to preach the holy Gospel, namely:

Master Augustin Marlorat for Paris

Master Martin to Biart

Master Gilles to Nérac

Master Jean Graignon, associate with the said Gilles.

Master Folion to Toulouse.

Master Prudhomme to Châteauroux

The pedagogue from Marin Maillet's house to Villefranche

August. For the land of Provence M. Ruffy has been elected and with him, as associate, master Jean Graignon.

For Tarascon, master Olivier.

For Valence, M. Brulé.

For Nantes, M. du Gué.

For Gien, Master Aignan the son-in-law of Perrière.

Master Jacques Vallier was elected and sent on the ... to preach the Gospel in Rouen with whoever it was that had been sent there earlier. At that time Master Jean Cousin was also sent to Caen to preach the Word of God.

Further, Master Elié to St Gilles.

Further, Master Geoffroy to Castres

Further, Master Jehan Graignon to Sommières

Further, de Rodés to ... [blank]

Further, Master Henry to ... [blank]

Pasquier to Montpellier.

The old man De Bosco was sent to Dieppe to preach the Gospel.

Further, Faget to go to Orleans.

Death of Master Lancelot D'Albeau, martyr. Further, Master Lancelot D'Albeau to go to Valence, in which place having faithfully preached the Gospel and being taken by its enemies, he sealed the doctrine of truth with his blood and with his death.

Source: *Registre de la Compagnie des Pasteurs* [G2], ii. 87-90.

17 The organisation of the Church. Extracts from the synods of Paris (1559) and Poitiers (1561)

The First National Synod, Paris, 25-28 May 1559

François de Morel de Colonges presided, and there assisted at it on behalf of the Reformed churches of France, the pastors of Dieppe and St Lô in Normandy, of Angers, Orléans, Tours, Châtellerault, Poitiers, Saintes, St Jean d'Angély, and Marennes.

[*The Discipline*][1]

1. Firstly, no church should aspire to any precedence or domination over another.

2. Each colloquy or synod should elect a president to preside over it. This office to come to an end at the conclusion of each synod or council.

3. The ministers should take with them to each synod an elder or deacon, or several.

4. General synods should assemble according to the necessity of the churches, and should hold an amicable and brotherly *censure*; and afterwards celebrate Holy Communion.

5. The ministers and at least one elder or deacon of each church or province should assemble twice yearly.

6. The ministers shall be elected by the elders and deacons of the consistory, and presented to the congregation to which they are ordained; if there is opposition, it shall be for the consistory to adjudicate. And in case of disagreement on either side, the whole matter shall be reported to the provincial synod, not in order to constrain the people to accept the minister elected, but for his justification.

[1] The text of the Discipline is taken not from Quick (who prints the text as amended by later synods), but from the *Histoire Ecclésiastique* [F3], pp. 215-20.

7. Ministers should not be sent from other churches without legitimate letters of attestation, and also not received without such letters, or due investigation.

8. Those elected must sign the Confession of Faith, both of the church to which they are elected, as well as any others to which they are sent. And the election is to be confirmed by laying on of hands, without any other superstitious practice.

9. The minister of one church may not preach in another without the permission of its minister, or in his absence, that of the consistory.

10. Anyone elected to the office of minister should be asked to accept, but not constrained. A minister who is not able to exercise his charge in the place ordained, if he is sent elsewhere and does not wish to go, should explain his reasons for refusing to the consistory, which will judge if these reasons are acceptable. If not, and if he persists in his refusal, the provincial synod should decide.

11. No one who puts himself forward as minister should be approved by neighbouring ministers if an objection is made by another church, even if he has the approval of his congregation; but before proceeding the provincial synod shall be called together as soon as possible to decide the matter.

12. Those elected to the ministry of the Word should understand that their election is for life.

13. And as for those sent for a certain time, if they see that the church cannot be provided for in any other way, they should not abandon the church for which Christ died.

14. It is permitted on account of the severe persecution to change for a time from one church to another, with the consent and approval of both churches. This may be done also for other proper reasons, reported and approved by the provincial synod.

15. Those who teach bad doctrine, and after having been admonished do not desist, those also of scandalous life meriting punishment by the magistrate or excommunication, or disobedient to the consistory, or insufficient in other ways, shall be deposed.

16. But as for those who, by reason of old age, illness or other incapacity, are rendered incapable of fulfilling their duties, they should retain the honour of their office, and should be recommended to their churches and maintained, and another should be found to perform their duties.

17. Ministers committing vices of a scandalous nature, punishable by the magistrate, and bringing scandal on the church, merit deposition, whether such offences are committed while they were still in ignorance or after. As for less scandalous vices, they shall be left to the

judgement of the provincial synod.

18. In the case of gross offences, the consistory shall order immediate removal, calling in two or three ministers to assist them. In the case of a written complaint or a calumnious accusation, this should be left to the provincial synod.

19. The cause of deposition should not be declared to the people if necessity does not require it, as the consistory shall judge.

20. The elders and deacons are the senate of the church, and the minister shall preside.

21. The duties of the elders are to call together the people, report scandals to the consistory and other such things; for which each church should have a written form, according to circumstances of time and place. The office of elder is not perpetual.

22. The duties of the deacons are to visit the poor, prisoners and the sick, and to go round the houses to catechise.

23. It is not the duty of the deacons to preach, nor to administer the sacraments, although they may assist. Their office is also not perpetual, although they should not depart without the permission of the church, the elders likewise.

24. In the absence of the minister, or if he should happen to be ill, or in any other necessity, the deacon should say prayers and read a passage of scripture without any preaching.

25. The deacons and elders are to be removed for the same reasons as the ministers, having been judged by the consistory. If they appeal they should be suspended until the next meeting of the provincial synod.

26. Neither the minister nor any other member of the church shall publish any book concerning religion, either of their own composition or by anyone else, without previously communicating it to two or three reliable ministers.

27. Heretics, despisers of God, rebels against the consistory, traitors against the church, those accused and condemned for crimes worthy of corporal punishment, and those who bring scandals on the church, are to be excommunicated and cast out, not only from the sacraments, but also from the whole assembly. As for other vices, it will be left to the discretion of the church to decide whether those excluded from the sacraments will be admitted to hear the Word of God preached.

28. Those excommunicated for heresy, schism, treason against the church, rebellion and other vices scandalous to the church, shall have their excommunication declared to the congregation with an explanation of the cause.

29. As to those who are excommunicated for less serious offences,

it shall be left to the discretion of the church whether they are openly denounced, until this shall be regulated by the next general synod.

30. If an excommunicated person should come to the consistory asking to be reconciled to the church, the consistory should judge whether they are repentant. If they have been publicly excommunicated, they must do public penitence. If not, they may do it in the consistory.

31. Those who have abjured their faith under persecution should not be admitted to the church until they have made an act of public repentence.

32. Following a time of persecution, war, famine, or any other great affliction, public prayers and fasting may be held without any scruple or fear of superstition; also before electing a minister, or at the beginning of a synod.

33. Marriages should first be made known to the consistory, together with the contract passed by a public notary, and announced to the congregation at least twice over a fortnight, after which time the vows should be performed in the assembly. This procedure shall not be broken save in exceptional cases, which the consistory shall judge.

34. Marriages and baptisms should be carefully registered by the church, together with the names of father, mother, and godparents.

35. As concerning degrees of affinity, members should not contract marriage from which scandals might result.

36. Any members whose spouses are convicted of adultery shall be urged to reconcile themselves with them. If they will not do so, they shall be at liberty, but churches should not dissolve marriages, in order not to impeach the authority of the magistrate.

37. Young people not yet of age may not contract marriage without the permission of their parents. If their parents are unreasonable, and will not consent to a proper marriage, then it is for the consistory to consider the matter.

38. Legitimate promises of marriage may not be dissolved, even by the mutual consent of both parties; such promises, if they are legitimately made, should be recognised by the consistory.

39. No church should do anything of great moment which might compromise or damage another church, without the advice of the provincial synod, if it is possible to bring it together. If circumstances prevent this, the church should at the least seek advice by letter from other churches of the province.

40. The articles concerning discipline decided amongst us may be changed if the needs of the church make this necessary. But it is not

in the power of any one church to do this without the advice of the general synod.

The Second National Synod, Poitiers, 10 March 1561

Le Baillier chosen Moderator.
Roland chosen Secretary.

[*Corrections to the Discipline*]
3. The sixth article was thus altered and amended: no minister shall be elected by only one minister or his consistory, but with two or three ministers together with the consistory of the vacant church, or if it may be by the provincial synod, or by the colloquy, ... and unto this the minister who is to be ordained shall make his address, and from the colloquy he shall be presented unto the people, to be accepted by them. But in case anyone opposes his admission, the colloquy shall judge hereof, and if neither party consents, the whole shall be referred to the provincial synod, which shall take cognizance of the minister's justification and of his reception, providing the consistory and the greater part of the people do approve and consent unto it.
5. Forasmuch as it is in no wise expedient that our people should hear popish preachers, or any others who are not lawfully called to preach the Gospel in those churches which have a settled and standing ministry, therefore all true pastors are to hinder their people from wandering after them, as much as in them lies.

[*New articles added to the church Discipline*]
11. All consistories shall be admonished by their ministers strictly to forbid all dancing, mummeries and tricks of jugglers.
14. The candidates for the ministry in all churches shall preach a trial sermon, and their text shall be some portion of God's Word, and this as time and place may conveniently bear.
15. Whatever shall be decreed by provincial synods concerning the suspension of vagrant ministers who intrude themselves into churches, it shall be as valid and effectual as if it had been ordained by the national synod.

[*General matters*]
1. It is thought needful that there should be a consistory in every church, consisting of ministers, elders and deacons, exercising their offices, who where affairs so require may call in whom they choose to

consult with.

7. This order shall be observed by him who begins to preach in public, and to gather a church, viz.: that as soon as possible he can, he shall take their names and number who will submit unto discipline, and who are to be regarded as sheep of that flock, so that all may not be received higgledy-piggledy without distinction to the Lord's Table. And over these shall be had a most diligent inspection.

8. All violences and injurious words against the papists, and also against chaplains, priests, and monks, shall not only be forborne but to the utmost of the church's power suppressed.

[Particular matters]

7. It being demanded, what course should be taken with such who having been a long time members of the church, do not communicate at the Lord's Table, lest they should be obliged to the total renunciation of idolatry. We answer, that if after some convenient time and admonitions given them they do not reform this conduct, they shall be cut off from communication with the Table.

25. It was thought meet to advise the churches, that in matters of general concern to them they should send from every province at the common expense some particular person, who follows the Court, to solicit the affairs of the churches in that province at Court. And all these representatives to communicate these counsels together, so that they might agree on those suits which they prosecute. They shall also carry with them the Confession of Faith, and consult of some means how to present it to the King in the name of all the churches.

27. It was demanded whether the Word of God might be preached publicly without authority from the civil magistrate? Answer was given, that special care be had of the times, and public peace, and above all that there be no tumults nor sedition.

28. The churches of Paris, Orléans and Rouen are deputed by this present synod to protest aginst the Popish Council now held at Trent, and of the nullity of all its decisions and decrees. And their protestation shall be done either by printed books, or oral remonstrances unto the King's Majesty, or by any other way as they judge needful.

30. Whereas divers persons solicit this national synod to supply the congregations who have sent them hither with pastors, they are answered, that at present we are utterly unable to gratify them. And that therefore they are advised to set up propositions[2] of the Word of God, and to take special care of educating hopeful young men in

[2] Trial sermons, a common form of ministerial training and examination in the Calvinist churches.

learning, in the Arts, Languages, and Divinity, who may hereafter be employed in the Sacred ministry; and they are most humbly to petition the Lord to send Labourers to gather in the harvest.

Source: Quick, *Synodicon* [F1], i. 2-30.

18 The conspiracy of Amboise

[Examination of the ministers concerning Morély's statement]

'Calvin said that it was true that Chandieu[1] had come here and that they had talked together about the tyranny which prevails [in France] at the present time and about what could be done to remedy the situation. He had argued with him and had pointed out that for all kinds of reasons the enterprise, in the form in which it was being planned, was not based upon the Word of God. He had agreed, however, that the time had now come when one could say that it was necessary, and one's duty, to do something, for the sake of justice and of the order established by the laws of France, but without the spilling of human blood … .

Afterwards the said Calvin, asked to repeat his statement, so that it could be accurately recorded in writing, said that he admitted that the aforesaid Chandieu had come here to talk to him in order to ask for his help in putting an end to the persecutions, but that he [Calvin] had not felt it in any way appropriate to communicate this to the Company of Pastors, and that for his own part he had tried in every way he could to put hindrances in the way of the proposed enterprise as it was described to him.

However, he did admit to having said something like this to Chandieu: that if some great man of the King's Council, someone who had the right to be at the head of the kingdom, in accordance with the laws of France, acknowledged this, and declared himself, and that if there was no question of proceeding in any way other than strictly according to the law, without violence or resort to arms, then it would be proper for such a man to take control, provided that all the Courts of *Parlement*, the nobility and the people were in favour of the cause. He admitted also that the aforesaid Chandieu argued with him, but that he would not go further, insisting that it was not licit to do so, according to the Word of God. And what is more, once a single

[1] Antoine de la Roche Chandieu, was alleged while minister of the Paris church to have told Morély that Calvin knew of the plot and approved it.

drop of blood was spilt, the gutters would run red with it everywhere, and that nobody would be able to prevent the most horrible disorder, and that it would be better for us all to die than to bring the Gospel into such disrepute ... .

The said sieur de Bèze admitted that the said sieur de Villiers [Morély] came to visit him in his house, after the sermon, together with a man called the sieur de Cheron, who was just about to depart, and that they talked about many things, but that they did not discuss whether or not, according to the Scriptures, the enterprise ought or ought not to be done in the way proposed, nor about whether or not it was right for them to take part, but simply about the best means to adopt if it did turn out to be God's will that the situation should improve and tranquillity return. He added that as far as the central allegation was concerned, it would be easy for him to prove, if necessary, that he had never advised anyone to take part in the enterprise. On the contrary, he had advised all those who consulted him on the matter to steer clear of it ... .

Antoine de la Roche Chandieu, on being questioned, stated and declared that the outcome of the enterprise had been pitiful, and that the sieur de La Renaudie had been one of the ringleaders. Asked whether to his knowledge the aforesaid enterprise had been in any way advised by the ministers of this city, he replied, no. He knew well that they had not approved it, in the way in which it had in fact been executed, and that the way in which the aforesaid enterprise had been carried out had displeased the said ministers, as he knew well.

The Syndics, having heard and understood the testimony given by Jean Morély on the matter in connection with which he had been charged and held prisoner, namely, that he had alleged that the ministers of the Church of Geneva had given their consent to a certain armed enterprise which aimed to put an end to the persecutions in France, and having also heard and understood the testimony of the said ministers, protesting their innocence in this matter, and claiming that it was wrongful and untrue to make those charges against them, and to involve them in that affair, having duly and thoroughly weighed one side against the other, have recognised and judged, and now recognise, judge and pronounce that the said Morély acted irresponsibly in speaking as he did, for it appears to them, even by Morély's own testimony, that the ministers never advised the use of force nor the taking up of arms for the sake of religion. What is more, it is clear to us that the ministers spoke out against it, and resisted all such suggestions as strongly as they could, and were opposed to everything that was being planned or was

[79]

carried out in this episode, and that if it had been in their power to do so, they would have prevented the whole affair. This being so, we find them pure and clean and beyond all suspicion of blame ... .

Morély is to recognise his fault, and to confess that he has done these ministers wrong in making these groundless allegations against them. Furthermore he is to engage to say no more of this matter in future. In order to ensure that this ruling is carried out, the Syndics have ordered the said Morély to pay bail and caution money of 500 écus, to secure his obedience to this judgement.'

Source: Archives d'Etat du Genève, *Régistres du Conseil de Genève* vol. 56; H. Naef, *La Conjuration d'Amboise et Genève* (Geneva, 1922), pp. 462-71.

19 Providential deliverance. Calvin and Beza on the death of Francis II, December 1560

Calvin to Sturm, 16 December 1560.

Did you ever read or hear of anything more opportune than the death of the King? The evils had reached an extremity for which there was no remedy, when all of a sudden God shows himself from heaven. He who pierced the eye of the father has now struck the ear of the son.[1] My only apprehension is lest some persons in the excess of their triumph defeat the hopes of an amelioration in our condition. For one can hardly believe how inconsiderately many people exult, nay wanton in their joy. They wish to transform the whole world in an instant, and because I do not countenance their folly they tax me with supineness. But to me it is enough that God approves of my diligence, and even more than enough to have in my favour the testimony of impartial and moderate men: these are not in a majority it is true, but I prefer their calm judgements to the noisy outcries of the multitude. They would wish me to act along with the King of Navarre in his turbulent projects, as if, indeed, supposing him to be the most sagacious and vigorous of mortals, it was in his power to grant what they so preposterously demand. I, on the contrary, am so opposed to this precipitancy that it gave me no small accession of joy to learn that his brother was unwilling to quit his prison.[2] I had

[1] Henry II died of a splinter in the eye, sustained while jousting; Francis of an abscess of the ear.
[2] Condé, in custody for his suspected part in the Conspiracy of Amboise at the time of Francis's death.

already previously given my advice to such an effect, so that I rejoice the more heartily that what I deemed the most salutary proceeding has spontaneously suggested itself to their minds ... .

Beza's verses

> Tool of bad men, Henry, thy thirst for blood
> Fit retribution found,
> From thy pierced eyeball gushed a purple flood
> Which crimsoned all the ground.
>
> Following thy father in his mad career,
> Francis, unhappy youth,
> Thou felt'st God's arrow cleave thy guilty ear
> Fast closed against God's truth.
>
> Ye crafty, foolish, dull-eared kings, to you
> These awful warnings cry,
> Or now prepare your evil deeds to rue,
> Or in your blindness die.

Source: Calvini Opera [C1], xviii. 270-2 (nos. 3293-4); *Letters of Calvin* [C6], iv. 152-3 (no. 579) and footnote.

20 Expansive growth. A letter from a minister in Normandy to Calvin, August 1561

Dearest and most honoured brother. I have no doubt that some report will have reached your ears of what occurred at the Guibray fair which began on 15 August. For this reason I wanted to write to you what I had personally seen and heard. Firstly it seems to me that there is nothing to compare with this fair, not only in Normandy but in the whole of France. People come from all over, even from abroad. I will tell you from my point of view what happened: when we met the previous Sunday, I had no intention of going there, even though our elders implored me to go there ... . I imagined a great multitude assembled from all corners of the realm, and it seemed to me that I had no business there. Moreover, I had more than enough work elsewhere, because requests for our services were coming in on all sides. Further than that, an apprehension of my own insufficiency prevented me from going voluntarily. I feared also the emotions that might be stirred up, and your last letters of 22 July admonished me that we should not take the law into our own hands, but wait for an official order. For these reasons, although I did not explain everything to the Council, I told them that I was not willing to go, but they told me that I needed only to sleep there one night, Saturday, and that it would only be a meeting in a private room, like last year, and not in public. On the Wednesday I was asked to go and visit a church three miles from our town and I rejoiced, hoping thereby to avoid the trip to Guibray. But the same day, while I was away, the merchants sent horses and instructions to bring me there to give a sermon on the Thursday, a feast day. So when I came back on Thursday morning someone was waiting for me. My horse was saddled and my wife waiting to depart. Seeing these things I resigned myself to God's will. Climbing down from one horse I mounted another, and we did not linger on the road, with the rain on our shoulders and the mud up to our knees. I arrived that evening in Falaise quite exhausted and with a headache, and we slept at a hostelry.

The following day, Friday, getting up with my headache still, I tried to shake it off. They urged me to eat, but the smell of food made my stomach turn. So they took me to the house of a good citizen, where I remained in bed until three o'clock in the afternoon. They asked me if I could preach that evening. I agreed, providing our elders and those of Rouen found a suitable room where it could proceed in orderly fashion. But it was not possible to find such a room because the crowd who wanted to hear the sermon was more than two or three thousand persons. Everyone was admonished to give nothing away [about the plans for the meeting]. The place chosen was close to Guibray, surrounded by walls, ample enough, with a single gate and outside the gate another large enclosure like the Molard.[1] The sermon was conducted in a seemly silence and with a psalm at the beginning and at the end. The following day the rumour spread through the whole camp that a sermon had taken place, and everyone wanted to find out about it, asking after the place and the hour. But we had no wish to tell them, fearing an ambush, and we were warned that we should raise a bodyguard of 200 men. The King's proctor in Falaise had closed all the bookshops this same day. The priests had complained greatly, because of the preaching and because they had been quite openly selling books from Geneva and because boys had been hawking through the streets with loud cries broadsheets denouncing

---

[1] The market-place in Geneva where Farel had preached in the early days of the Reform.

the mass. The broadsheets began thus: 'True articles on the horrible, great, and insupportable abuses of the papal mass, etc.' I believe it was written by M. Farel (the style suggests this). It ran as follows: 'I call the sky and earth to witness the truth against this pompous and arrogant Mass, which, if God does not soon provide a remedy, will soon bring total ruin on the earth.' As far as the boys' shouts were concerned, I kept in the background, not wishing to damage what I had begun. I said only this: 'They are calling boldly for the abolition of the Mass.'

To return to the matter in hand, we were also threatened with the arrival of the Bishop of Sées, M. du Val, a learned man, they said, who would arrive on Sunday. I will say more of this Bishop later.

I will return now to the first disturbances. Instead of a bodyguard of 200 armed men there were no more than sixteen or twenty, poor artisans with borrowed staves. They said they would come at seven or eight o'clock to the meeting place, but in fact they arrived at five or six. Our people were already assembling, but the bodyguard was turning them away. Meanwhile some of our leaders consulted together, and decided it would be better to continue, for fear of a tumult. When the people were gathered, they came to fetch me. I wondered whether I ought to go; but I went and all went well. As for the booksellers whose stalls had been closed up, they appeared the same day at the appointed hour. They found neither the King's proctor nor anyone else with whom to speak. They asked for a certificate to prove that they had appeared, which they were granted, and they returned to their books more impudent than before. And all this occurred on the Saturday.

On Sunday morning a huge number of our people gathered together at five o'clock in the morning. The meeting place was changed to a place out in the open country, which was felt to be better so that any enemies could be seen from whatever direction they came. There was not the same silence as on previous days, yet everything passed off in a most edifying way, and after the preaching everyone went off peacefully. After dinner the bell was rung for the sermon of the Franciscan friar at the Guibray church. Some of our people went, and while he was speaking blasphemously about images a cut-purse was taken in the act and beaten up. Others cried out at the friar that he lied and was a false prophet. Thus there was a certain disturbance, but it passed off without any more trouble. The friar on his journey back to town was struck a blow on the cheek, but that was not approved by us: we protested that such vehement behaviour was excessive (I am speaking now of public demonstrations at their sermons) and that it played into their hands.

For our part our people assembled at five that same evening ... . I believe that something more than five or six thousand people were present. I was in considerable doubt what text to take for my sermon, but my mind was suddenly made up to speak about the Communion. I took as my text 1 Corinthians 2. My preface went as follows: Now that we have spoken of doctrine and how our Lord Jesus has united the sacraments with his Word, we should talk of how to remedy the controversies which have grown up today between men. And I spoke as gently as I could so as not to give offence to anyone, attributing to Christ alone all authority. But very suddenly a disturbance arose, so that everyone sprang up, clutching their swords, and crying, 'What is it, what is it?' For my part, I did not move from my place (thanks be to God, for giving me courage). But I did not have the wit to remove my beret, which I was wearing to distinguish me from the rest. Then I called out, 'My friends, it is nothing', and this cry was soon on everyone's lips. Daggers and swords were put back in their sheaths. Many said to me, 'Fear not, monsieur, if you die we die with you.' And suddenly the tumult passed; one had lost his hat or coat, another a shoe, another a book. A girl had a gold chain torn off, but as God would wish for the glory of his Gospel, everything was recovered. There was a great heap of all of these things in front of my feet. Even the papists were forced to admit, 'these Lutherans are as honest as the clock, nothing is lost in their midst'. And silence having been restored, I exhorted the people to listen to the words of the Gospel, and said that it was Satan who had caused this disturbance to prevent the coming of Christ's kingdom. Then I returned to my theme without (thank God) further trouble, and continued to the end, showing the difference between the Communion of Christ and the priestly mass. And this was what happened on Sunday.

Several theories have been advanced to explain the cause of this disturbance. Some of the papists who looked on from afar thought a great thunder-clap had descended among us, on account of the great sound of voices. Others said that two priests, hearing me speak, had begun to grumble, saying, 'this blackguard will ruin the body of Christ'; and some replied to them that I was speaking the truth. Others have said that some of the Bishop's servants have since boasted of having caused it by crying out: 'enemies are here!' But I have not heard that any blood was spilled.

This same day after supper, between nine and ten o'clock, the stall holders were sitting around singing psalms with great gusto. And a number of makers of rosary beads from Paris called them *maillotins* [rebels], and mocked them by singing bawdy songs. They were told either to shut up or join in singing the Lord's praises. And since they took no notice a fracas arose, and voices were heard crying 'Rouen, Rouen' [a rallying cry], and a great crowd of two or three hundred found themselves at sword-point, and the cry went up, 'Long live the Gospel!' The rosary-sellers took fright, and started shouting 'Long live the Gospel!' with the rest. And the crowd moved through the camp, reforming all the singing and dissolutions they came across. That done, they put up candles at the junctions of the main roads and knelt down to pray before they went to bed, and this practice was continued until the end of the fair.

On the Monday morning the Bishop preached a sermon at Falaise, close to Guibray. He took as his theme *Non est confusionis autor Deus sed pacis*, 1 Corinthians 14 [the Lord is the author not of confusion but peace]. Some good-natured person gave me a summary of what he said. He began with a *Pater* and *Ave*. Then he said, I have two points to make, the first concerning faith, the second works. And having discussed these themes he said that those who preach today [i.e. the Reformed] do not disagree with us on these two matters. It is only certain ceremonies which divide us. He said that there were good things in the Mass, like the Epistle and Gospel, but also things of which he did not approve. In sum, the papists are by no means happy with him, thinking that he was preaching in our favour. And this same day he departed without doing anything else, so that his visit has been quite helpful, not least in causing the priests amazement.

Our people, seeing that the bishop was going away again, took great courage, and made preparations for an evening meeting at five o'clock, sending boys around the camp shouting, 'Any who wish to hear the Word of God should come now.' The meeting took place at the walled meadow. The door was guarded by about forty men, including half a dozen with halberds, so that when people had come in they could not leave until the end. In this sermon I denounced the Mass, yet in temperate terms and without invective. And when some failed to remove their hats for the prayers, I began by saying, 'We are worshipping the living God, and if any do not wish to worship him they should leave.' And everyone took off their hats. The priests feared to show their crown.

On the Tuesday, when I was about to leave, I was told of an issue that was causing some disquiet among the people. Many were saying, 'what shall we do now? We can no longer go to mass: how do we live now?' I remained there this day also, and important people, principally the local nobility, began to arrive. For it is the custom that the seigneurs come with their ladies for the last days when the merchants have done their deals. In my sermon on this day I took as my text Colossians 2: when you have received Christ, follow him. And I gave many suggestions what each should do while they were waiting for the Gospel to be preached in public. How each might teach his family, read scriptures, reform his life, pray for the King and the princes, that God might bring them to an understanding of his Holy Gospel. Also that each should attempt to join themselves to our secret assemblies. I took this opportunity to talk of our meetings and what was done in them, and answer the calumnies spoken about us ... . I spoke briefly of the articles of faith, and how ours is not a new faith but that of our forefathers, like the prophets and all those who have known the Gospel. Briefly I enumerated the commandments one by one, denouncing vices, particularly idolatry, blasphemy and other most common faults.

This was what happened on Tuesday evening. Immediately after the sermon was finished, the man who had been President [of the local court] at Caen came to speak to me, although I did not recognise him. Some thought that he was going to arrest me, but he was no longer in office, and, in any case, we were under the eyes of more than a thousand people. So that was a rumour without foundation. He began to ask me how it was possible to guard against false prophets. I replied that it was necessary to have good guarantees of the life and doctrine of those who teach, and that the church discipline we have adopted should be observed by them, and that they should have written authorisation from those who sent them. He asked how I came to be in this land. The faithful, I replied, made a request to the church at Geneva, which sent me with its recommendation. He asked me how I came to Guibray, and if the merchants of Rouen had sent for me. I replied that they and others had asked me to come. (At this point when he mentioned the merchants of Rouen specifically I began to suspect something.) Then he asked me my name, and if I was La Barre [one of the ministers to the Caen community]. I replied that he would learn my name another time but that no, I was not La Barre. 'Ha!,' he cried, 'do not defy me!' 'Monsieur', I said, 'I do not know who you are.' 'I am,' he said, 'the man who last year was President at Caen.' And then, taking off my hat, I said, 'I thank you for the hot time you gave me last year.' (I imagine, my brother, that you have heard the great affliction that my congregation has suffered through this man when he was in office.) He replied, 'I have never attempted to apprehend you, although I knew where you were.' 'As for your wishes,' I said, 'that I do not know. What I do know is that it is the Lord who has prevented you.' Then he protested that it had never been his intention to afflict the church and its members. I retorted that the prisoners who had been languishing so long in jail would not see things in that light. He had, he said, to do something for political reasons, but nothing was done out of malice. To which I replied, 'God will judge your actions and your conscience.' As I was saying this a merchant from Rouen came up and said in my ear that the company did not think it a good idea that I should linger much longer. So having taken my leave of the former President, about an hour and a half later I got on my horse and, well accompanied, I arrived back at my home after midnight. And that was my trip to Guibray.

These were the books that the book-selling boys were advertising at the fair: *A Just complaint of the Faithful of France against the Papists and other Infidels. The Commandments of God compared with those of the Papal Antichrist. A Treatise on Relics. The New Doctrine and the Old. Epistle sent to the Tiger of France.*[2] And flourishing the broadsheets denouncing the Mass in front of the priests and monks they shouted these words, 'The abolition of the Mass! Down with the stinking Mass! The Mass abolished by law, who wants it! Here is the ruin of the players in this farce with which they deceive the world! Here's how the merchants who sell this fine merchandise will be done away with!' There were one or two priests who wanted to argue the toss, but everyone shouted after them things like, 'Go to work, it's high time! Go and carry baskets at the grape harvest! You fine merchants, learn to work: you have eaten too long without doing anything!' And sometimes they were pushed in the mud in the middle of the road. Also, it was usual for prostitutes to set up their booths around the camp at Guibray; this year all had been abolished. The merchants selling chasubles, rosaries and wax have not much profited by this fair.

After the fair news arrived that the following Saturday a papist called one of our people a Lutheran, which is forbidden by the King's edict, and he was fined 25 francs. The following Monday some priests caught and beat up one of the book-selling boys who was carrying *The commandments of God and the Pope*, but the people set upon them, and having roughed them up they were clapped in prison, and since then they have been charged.

So that is the state of things at present. We continue our services in private houses, waiting the moment to show ourselves in public. In

[2] 'The Tiger of France': the Cardinal of Lorraine, brother of the Duke of Guise.

Dieppe, Rouen and St Lô they speak in the open; it is rumoured that a further tumult has taken place in Rouen but accounts of it vary. I can tell you no more.

Unsigned (August 1561).

Source: 'Une Mission à la Foire de Guibray', *Bulletin de la Société d'Histoire de Protestantisme Française* 28 (1879), pp. 455-64.

21 Preparing for war. Extracts from the *Commentaries* of Blaise de Monluc

Some months after my return, I heard on all sides the terrible language and audacious words used by the ministers of the new faith, even against the authority of the Crown. I heard it said that they were imposing taxes, that they were appointing captains, raising troops, holding assemblies in the houses of noblemen in those regions where the new religion prevailed; all of which was to bring about all the troubles and the massacres which each side inflicted upon the other. From day to day I beheld the evil spreading, and I could see no one who spoke out in the King's name. I heard it said also that most of the officials who concerned themselves with affairs of finance were of that religion; well, it is human nature to run after novelties; but the worst aspect of it all, and the one which led to the greatest misfortunes, was that the men of justice in the *parlements*, and in the *sénéchaussées*, and the other judges, abandoned the old religion of the King to take up the new one. I also heard strange words like 'elders', 'deacons', 'consistories'. 'colloquies', 'synods'. I had never dined before off such peculiar meats. I heard it said that the elders had bull-sinew whips called 'johnnies' with which they thrashed and ill-treated the poor peasants if they refused to go to the sermons; people stopped taking cases to court, because, they complained, all they met with there was insult; and no sergeant was to be found who dared to carry out the orders of Catholics, but only of 'Huguenots' as they were called, I don't know why. Those of the King's judges and officials who remained Catholic were so intimidated that they dared not initiate any prosecution for fear of their lives. All this seemed to me to be a clear presage of what did in fact ensue. On the way back to Estillac from another of my properties, I found the town of Laplume besieged by three or four hundred men. I had the captain Monluc, my son, with me, and I said to him that he had better speak to them with gracious words, because we had only ten or twelve horses with us. He did this so well that he was shown into the company of the Brimonts, who were in charge of this operation, and learned from them that what they were after was the return of two prisoners of their religion who were being held by the judicial authorities in Laplume. My son promised them that if they would withdraw their troops, I would arrange to have their prisoners released. They agreed, and the next day I went and parleyed with the officers of the town, arguing that for the sake of two prisoners it was not worth allowing the others to create a sedition; they saw my point, and let the men go … .

Well, to get back to what I was saying: once I had seen all these happenings and all these novelties, which increased after my return and after the death of the King (because by that time it was all being talked about openly) I decided to go back to Court, and not to budge from the Queen Mother's side, and that of her children, and to die at their feet, standing up against anyone who came against them, exactly as I had promised the Queen; and so I set out on my way. The Court at that time was at St-Germain-en-Laye: I stayed in Paris for no more than a couple of days. No sign there of anyone of the house of Guise nor indeed of any other, but at Court where I was made welcome by all I found the Queen, the King of Navarre, the Prince of Condé, and the Cardinal of Ferrara. The Queen and the King of Navarre took me on one side and asked me how things were in Gascony. I told them that so far the situation there was not too bad, but that I feared that things were going from bad to worse; and I told them why it seemed to me that it would not be long before the two sides came to blows. I stayed at Court only five days, during which time the news came in that the Huguenots had risen at Marmande and had killed the Franciscan friars and burned down the convent. Before very long news came in of the massacre inflicted by the Catholics on the Huguenots of Cahors, and of Grenade near Toulouse. A little later we heard the news of the death of M. de Fumel, cruelly slain by his own subjects, who were Huguenots. This upset the Queen more than all the rest of the news, and she began to realise that I had been right in predicting that it was inevitable that we should soon be at war … .

The entire city of Bordeaux had taken sides, one against the other, and the *Parlement* too, because the Huguenots were demanding open preaching within its walls, saying that this was permitted to them since the Colloquy of Poissy, and the Catholics were denying this. M. de Burie and I were occupied for a whole day in keeping them from coming to blows, and we announced that we would raise some troops, and that when the commissioners had arrived we would march straight to Fumel, because our orders stated that we should start from there. For I had the right to raise troops and to command them. We announced that we were raising 200 foot armed with arquebuses, and 100 mounted and similarly armed. In charge of them I put young Tilladet, who is now Seigneur of Saint-Orens. I had hardly been more than four or five days in my house at Estillac when a minister called La Barelle came and called on me on behalf of their churches. He said that the churches had been very glad to hear of my arrival and of the commission I had been given by the Queen, and that now they felt that they could rest assured that they would see justice done towards those who had perpetrated the massacres. I replied that they could be quite certain that wrongdoers would be punished. Next he said that he had been charged by the churches to give me a handsome present, with which I would have good reason to be content. I said to him that in my case there was no need to resort to presents, because with all the presents in the world no one could make me act contrary to my duty. Then he told me that the Catholics were saying that they would not tolerate anyone trying to bring them to justice, and that he had been charged to present me, on behalf of the churches, with four thousand paid-up infantry. At these words I began to get very angry. I said to him, 'Who are these four thousand men, and what nation do they come from ?' He replied, 'They are local men, from this area, and they come from the churches.' At this I demanded to know whether he had the right to 'present' subjects of the King in this way, and to put them in the field without any orders from the King, or from the Queen, who was governing the kingdom at that time, in accordance with the decision of the States which met at Orléans. 'You crooks!' I said to him, 'I can see what you are up to - you are deliberately opening up divisions in the kingdom, and you lot, the ministers, are doing it all in the name of the Gospel!' I began to swear, and I got hold of him by the collar, and I said this to him: 'I don't know what is stopping me personally hanging you from that window, you villain, because in my time I have strangled with my own hands twenty better men than you.' Trembling with fear, he said, 'Monsieur, I beg you, let me go and find M. de Burie, because I have been charged by the churches to go and speak to him. Don't attack me, just because I am the spokesman. We are only trying to defend ourselves.'

I told him to go to the devil, him and all the other ministers. And so he left, having had more of a fright than he had ever had before. That incident put me in very bad odour among the ministers, because it's the crime of *lèse-majesté* to lay hands on one of them.

Source: Commentaires de Blaise de Monluc [F9], vii. 211-12, 213-14.

(c) The organisation of French Calvinism, 1562-71

22 The end of the First War. The Edict of Amboise, March 1563

Charles by the grace of God King of France: To all those who see these letters, greeting … . Having willingly taken the good and prudent advice of the Queen our most dear and most honoured lady and mother, and of our dearly beloved cousins the Cardinal de Bourbon, the Prince de Condé, the Duc de Montpensier, the Prince de la Roche sur Yon, princes of our blood; also of our dearly beloved cousins the Cardinal de Guise, the Duc d'Aumale, the Duc de Montmorency, constable peers of France, the Duc d'Estampes, the marshals de Brissac and de Bourdillon, the sieurs d'Andelot, de Sansac, de Cipierre and other great and good personages of our *Conseil privé*, all of whom support the common good of this our kingdom, we enact and proclaim the following:

I. It is our will and pleasure that from this time forward each and every gentlemen who is a baron, a castellan, who has the right of high justice, or who is a lord holding *plein fief de haubert*, may live in his house where he dwells in full liberty of conscience and in exercise of the religion which is called Reformed, together with his family and subjects, who may live there freely and without any constraint.

II. And the other fief-holding noblemen, also in their households for themselves and their families only, provided they do not live in a town, borough or village belonging to a lord with high justice, ourselves apart, in which case they have no right in such places to practise the said religion except by permission and leave of their aforesaid lord with high justice, and not otherwise.

III. That in each *bailliage*, *sénéchaussée* and area of government equivalent to a *bailliage*, such as Péronne, Montdidier, Roye and La Rochelle, and others of similar nature, having resort to our courts of *Parlement*, we will designate, at the request of those of the said religion, one town in the outskirts of which the said religion may be practised by all those of that administrative area, who may go there [to practise their religion] but not in any other manner and not to any other place.

IV. Despite this, every man may, within his own house, live and dwell entirely freely, without being investigated nor molested, forced or constrained in matters of his conscience.

V. That in all towns in which the said religion was practised, up to the 7th of the present month of March, as well as the other towns which (as laid down here) will be specifically designated in each *bailliage* and *sénéchaussée*, the same practice shall be continued in one or two places named by us within the said town: this does not allow those of the said religion to help themselves to seize or continue to hold any temple or church belonging to the clergy, whom we intend to see reinstated in their churches, houses, goods, possessions and revenues, to enjoy and use them exactly as they did before the outbreak of the present troubles, and to hold and to continue to hold divine service in their accustomed manner in their churches, without being impeded or molested by anyone, and without anyone being able to claim anything resulting from the demolitions which have taken place.

VI. We intend also that the city of Paris including the area of resort of its *prevoté* and *vicomté* shall be and shall remain exempt from any practice of the said religion, but that despite this, those who have their houses and property within the said town and area may go inside their houses and there enjoy peacefully their said rights, without being forced or constrained, investigated or molested with reference to the past or to the future, in matters of conscience.

IX. And so that no doubts persist about the sincerity and straightforward intentions of our cousin the prince de Condé, ... we proclaim and declare that we take our said cousin to be our good kinsman, faithful subject and servant, as we take also to be our good and loyal subjects and servants all those lords, knights, gentlemen and other inhabitants of towns, communities, villages and other places of our kingdom and the territories of our obedience who have followed him, and succoured, aided and accompanied him in this present war, and during the tumults which have taken place in our kingdom, believing and reckoning that what was done at that time by our subjects, whether it was done by force of arms or by recourse to justice, was well-intentioned and done for our service.

XIII. And because we fervently desire to see an end to all the occasions of these troubles, tumults and seditions, and to bring about reconciliation and to unite the wills and intentions of our subjects one towards another, and in that unity secure more easily the obedience owed to us by each and every one of them, we provide ... .

XIV. That all injuries and offences caused among our subjects by the iniquity of the times and the situations which have arisen therefrom, and everything else which happened in or was caused by the present tumults shall remain extinguished, as if it was dead, buried, and had never occurred: most strictly, and on pain of death, forbidding all our subjects of whatever rank and quality to attack or to injure one another, or to provoke one another by reproaches about what has passed, or to dispute or quarrel among themselves about matters of religion, or to offend or outrage one another by word or deed, but to restrain themselves and to live peaceably together like brothers and fellow-citizens: those who contravene this ... shall be punished on the spot and without any other form of trial, in accordance with the rigour of this present edict.

Given *en mandement*, at Amboise the 19th day of March the year of grace 1562 [1563] and of our reign the third. Signed, Charles. By the King in his Council, Robertet, etc. Sealed in yellow wax. *Sic signatum*, Du Tillet.

Source: Haag, *La France Protestante: Pièces Justificatives* [F5], pp. 61-5 (no. 21).

23 Organising a national church. From the Synod of Orléans (1562) to La Rochelle (1571)

The Third National Synod, Orléans, April 1562

Anthoine de Chandieu, chosen President.
Robert le Maçon and Pierre Sevin, chosen Scribes.

[*General matters*]

2. The Princes and other great Lords following the Court, in case they would have churches instituted in their houses, shall be desired to take for their pastors such as are ministers in churches truly reformed, bringing with them sufficient testimonials of their lawful calling to the ministry; and who shall before their admission subscribe the Confession of Faith of the churches in this kingdom and our church discipline. And that the preaching of the Gospel may be more successful, the said protestant Lords shall be requested, every one of them, to erect a consistory, composed of the ministers and other persons most eminent for piety in their said family, by which consistory all scandals and vices shall be suppressed, and the rules of discipline observed.

4. If it happen that a bishop or curate desires to be promoted to the ministry of the Gospel, they shall not be received until such time as they are first admitted members of the Church, renounced all their benefices, and other rights depending on the church of Rome. Professing also public repentence for their past sins, as shall be ordered

by the consistory; and after long trial and proof of their repentance, and godly conversation, they may be chosen to the ministry of the Gospel according to the canons of our church discipline.

12. The churches shall admonish the faithful of both sexes to be very modest in their apparel, and to avoid all excesses and superfluities. However the churches shall make no decrees concerning this, because it is a matter pertaining to the civil magistrate, but rather cause the King's ordinances relating to this to be diligently observed. Nor may the churches excommunicate any man or woman for using such habits and fashions as are common and customary in this kingdom.

21. Concerning names imposed on children, ministers shall reject those which remain from the old paganism. Nor shall they give to infants such as are attributed to God in Holy Scripture, nor names of office, as Baptism, Angel, Archangel. Moreover parents and godparents shall be admonished as far as possible to take those which are approved by God's sacred Word.

26. Churches having printers and booksellers shall carefully advise them to print no books concerning religion, or the discipline of the Church, before they have referred them to their consistories, because of the inconveniences which have arisen. Nor may any booksellers or hawkers sell scandalous books, nor may they in the sale of their books take unto themselves immoderate gains.

The Fourth National Synod, Lyons, 10 August 1563

Pierre Viret, chosen Moderator.

[*Observations, additions and annotations to the Church Discipline*]

6. Although it may be convenient in weighty and important business of the Church to call together with the consistory some of the most discreet and judicious members of the Church, though they be not in actual office in the consistory; yet nevertheless, there ought not to be any other ordinary assembly or form of council for church matters, excepting the consistory, which has been chosen and settled by the Church for this very purpose.

11. If any officer of our Reformed churches has committed idolatry in times of persecution, they shall be deposed from their office and do public penance before they are admitted to communicate at the Lord's Table. And private persons who have offended in the same manner shall undergo such penance as the consistory judge fit. The

whole to be managed with Christian moderation according to the Discipline.

14. Ministers, though settled in one church, may be lent to other churches for a time, for their instruction and comfort. When proponents are called to the ministry, they too shall be settled in one church. Synods shall have power to remove ministers from one place to another, for some certain reasons and considerations, providing the churches consent to it, according to the Discipline.

[Particular matters]

3. The brethren of Normandy requested that the article of the synod of Paris might be altered where it was ordained that no beneficed person should be received into the ministry without long experience both of their life and doctrine. The present assembly decrees that the said article shall remain entire and in its full power without any relaxation or alteration, and that it may be more diligently observed.

24. The churches shall be advertised not to celebrate the marriages of unknown persons unless they bring certificates from the churches where they belong.

36. A gentleman troubles the church, and wills that his wife should come up to the Lord's Table immediately after him, before any of the men. And although it had been ordained by the synod of Caen that he should follow the general practices of the churches, yet nevertheless he will not consent thereunto. This assembly orders a letter in their name to be sent to him, advising him to walk with more humility.

43. A certain abbot in Limousin professes himself a doctor and preacher. The people hear him gladly; nevertheless he maintains his monks, goes in person to the mass, and does not join himself to a Reformed church. Asked whether the people may be permitted to hear him; and whether those ministers who exhorted him to read his lectures have done well, it is answered that those ministers who have been present at his sermons, or exhorted the people to become his hearers, or him to teach, ought all of them to be grievously censured. And the people shall be admonished to content themselves with their own preachers; and that my lord abbot be desired to forebear his lectures, and subject himself to the order of God's church, and tarry until he be called unto such an office.

[Memorials drawn up by the present synod]

1. The churches shall be admonished to make a faithful collection

of all notable and remarkable passages of divine providence which have happened in their localities, and to send them to our brethren of Geneva with all possible speed and diligence.

5. Our brethren the pastors of Geneva shall be entreated to write us their judgement about some principal points of church discipline, as about election of church officers and the sentence of excommunication, and to send copies of this judgement to the church of Lyons, which is ordered to distribute them among the provinces of this kingdom, that the deputies may come prepared with well-digested thoughts about those articles to the next synod.

Distinction of the provinces of France.
1. The île de France, Picardy, Brie and Champagne.
2. Burgundy, Lyonnais, Forez, and Auvergne.
3. Dauphiné, Languedoc, and Provence.
4. Poitou and Saintonge.
5. Gascony, Limousin and Agenais.
6. Brittany, Touraine, Anjou and Maine.
7. Normandy.
8. Berry, Orléans and the county of Chartres.

The vagrant and deposed ministers.
1. Marmande, who was minister near Chartres.
2. Jacques de Vernueil, or Berneil, employed in Normandy.
3. Beaujean, Beraud, or Bergard, for he is known by all these names. He was an Augustinian friar and prior of their house at Poitiers ... .
6. A great lubberly Franciscan friar, who abandoned his flock in the house of the Lord de la Martinière. He is called La Motte ... .
20. Jacques Courtain de Calaux, a fellow boasting himself a prophet, and to be endowed with a prophetic spirit.
22. Jérôme Bolsec, a most infamous liar and apostate.
[24 names in all].

The Fifth National Synod, Paris, 25 December 1565

Nicolas des Gallars, minister of Orléans, chosen President.
Louis Capel, minister of Meaux, and Pierre le Clerc, elder of Paris, scribes, after the invocation of the Word of God.

6. Whereas certain churches, and in particular that of Sens, earnestly demand that it may be permitted them to establish a council in

their city, composed of wise and experienced persons, not being officers of the Church, urging for it, the multitude of their enemies necessitating them to stand upon their guard, and that hourly diverse affairs of great importance occur, calling for prompt and speedy assistance to the conservation of the Church ... . The assembly is of the opinion that no such council should be established, excepting that composed of ministers, elders and deacons, being confident that God will always bless their labours and counsel, whom he has called to office in the Church, and better serve himself by their simplicity than by the prudence of worldly politicians. Besides, it shall always be lawful for the pastors and elders on any great and difficult affair to call unto them such persons as by whose counsel they may be any way aided ... . But we do not hereby intend to authorise any company of men, besides the Consistory, to be styled the council of the Church.

7. Because in the ninth article of the Discipline it is said that when ministers are confirmed there shall be imposition of hands upon them, yet not of pure necessity, it is demanded whether the churches that have no such custom should for time to come submit to this usage? The reply was, that there being neither precept nor promise touching this matter, therefore no necessary obligation shall be established about it. However this ceremony being of ancient usage in the Church, practised by the Apostles and tending to edification, the churches shall endeavour to promote conformity to it, as far as possible they may.

[General Advertisements to the Church]
28. Because there is everywhere a visible decay and a great want of ministers, and that some provision may be made for a succession, the churches shall be admonished by our brethren the provincial deputies, that such as are rich would maintain some hopeful scholars at the universities, who being educated in the Liberal Arts and Sciences, and other good learning, may be fitted for and employed in the Sacred Ministry.

The Sixth National Synod, Vertueil, 1 September 1567

M. de L'Estre, chosen Moderator.

[General advertisements to the churches of France]
2. Explaining the second article of the Discipline under the head of particular orders, it is resolved that all carpenters, masons, glaziers

and other artisans shall abstain from all manner of work in their respective trades, that may in the least favour idolatry; and if after admonition they continue in such practices they shall be subjected to censures.

13. This assembly is informed that the members of some churches being disgusted at their consistories, declare that they would not subject themselves to their censures, and therefore to calm and pacify them they thought good to leave the election of the new consistory to the body of the people. But this national synod does not in the least approve their action, as being a very evil matter and of dangerous consequence: and judges that the said church shall be advised to conform itself with the other churches of this kingdom unto the canon of the Discipline, viz. that elders and deacons shall be chosen by the Consistory and then presented to the people.

[The Roll of Vagrants]

1. One Charlir, or Charles, who says of himself that he was a Counsellor of Grenoble, ... a man of mean stature, his beard waking grey, deposed from the ministry of Uzerche by the brethren of Limoges for lying, cheating, forgeries, roguish tricks, drunkenness, unchaste kissings, and at Pamier for dancing and contumacy against the Church. This fellow intrudes himself into all places where he can get admittance to preach.

2. Simon du Plessis, going by the names of Mr Peter Grueill, La Mulle, Nevill, Grand-champ, La Jaunière, formerly a Franciscan friar, deposed at Orbec by the *classis* of Eureux, because without any call or ordination he had usurped the ministry of the Gospel, quitting and retaking at pleasure his friar's weeds. Convicted of and condemned for adultery by the provincial synod of Normandy, accused also of being confederate with robbers, he came into Saintonge, but is now at Avranches; a fellow of great stature, yellow beard and hath lost two of his front teeth.

5. Jean Clopet, alias Child, a wretch full of heresies, a champion for the Mass asserting its goodness, in two points only excepted, viz. prayers unto the saints and for the dead. Maintaining that the good and bad have equal privilege to communicate in the body of Christ, as also celibacy and praying towards the East; and that the commentaries upon the Scripture are needless: and that Calvin did very ill in writing of predestination; and that man may keep perfectly all the commands of God. He is a fellow of mean stature, of yellowish beard, and speaks somewhat thick, plain in his looks, and tawny face, aged twenty-five, a Savoyard, born in the country of Bresse.

The Seventh National Synod, La Rochelle, 2-10 April 1571

Theodore de Bèze, minister of Geneva, chosen Moderator.
Nicolas des Gallars and de la Rougeraye, chosen Scribes.

[General matters]
  [Observations upon the Confession of Faith]
  2. Forasmuch as our Confession of Faith is printed diverse ways,
the synod declares this to be the true Confession of Faith of the
Reformed churches in France, which begins with these words, 'We
believe that there is but one God ...', which confession was drawn up
in the first national synod held at Paris, 25 May 1559.[1]
  8. When the Confession was read and ended, the whole synod
agreed that there should be three copies fairly written in parchment,
whereof one should be kept in this city of La Rochelle, another in
Béarn, and the third at Geneva, and all three should be subscribed by
the ministers and elders, deputies of the provinces of the kingdom, in
the name of all the churches. Moreover, her Majesty the Queen of
Navarre, and my Lords the princes of Navarre and Condé are also
requested to subscribe it with their own hands.
  [Observations on the Discipline]
  4. On the thirty-eighth article, M. de Bèze having propounded
according to the commission given him by our brethren of Geneva
that there might be some certain person chosen to answer the many
books published against our doctrine, and that those answers might
be brought into the provincial synods, and there perused by them,
and so to be printed either with, or without the author's name, as the
synod should judge most convenient. This motion was well approved
by the whole assembly.
  [Concerning particular orders]
  4. On the fourth article, the Queen of Navarre demanded our
advice, whether through want of others she might with a good conscience receive and establish Roman Catholic officers in her dominions, as also in her Court and family. To which the synod humbly
replied that her Majesty should take special heed about her domestic
officers, and as much as possible only to employ persons fearing God
and of the Reformed religion; and that she should cause the papists
that are peaceable and of unblameable lives to be instructed, and
that she should utterly discard those traitors who forsook her in her
necessities, and cruelly persecuted God's saints in the last troubles.

[1] This declared the supremacy of the Paris version over the text supplied by the
Geneva church and still preferred by Geneva's printers.

9. According to the twelfth article, the colloquy of Beauvoisin is ordered to receive books from all parts of the kingdom, and all other ministers shall send controversial books, written by their adversaries, unto them, that they may be answered. To this purpose are named Messieurs de Saulete, de Chandieu, de l'Estre. des Bordes, Houlbec, Despina, Daneau, Daniel Toussain, de Villefort, de St Paul and Merlin. And these books shall be sent from all the provinces unto the said M. d'Estre. And the said colloquy of Beauvoisin shall determine which of the eleven deputies is to undertake an answer, and what may be needful or convenient for them.

There were present at this synod of La Rochelle, Jean by the grace of God Queen of Navarre, the high and mighty prince Henry, Prince of Navarre, the high and mighty prince Henri de Bourbon, Prince of Condé, and the most illustrious prince Louis, Count of Nassau, and Gaspard, Count of Coligny, Admiral of France, and divers other lords and gentlemen, besides the deputies, who were members of God's Church.

Source: Quick, *Synodicon* [F1], i. 22-101.

24 The Morély affair

The Synod of Orléans, 1562

[Particular matters]

7. As to that book entitled *A Treatise of Christian Discipline and Polity*, composed and published by Jean Morély, the council judges that in the points concerning the discipline of the Church, by which he claims to condemn and subvert the order received in our churches, founded upon the Word of God, that the said book contains wicked doctrine, and tends to the confusion and dissipation of the Church. And therefore the council cautions the faithful to take heed of the aforesaid doctrine.

Source: Quick, *Synodicon* [F1], i. 27.

[Morély before the Geneva Consistory]

Tuesday 31 August 1563. M. de Villiers alias Morély summoned to state whether or not he still wishes to stand by his book in which he rejects the church-order of this city, including its Consistory, and even goes so far as to challenge the powers of the civil magistrate. The principal points having been put to him, he asked for time to reply to each one in turn and to reflect on the matter. This response having been heard, it was decided that he had not replied pertinently and that he knew very well just how to uphold his errors, it being notorious that he was convinced that he was right. It was decided to excommunicate him, and to send him back to their Lordships on Friday so that they can use their discretion in proceeding further with the matter. Furthermore it was resolved that the Honourable Ministers should make representations on the affair to their Lordships, M. Calvin and M. de Bèze being entrusted with this task.

Source: *Calvini Opera* [C1], xxi. 807-8.

The Synod of Paris, 1565

[*General matters*]

1. Forasmuch as the Church of God ought to be governed by a good and holy discipline, and that no other may be introduced but what is grounded upon the Word of God, the ministers and elders deputed from the provinces of this kingdom to confer about ecclesiastical affairs, ... after diligent perusal of the book and other writings of Jean Morély, concerning the polity and discipline of the Church, and sufficient conferences had with him from the Holy Scriptures about it, do by this present act condemn his said books and writings, as containing evil and dangerous opinions, subverting that discipline which is conformable unto the word of God and at this day received in the Reformed churches of this kingdom: and whereas delivering up the government of the Church unto the people he would bring in a new tumultuary conduct, and full of confusions, upon it, and whence would follow many great and dangerous inconveniences; which have been remonstrated to him, and he once and again admonished to abandon these matters, which yet he will not do, but persists in his assertions, saying that he is persuaded that his opinions are built upon God's Holy Word.

Source: Quick, *Synodicon* [F1], i. 56-7.

Morély to de Bèze, Paris, 4 February 1567

Monsieur, and Father in our Lord, I have received your letters dated 15 January and have found in them what in good devotion and no less hope I have long been waiting for, namely to learn that you have now trodden underfoot all recollection of my insults to you in my letters to M. Du Rosier; I pray that God will forgive me for them ... .

Following your advice, I have written to their honoured Lordships of Geneva and to the Consistory and I beg you to intercede on my behalf with them so that in the end I may make peace with them and return to their good graces. With that end in view I have asked Messieurs the Pastors of that church to inform you how things have gone with regard to myself, as I have asked them to do. And because you have found some contradiction between what I have written about the Discipline and what is contained in my letter of recognizance, namely that what is received now in this kingdom is good, holy, and founded on the Word of God, I would add the qualification which I have everywhere declared and written, namely, that this order is salutary and good for the churches at present, but that the order I have written about belongs to the realm of assurance and of foresight for the future. And, subject to your correction, I have nowhere written otherwise with respect to the authority of the synods. Summer fruits are beautiful, wholesome and good to eat, but their season is short; yet it would be a foolish man who refused them on that account. For my part, I have merely wanted to supplement the present short-term order of things with what seemed to me to belong to the hopes we may have of it in the future.

In the same way I will add a word about some thoughts I wanted to advance when I wrote to M. du Rosier on the subject of prophecy. What I wrote was at his request, and I insisted that it should never be published. The fact that I wondered whether I ought to adduce some authorities in favour of this argument in the treatise I presented to Messieurs the Pastors of Geneva shows how doubtful I was about the advisability of letting it be read more widely. I have asked Messieurs the Pastors to send you a copy of the propositions I hold concerning eternal election and reprobation, which have been countersigned by three excellent persons [pastors and elders of the Church in Paris]. I have no doubt that you too will find them satisfactory and that you will acquiesce in the peace which (thanks be to God) I enjoy in these churches, within which I hope that God will permit me to persevere for the rest of my life, and that I shall accord to you all honour and friendship due.

And now I, dear Sir and Father, I pray to the Lord our God, to augment in you the gifts of his Holy Spirit and to preserve you for a long time yet in his Church and under his blessing. From Paris,

4 February 1567.
Your most humble son and servant, J. Morély.

Source: *Correspondance de Bèze* [F7], viii. 59-60 (no. 535).

De Bèze to Viret in Béarn, 1 March 1567

Dear Sir and Brother, I believe that by now you will have received my last letter. When you can, please write to us and tell us how things are getting on down there. I do not know whether you have heard what happened in Montpellier after you left, about the arrival there of that good and holy person (and, unfortunately, the simultaneous arrival with him of the spirit of division), and about the events which ensued. These people who argue all the time about forms of church discipline remind me of priests and monks talking about celibacy. For if there is anything they hate and fear and cannot abide it is discipline of any sort, as their lives demonstrate.

Morély wants pastors to be elected by the express suffrage of all the people. What is more, although he has no vocation whatsoever, he has taken it upon himself to overturn the entire order of the Church, despite all the condemnations of him by the synods. He has been endlessly stirring up trouble in our midst over the last five or six years. If we excommunicate him on account of all this, or even make it clear that he is not very welcome, La Haye cries blue murder, as if we were intent upon restoring papist tyranny. And if what Morély seeks were to come to pass, where would we be? Morély has attacked the discipline which has been established with such care, and which enjoys God's blessing, as everyone knows. There are those who think one should not condemn his book, although they cannot deny that a thousand mad ideas are to be found in it, even when they want to approve of the rest of it. Take the case of a faithful servant of God who has answered all Morély's arguments in the most modest possible manner – even that is thought to be unacceptable, as if one ought to stand idly by, not only when the house of God catches fire but until it is all consumed in the flames.

They want something more perfect than what we have. And the Lord wants us to give it to them. Oh, the poor Church of God, if to be perfected it has to rely on the advice of people like that, of whom it may be said, 'By their fruits you shall know them'! I cannot see why they should be tolerated within the Church, however much they insist that the Church cannot do without them. One has seen how

[103]

difficult it is to make men submit themselves to the reprimands of other individuals; it is more difficult again to lead them to see that they can benefit from consistorial corrections. What would the situation be if a whole multitude of people had to hear all the cases and to deliver their verdict? In an entire town one can just about find, with great difficulty, a dozen tolerable elders fit to hear and judge cases adequately. What would it be like if the right to judge lay with everyone in common? Take a question of doctrine: if they want everyone to judge it all together, what would become of the good men, and what better could all the heretics wish for? It is only with great difficulty that one can find in entire regions a single man suitable for the ministry. If the practice was for every man to cast his vote, straight off, what procedure could be adopted when it was necessary to call the minister from another place? And if one fears scandals, what better way to bring them about than to stuff into the Church all the world's garbage?

You are entirely familiar with the characteristic process by which the churches out there were planted and afterwards kept in being. And if elections and ecclesiastical judgements had been regulated in this fashion, you know very well what the result would have been. You are not unaware of the means by which Satan has little by little brought about the ruin of the church in Strasburg, and, more recently, of the church in Frankfurt. For my part I have no doubt at all that we will see the entire ruin of the churches here there and everywhere when we follow the procedures these people want to establish. I pray to God that he will not let me live to see such desolation. God be praised, I do not think we are in any such danger here. As long as God grants me life and wants to make use of me in his Church, I will set myself against all this, from my head to my feet. I cannot bear to see such destruction masquerading under the name of edification, and being carried out by such people, in the churches for the benefit of which God has given me the grace, with others, to devote my life ... .

As far as I myself am concerned, God willing, no more difficulty will arise, when after all there are a hundred thousand worse things to worry about. But the main issue lags behind – what are we to do about that? And when, instead of recognising his many, many faults, he pleads his simplicity, and forgets himself so much as to take for the basis of his justification the very letters in which he has shown himself guilty of so many cowardly propositions unworthy not only of a Christian but of any frank and honest man, what can I say, except that he goes from bad to worse? You can see why, since it has pleased the Queen [of Navarre] to ask my advice about whether or not she should retain him in her service, I cannot counsel her to do so. And because her Majesty added in her letters that we should send her some suitable person as a replacement for Morély, we have approached M. Masseillan, who has, in the end, agreed to accept the post if no one else can be found. As far as I know him, I estimate that he is entirely suitable in every way. I believe that you are acquainted with him, so perhaps you too can provide a testimonial for him.

Source: Correspondance de Bèze [F7], viii. 78-9 (no. 341).

25 Guidance from Geneva. Two further letters from Théodore de Bèze

Letter from Théodore de Bèze to Nicolas Pithou for the church in Troyes, 26 March 1566

My very dear brother, I hope that you and all the company in Troyes will not to take it in bad part if I warn you frankly about two points which must be appreciated if you want God's reign to prevail among you. One concerns the coldness, or icy indifference, which grips the hearts of many. The other concerns various kinds of games, to which some people are too much addicted.

With reference to the first: to have tasted the doctrine of life and then to have become disgusted with it is a most dangerous sign of spiritual death. I beg each one of you in God's name most carefully to weigh in the balance the grace which you have been given, and to consider well the implications of an equivalent weight of divine malediction. We have it from the mouth of the Son of God himself that the people of Sodom and Gomorrah got a better deal (if one can use these commercial terms) than the one which will be available to those who refuse the proffered Word of the Lord. What reward can be expected, then, by people who, after having received the Word, dishonour it by their idleness and contempt ? I wonder what kind of an answer such people would give to our brethren who have bought with their blood such liberty as we now enjoy? If such people will stop for a moment and remember what they used to be like in the times of the great persecutions, when they burned brightly with the zeal of the house of God, and if they will compare this with what they are like nowadays, when although some of them feel chastened, others let themselves succumb to temptations which once they would have overcome, it will be astonishing if they do not feel ashamed of themselves. I sincerely hope they will, so that, by checking themselves in good time, they will not at any time fall under the condemnation of the Lord.

With reference to the other point, the question of games: I cannot express my amazement that in such terrible and calamitous times, when we hear on the one hand of so many blasphemies against God, and on the other of so many poor brethren afflicted, and when there is such howling even from unbelievers oppressed by hunger and poverty, there should be people so stupid as to be thinking about things like games instead of being continually in tears and at prayer. I am fearful that the Lord, faced with this, may soon bring it all to an end as he did in the days of Noah; if he does so no one will be more surprised than those who mock. However, we do realise that people's spirits cannot be kept up unless they have some form of recreation, and that extreme severity is not to be recommended in this matter, or indeed in any other. There is room for a great deal of discretion here, even though the times call rather for sorrow than for play. But we should bear in mind all the time that Satan, under the guise of giving us a pastime, is subtle in the way he deliberately brings us to ruin.

Some games are entirely forbidden; these include games which are based entirely on luck, and which do not demand any praiseworthy effort of body or of mind, like games of dice and of cards, and other games forbidden by the civil law. For the truth of the matter is – whatever people try to pretend – that such games are simply inventions to take money away from others. It is no use people trying to excuse the evil involved by claiming that they are not playing out of greed. Because if they follow their conscience they will have to admit that even if no money is lost, something else more precious even than money, namely time, is wasted. They cannot deny that time is illspent on pursuits which are no use to soul or to body, and that it would not so be spent were it not for the bad habit of taking pleasure in vain things. Also they know perfectly well what is the view taken by respectable and moderate people about such games.

There are other games, based upon bodily activity or upon the use of the mind, like chess, or upon a mixture of luck and skill, like backgammon. I will not condemn these outright, since they do provide refreshment for body or mind, or for both at once, but I do assert that in using them properly one must have regard to two questions in particular. First, that such games are not to be played professionally, for a living, for that is not how we should employ our talents; God has not made us so that we may play, but so that we may serve him, and, with due deliberation, help our neighbour. Second, that God is not dishonoured nor our neighbour in any way harmed by the way the games are played.

Here, briefly set out, is the best ruling I can give you on this matter. If anyone demands to know upon what passage in Scripture it is founded, I refer him to the commandment *Thou shalt not steal*, according to which I believe all those who play to take money, however small the sum, from anyone else, to stand condemned, unless they can demonstrate to me that gambling is one of the ways in which God has ordained that it is legitimate to acquire the goods of your neighbour. I do not think anyone will ever succeeding in convincing me of that. The other foundation in Scripture is the continual condemnation found there of idleness, frivolity and everything that arises from these, in short of everything that does not render our minds or our bodies better disposed to acts which redound to the glory of God and to the edification of one's fellow-man.

In a word, I hope that the memory of recent calamities and the warning signs of calamities yet to come will teach those who call themselves Christians and children of God to think about the things that touch them most nearly, rather than to amuse themselves with such vanities, which is the best name I can give them at this time. I have written to you in this way, not to reprove you personally, but because I know that you will know very well how to pass on what I say to those who have need of it.

Your devoted brother, Th. de Bèze

Source: Correspondance de Bèze [F7], vii. 59-61 (no. 456).

Response of Théodore de Bèze to a letter from his Lordship the Admiral, 1570

There are some who complain about the ministers, saying that far from contenting themselves with their calling, itself only too heavy a charge, they are taking on the management of matters of State and of the regulation of conduct, and that they also want to be informed about the private affairs of every household. In view of this, it has become necessary, in order to hold back the more officious of the ministers, and in order to shut the mouths of the slanderers – in short, to offer guidance to all concerned – to ensure that the boundaries and limits of government both civil and ecclesiastical, within which office-holders should be well content, are clearly observed.

Nowadays all men of good sense and of good conscience are resolved upon two points. First, that the two forms of government are so distributed by the will of God, that anyone who is involved in the one should on no account involve himself in the other. Secondly that human policing, that is to say matters which directly concern law and order in this world, belong to the politic arm, whereas those which are directly connected with men's consciences and with eternal life belong to the ecclesiastic. But the difficulty lies in discerning correctly which is the temporal and which the spiritual sphere, for the difference between the two is more obvious in some matters than in others. When it is a question of invoking force, giving judgement in trials, sentencing, assuming judicial authority, and running matters of that kind, everyone can easily recognise that all this belongs to human policing, as one can see from the fact that ecclesiastics of the Roman Church claim when they mix themselves up in this sort of thing, that they do so because the temporal sword belongs to them as well as the spiritual. In this they greatly delude themselves. Similarly, preaching the Word of God, administering the sacraments, awarding ecclesiastical censures, and other things of this kind belong, quite obviously, to spiritual government.

But there are certain questions which present the kind of difficulty we will here set out; for some people, while they are happy enough for the ministers to preach, to administer the sacraments, to point out abuses of doctrine, and to censure certain vices, such as contempt of the Word of God, blasphemy and such scandals, argue that ministers exceed their functions the moment they begin to involve themselves in government of any kind, whether it be public or private. However, it often happens that the truth of the matter is just the opposite from what these critics infer.

In order to form a correct view of the difference, we must note that the aim of well-regulated ecclesiastical government is the repose and tranquillity of conscience for every man whoever he may be, just as the political good is concerned with peace and tranquillity in this present life.

From this follow two conclusions, which can and should exhaust the question of the difference between the two spheres. The first is this: since all actions, public or private, ought to be done in good conscience, there is no action over which, in this regard, pastors do not have a duty to watch, to render an account of it to God. The second is this: since public tranquillity rests above all upon the peaceable honour and service of God, the politic arm should so watch over everything that involves one's duty to one's neighbour that above all it is on the look-out for perturbers of true religion, who are the most dangerous enemies of the public good. Behold how the Lord has defined and distinguished these two different kinds of government so that each has its own aim, which he has intended to support and uphold each other, as the passage above clearly shows.

Let us take the first: I will show you what it rests upon, and how I interpret it. Saul was rejected because before giving battle he did not wait to hear what the Lord had to say through the mouth of Samuel. Jehosophat, through Ahab, enquired of Micah the prophet if he should make war on the Syrians, and later was bitterly reproved and chastised for not having believed him. The same king fell into great difficulty because he had made an alliance with Ahab, which he would not have done if he had consulted the prophets of the Lord, and these prophets reproached him with this ... . The prophets cried out against the alliances with Egypt and with Assyria. The prophet Jeremiah warned that if the city was not given back all would be lost. Can we say that these prophets had exceeded their bounds? No, certainly we cannot. Nor will it do to claim that the age of prophetic revelation is past. For even though individual and extraordinary visions are no longer vouchsafed, the Word of God endures for ever and its ministry likewise, and it will endure with the same authority until the end of the world.

For howsoever much it may be said that giving orders for a battle, making an alliance between one kingdom and another, receiving ambassadors, besieging or defending a city, and all such matters are really political in nature, the involvement of ecclesiastical government has indeed been necessary in order to make certain that their outcome was in accordance with the will of God. However, that involvement has not been on the same level as the political, but merely with regard to the question of conscience, in order to decide whether or not a course of action could be or should be taken, in the light of the will of God. And if this ought to be done in the greatest matters of State and in areas which touch public affairs and government, as something commanded by God and practised in olden times by all true prophets and servants of the Lord, *a fortiori* it will be admitted that the pastor is bound to watch the actions of individuals, whoever they may be. Why otherwise do the whole of the Scriptures contain such clear signs that reproof is due, not only to idolators, blasphemers and the other transgressors named in the first table of the law, but also to all seditious men and rebels, all murderers, all thieves, all cheats, in brief all those guilty of any vice or crime? Are these signs put there to teach ecclesiastics how to go beyond their due bounds and to trespass on the territory of statesmen? Nothing is further from the truth. For they each have different jurisdictions in relation to the same facts. Political government is concerned with public peace and with handing out to disturbers of that peace civil punishment, pecuniary or corporal. Ecclesiastical government, being concerned only with the conscience, so that the sinner may be made to recognise his fault and amend it, and so that scandal may be avoided, proceeds by purely spiritual censures, as the Apostle teaches us, not saying that such people shall be punished by being fined, or flogged or hanged, but that if they persist in offending they will have no part in the Kingdom of God, and even that they should be cast out from the company of the faithful to make them feel ashamed.

Therefore, to conclude, the civil magistrate will enquire into anything he sees fit, enter houses with impunity, imprison, take oaths, torture if need be, judge according to laws and edicts which he has perhaps himself framed, even sentence to death, if the case requires it. But the ecclesiastic does not enquire into anything he likes, he guards against mere curiosity, contenting himself with that which is necessary in order to prevent an anticipated evil or to remedy an evil which has already come about. If he has to resort to threats, they will be purely spiritual and founded on the Word of God. If the matter merits the attention of the Church, it will be judged with care and discretion, not by a single man, whoever he might be (for in the Church of God there is no monarch but Jesus Christ), but on the advice of the assembly of elders established to take cognizance of such things, in no way in accordance with human laws, but following the Word of the Lord, by which all consistorial and canonical ordinances should be regulated. Such a judgement will not seek to damage the guilty party in his goods or in his body, and certainly not in his soul, but rather it will seek his salvation and the edification of the entire Church.

Similarly, when it is a question of deliberations and enterprises which are of their nature political, but which at the same time, as we have seen, raise matters which are the responsibility of ecclesiastics, it is not said that ministers ought to sit in on the councils of princes and magistrates, nor that they should know their secrets, but it is said that nothing should be undertaken without the rights and wrongs having been examined in the light of the Word of God, and if the said lords and magistrates feel that they are not sufficiently well instructed already to take a view on this, they must have recourse to the Word before all else, it being a matter for their discretion to decide whether to call in advice, how to listen to it, how much of their affairs they need to disclose, what to make of the replies they are given, without deluding themselves or becoming angry. And when the civil magistrates do not carry out their duty of interrogating the Lord, then the pastors must not forget theirs, admonishing or reproving the magistrates with gentleness or severity as the case requires, following the example of the prophets of old. On him who casts scorn on them, evil will surely befall.

Source: Correspondance de Bèze [F7], viii. 270-2 (annexe 7).

(d) Weathering the storm. From the massacre of St Bartholomew to the Edict of Nantes

26 Beza passes on news of the massacre, 4 September 1572

Bèze to Christopher Hardesheim in Nuremberg, 4 September 1572

I write without collecting my wits, stricken in spirit, and with a sense of tragic foreboding, to inform you of the events which have taken place, as they were reported to me, and which I can hardly grasp in my mind, let alone describe in writing or in speech.

On the fourth day after the wedding celebrations of the King of Navarre, which passed off peacefully enough, the Lord Admiral (whom even his enemies admit to have been the wisest and most outstanding of men, on account of the integrity of his mind) was returning from the King's Court to his lodging, reading on the way certain letters that had been handed to him, when two bullets fired by a hired marksman from the window of a house wounded him in such a way that although his body was not injured, one of the bullets took away his right thumb and the other went right through his left arm.

When this happened there was complete confusion, some of those present being in a state of shock, others breaking their way into the house to find the marksman, who made his escape, however, through a small doorway. A maidservant and a boy were taken for questioning, and the Admiral was carried home. The King himself, together with his brother and several leading noblemen, hastened to call on him and pretended to show concern. No effort was to be spared, it was said, to track down the evildoer as speedily as possible, the King swearing that if such a deed was not punished with the greatest severity, he was no King. The very next day (the 23rd of last month) he himself ordered his very own bodyguards to watch the Admiral's house day and night so that he should not be attacked by his enemies.

During the evening of the 23rd it became clear that the wounds were not going to prove fatal, and it was after this that assassins were sent, before dawn on the 24th, from the town to the lodging of our people, an easy way for them to get in having been planned in advance. They cruelly hacked many to death as they slept, and then they all fell at once upon the Admiral, inflicting upon him so many wounds that he fell to the floor semi-conscious. As for the guards posted by the King, not only did they fail to resist, they made the assassination possible, and took a leading part in it, killing without exception all those who did not manage to escape, noblemen, domestics, and others. They hacked the Admiral, inflicting many wounds. Not content with this they threw his body out of the window for the crowd to tear apart. Then the whole town became a scene of massacre. So great was the mad rage that no distinction was made of age, sex or condition. Navarre and Condé[1] only just managed to escape, and there is a rumour, still unconfirmed, that they have been poisoned. Some of the assembled noblemen tried to put up a resistance but in the end a great many were killed, only a very few escaping by making their way into the suburbs and taking flight. It is reported that thirty-two noblemen of the first rank, the most prominent of the leaders of our party, as well as eighty gentlemen of lower rank lost their lives: simply because they attended the wedding festivities of the King of Navarre. And out of the rest of the population, if what is being said is true, no less than 8,000 were slain.

As the news of this atrocity spread rapidly through the provinces, city-gates everywhere were closed, and in case someone resorted to treachery our people were assured in solemn proclamations that they had no need to be afraid (for in many places they could have overcome their enemies in an open fight). And then, that very same night, in almost every town, our people were detained without warning and cast into prison. We still do not know what will happen in most places. They say that in Lyons at least 3,000 people have died, some cruelly put to the sword, some strangled. Others were thrown into the Saône to drown, but some of them managed to struggle ashore and to make their way here.

It is said that the King's brother was not merely a spectator of this horrific tragedy but an actor in it, and that he is soon going to ride with an army to join the Duke of Alva. Many believe that the French fleet, recently assembled at Bordeaux, has sailed to England to commit similar atrocities there, using the money recently injected into

[1] The young princes: Henri of Navarre (then aged nineteen), son of Antoine de Bourbon, who was killed at the siege of Rouen in 1562, and Henri de Condé, heir to Louis de Conde, who had been murdered after the battle of Jarnac in 1569.

the sworn confederation and with greater help from the Pope than has been available before. No one can doubt that these events are the result of a plot worked out at the Council of Trent. In this city, hated as it is by everybody and especially by its neighbours, we have no choice but to behave as if we were in the front line of the battle. I am afraid that all one can hope is that we will go down bravely, unless the merciful Lord makes his presence known to us in some special way and fortifies our inadequacy and our weakness. My thoughts run more upon death than upon life at this time, and I write to you, most honoured friend and dear brother, for what may well be the last time.

The papers you entrusted to me, more precious than any treasure, I am returning to you since it is impossible to have them printed here at the moment because of the unexpected death of Crespin. I will take care somehow, if I can, to see that they get back either to you yourself or to our brother Master Bullinger in Zurich.

I have told you a story of unprecedented perfidy and cruel barbarity; from such events may our Lord God preserve us.

Farewell, my brother. Continue to pray to the Lord for us all. May I ask you to communicate to my esteemed brethren Masters Durnhofer and Camerarius the news of all this for it hurts me to describe repeatedly all this sorrow. One thing only consoles me, the hope that my future life will be but brief, so that I may soon draw nearer to my God.

Geneva, 4 September 1572. Your Beza.

Headed: To the distinguished learned and pious Doctor Christopher Hardesheim, Juriconsult and Councillor of the Illustrious City of Nuremberg.

Source: Correspondance de Bèze [F7], xiii. 180-2 (no. 939).

27 New peace negotiations. Beza and Condé, 1575

On 4 [June 1575] we being assembled read the letters to their Lordships and to M. de Bèze of the Prince of Condé, who is in Basle, in which he demands that M. de Bèze travel to see him in Basle to advise him on the articles of peace proposed by the King of France.[1] The Company has decided that it cannot refuse the request if their Lordships approve it, as in fact they have done. Monsieur de Bèze departed

[1] A peace eventually agreed a year later, on 6 May 1576 (the Peace of Beaulieu, usually known as the Peace of Monsieur because of the role of the King's brother, Anjou).

on this journey on the following Thursday, 9 June, and was back by Sunday the 26th of the same month.

Source: *Registre de la Compagnie des Pasteurs* [G2], iv. 26.

28 The Synod of Ste Foy, 1578

Pierre Merlin, minister, and pastor in the house of Guy, Comte de Laval, was by general suffrages chosen Moderator, and M. François Oyseau, minister of the church of Nantes, and M. Guillaume de la Jaille, minister of the church of Saujon, were chosen Scribes.

There were present and voted in it the most noble and illustrious lord Henri de la Tour, vicomte de Turenne, representing as Lieutenant General his Majesty the King of Navarre, in the province of Guyenne.

There sat also in this synod the judges, magistrates and consuls of the said city of Ste Foy.

General matters

6. The synod of Upper Languedoc shall ordain two or three of their assembly, and such as they esteem best fitting for that service, to answer the public writings of our adversaries; and in their replies and refutations they shall deport themselves according to the canons of our Discipline in that case, with all gravity, piety, civility and moderation.

7. Churches shall be admonished more frequently to practise catechisings, and ministers shall catechise by short, plain and familiar questions and answers, accommodating themselves to the weakness and capacity of their people, without enlargements or handling of commonplaces. And such churches as have not used this ordinance of catechising are hereby expected to take it up. Yea, and all ministers shall be obliged to catechise their several flocks at least once or twice a year, and shall exhort their youth to submit themselves to it conscienciously. And as for their method in preaching and handling the Scriptures, the said ministers shall be exhorted not to dwell long upon a text, but to expound and treat of as many in their ministry as they can, fleeing all ostentation and long digressions, and heaping up of parallel places and quotations. Nor ought they to propound diverse senses and expositions, nor to allege, unless very rarely and prudently, any passages of the Fathers, nor shall they cite profane au-

thors and stories; that so the Scriptures may be left in their full and sovereign authority.

An act for a national fast

For as much as the times are very calamitous, and that our poor churches are daily menaced with many and sore tribulations, and for that sins and vices of all sorts are risen up, and growing in upon us in a very fearful manner, a general day of prayer and fasting shall be published, that our people may humble themselves before the Lord, and all the churches of this Kingdom shall observe it on one and the same day, which shall be Tuesday 25 March next following. And if it may be done the Lord's Supper shall also be administered in all the churches on the ensuing sabbath.

Cases of conscience

20. That article concerning the immodest habits and fashions of men and women shall be observed with the greatest care imaginable. And both sexes are required to keep modesty in their hair, and everything else, that no scandal may be given to our neighbour.

23. Fathers and mothers are exhorted to be exceedingly careful in instructing their children, which are the seed and nursery of the Church, and those who send them to the schools of priests, Jesuits and nuns shall be most bitterly censured. As also the gentry shall be reproved, who place pages or domestics in the houses of lords and noblemen of the contrary religion.

26. The churches and particular persons shall be admonished never to depart from the sacred union of the Church, whatever persecutions may befall them, nor shall they procure for themselves a separate peace and liberty distinct from the whole body of our churches. And in the case of failure herein, they shall be censured as the colloquy or synod shall judge expedient.

Appeals and particular matters

His Excellency the Prince of Condé appealed from the consistory of La Rochelle, for dissuading him from communicating at the Lord's Supper, because of a prize taken at sea by his commission after publishing the last edict of pacification, embraced by the said prince. Unto which his Excellency made this answer, that the said prize was taken before the forty days for divulging the said peace were expired, and it was from the sworn enemies of the King of Navarre, and of himself also. And that it being a mere civil state matter, the consistory had nothing to do with it. To which the consistory replied, that the whole church and city of La Rochelle were greatly scandalised here, because they were accounted infractors and violators of the public peace of the kingdom, and that they were commonly taxed and reproached for such prizes as harbourers and concealers of pirates and piratical goods. And they most humbly beseech his Excellency the Prince to take kindly this their admonition ... . This assembly, having maturely considered the whole affair, doth acknowledge and approve of the zeal of the church and consistory of La Rochelle, especially in opposing itself against scandalous sins, and that herein they have not acted beyond the line of their duty ... . Yet nothwithstanding, this assembly could have wished that the said consistory had suspended and deferred their judgement in an affair of so great importance, and had not been so hasty and precipient about it, that so all suspicion of animosities on either side might have been avoided. And as for his Excellency the Prince, this assembly doth earnestly beseech him not to misconstrue those remonstrances made him in the name of God, which we judge were but just and needful, and grounded upon the Word of God, and therefore we desire his Excellency that he would be pleased to remove the occasion of the said scandal ... and this being done we decree that his Excellency the said Prince shall be received into communion at the Lord's Table.

Source: Quick, *Synodicon* [F1], i. 116-23.

29 Geneva and France, 1585

Conference between the Geneva pastors and the French pastors who have taken refuge in the town

Those who have retreated to this town from France sought advice on how they should conduct themselves with regard to a certain royal edict which informs those who have left the kingdom because of religion that, on pain of forfeiting all right to their property, they must inform the authorities how much stay of residence they have been granted in the places where they are, and also that they are under an obligation to undertake to offer no favour to those who have risen in arms against the King's authority. The Company agreed that this was a matter of great consequence and requested the brother ministers from France who were in the town to come to a meeting with the pastors and professors of Geneva on the following Monday, so that by mutual agreement a firm line could be taken on the matter, to satisfy and reassure those who had asked for this advice.

The next Monday nine ministers from France met with the pastors and professors of the town and having debated the issue lengthily and carefully among themselves, they agreed that those to whom the edict applied could give some kind of a reply to the King, on condition that the reply was in no way prejudicial to the glory of God nor to the duty of a truly Christian conscience. Messieurs de Bèze, Rotan, Caille and Constant were charged with the task of drafting such a reply, to be brought before the Company the following day straight after the sermon to see if it was in accordance with the Company's intentions. It was decided also to instruct the ministers of the Church of France to tell as many of their acquaintance as they could find, at the same hour or soon after, just what was in the said reply, to console and encourage them.

It was decided also that once the wording of the reply was agreed upon and approved, the text would be communicated to those who had taken refuge in Montbéliard and in Basle as well as to those who are still in France, as far as this proves possible ... .

Declaration to be made by the said foreigners on the proposed edict:

On Tuesday after the sermon the four who had been charged with drawing up the response in question brought it to the Company, where it was read, corrected, and agreed in the following form: 'I, N., in obedience to the letters-patent of His Majesty dated 26 November 1585, certify to all concerned that since I cannot and should not do otherwise without forcing my conscience and since His Majesty himself gives me the choice, either to follow the Roman religion or to leave his kingdom within the time agreed, first for six months, then for fifteen days, I have retired to this place of N., well-disposed to His Majesty and to the Crown of France, in order to serve God here, according to the religion which I hold to be true, and in this religion I wish to live and die, unless by a legitimate and Christian council, general or national, or by some other means consistent with the Word of God, I come to be taught that I am in error, in which case I will always be ready to give glory to God and to follow another and better path. And as for the carrying of arms mentioned in the aforesaid letters-patent of His Majesty, I declare and promise that, subject to the grace of God, I will never favour nor aid anyone whom I know or believe to be carrying arms against His Majesty or his estate or against public quiet in France, but that, on the contrary, I will always be ready to employ my body and my goods to the best of my ability, in accordance with the duty of a good, natural and loyal subject and servant of His Majesty, for the preservation of His Majesty, of his Estate, and of the Crown of France, my fatherland, in testimony of which I hereby give my signature.'

This having been done, the refugees from the troubles, noblemen as well as others, were invited in to the meeting, and M. de Bèze made them a speech of consolation and encouragement, exhorting them despite all kinds of temptations to persevere constantly to the very end in the grace which it had pleased the Lord to bestow upon them. Then they were shown the above form of words and given a copy of it so that they could confer together at their leisure, going over it word by word to see whether they could accept it with a clear conscience. They were also told the reasons why it had been decided that some kind of a reply was advisable, and why it had been decided that it should take this form.

Source: Registre de la Compagnie des Pasteurs [G2], v. 95-6.

30 Changing circumstances. The Synod of Montauban, 1594

M. Michael Berault, chosen Moderator, M. Jean Baptiste Rotan, Assessor, M. Jean Gardesy and Jacques Thomas, Scribes.

Deputies

For Provence there appeared no one. And the exiled ministers of the churches there, who had taken refuge in Lower Languedoc, excusing themselves by the deputies of that province, the synod resolved that letters of consolation should be written to them.

[Resolved to censure provinces which had sent no representatives: Vivarais, Velay, Dauphiné, the Île de France, Normandy and Burgundy.]

General matters

15. All ministers are exhorted to be earnest with God in their public prayers for the conversion, preservation and prosperity of the King. And whenever they are at Court, and have access to his Majesty, they shall do their duty in reminding him seriously of the great concerns of his soul's salvation. And the pastors ordinarily residing at Court, or in its neighbourhood, shall be written to by this synod more especially, to put this counsel into practice.

16. Letters shall be sent from this synod to Madame the King's sister, congratulating her perseverance, and advising Her Highness to continue faithful unto the last.

18. Whereas diverse persons would compel consistories to depose before the civil magistrate matters told in consistory; a memorial shall be prepared and presented by the General Assembly of Ste Foy, to take this matter into their most serious consideration, and to procure a grant from His Majesty, for the conservation of the liberties of consistories.

22. Churches that have neglected their duty of paying the quota towards the last assembly held at Mantes, and other assemblies elsewhere, and to this also, which is shortly to be held at Ste Foy, shall be summoned once more by the deputies of their provinces to bring in out of hand their respective proportions, and in default hereof, their said deputies shall immediately upon their return, by the authority of this synod, deprive them of the ministry of God's Holy Word and sacraments, with an interdiction unto all ministers from officiating among them.

49. The present synod returns thanks unto M. Berault, Rotan, and the other pastors, for their pious endeavours in maintaining the truth at the conference held at Mantes with M. de Perron and other popish theologians, and ratifies their whole proceedings, and that offer made by them to continue the said conference at the pleasure and commandment of His Majesty. In pursuance whereof the synod has nominated twenty pastors, out of whom twelve shall be chosen to confer with those of the Romish Church, that so the provinces may have notice, and come prepared for the said conference.

Particular matters

4. Those of the Île de France shall be severely censured for proposing to this assembly a politic union with those of the Romish Gallican

[119]

E

Church, in defence of the liberties of the Gallican Church against the Pope. And letters shall be despatched unto those aforementioned persons, to acquaint them that their proposition was judged utterly unworthy of our consultation, and they shall be further censured for demanding competent judges both of the one and the other religion, to decide the points in controversy between us; as also for demanding that neither national nor provincial synods be convened, unless on very great and weighty occasions, and that very rarely.

Source: Quick, *Synodicon* [F1], i. 157-69.

31 The Edict of Nantes, April 1598

The Edict of Nantes

Henry by the Grace of God, King of France and Navarre, to all present, and to come, greetings ... .We have by this edict or statute perpetual and irrevocable declared and ordained, saying, declaring and ordaining:

1. That the memory of all things past on the one part and the other, since the beginning of the month March 1585, until our coming to the Crown, and also during the other precedent troubles, and the occasion of the same, shall remain extinguished and suppressed, as things that have never been.

3. We ordain that the Catholic Religion shall be restored and re-established in all places and quarters of this kingdom and country under our obedience, and where the exercise of the same hath been intermitted, to be there again, peaceably and freely exercised without any trouble or impediment.

6. And not to leave any occasion of trouble and difference among our subjects, we have permitted and do permit to those of the Reformed Religion to live and dwell in all the cities and places of this our kingdom and countries under our obedience, without being enquired after, vexed, molested, or compelled to do any thing in religion, contrary to their conscience, nor by reason of the same be searched after in houses or places where they live, they comporting themselves in other things as is contained in this our present edict or statute.

7. We also permit to all Lords, Gentlemen and other person making profession of the Reformed Religion, having in our kingdom and countries under our obedience high Justice as chief Lord ... to have in such of their houses ... the exercise of the said Religion as long as they

are resident there, and in their absence, their wives or families, or part of the same.

9. We permit also to those of the said Religion to hold, and continue the exercise of the same in all the cities and places under our obedience where it has been established and made public by many and diverse times in the year 1586 and in 1597, until the end of the month of August, notwithstanding all decrees and judgements whatsoever to the contrary.

10. In like manner the said exercise may be established and re-established in all the cities and places where it has been established, or ought by the Statute of Pacification made in the year 1577.

12. We do not understand by this present statute to derogate from the laws and agreements heretofore made for the reduction of any prince, Lord, Gentleman or Catholic city under our obedience, in that which concerns the exercise of the said Religion, the which laws and records shall be kept and observed upon that account, according as shall be contained in the instructions given the commissioners for the execution of the present edict.

13. We prohibit most expressly to all those of the said Religion to hold any exercise of the same as well by ministers preaching, disciplining of pupils, or public instruction of children, as other ways, in this our kingdom or countries under our obedience, in that which concerns religion, except in the places permitted and granted by the present edict or law.

14. As also not to exercise the said Religion in our Court, nor in our territories and countries beyond the mountains, nor in our city of Paris, nor within five leagues of the said city.

20. [Those of the Reformed Religion] shall be obliged to keep and observe the festivals of the Catholic Church, and shall not on the same days work, sell, or keep open shop, nor likewise the artisans shall not work out of their shops, in their chambers or houses privately on the said festivals, and other days forbidden, at any trade the noise whereof may be heard outside by those that pass by, or by the neighbours; the searching after which shall notwithstanding be made by none but the officers of justice.

21. Books concerning the said Reformed Religion shall not be printed or sold publicly, save in the cities and places where the public exercise of the said Religion is permitted. And for other books which shall be printed in our cities, they shall be viewed and visited by our theological officers, as is directed by our Ordinances.

27. To the end to reunite so much the better the minds and good-will of our subjects, as is our intention, and to take away all com-

plaints for the future, we declare all those who make or shall make profession of the said Reformed Religion to be capable of holding and exercising all estates, dignities, offices and public charges whatsoever, royal, seigniorial, or of cities of our kingdom, countries, lands and lordships under our obedience, notwithstanding all oaths to the contrary.

30. To the end that justice be given and administered to our subjects, without any suspicion, hatred or favour, as being one of the principal means for maintaining peace and concord, we have ordained and do ordain that in our court the *Parlement* of Paris there shall be established a chamber, composed of a president and sixteen councillors of the said *Parlement*, which shall be called and entitled the Chamber of the Edict.

34. All the said several Chambers [Paris and the other *parlements*] shall have cognizance and by decree shall judge in sovereignty and last appeal, exclusive to all others, the process and differences that are already, or shall arise, in which those of the Reformed Religion are or shall be parties.

58. We declare all sentences, judgements, procedures, seizures, sales and decrees made and given against those of the Reformed Religion, as well living or dead, from the death of the deceased King Henry II our most honoured Lord and father-in-law, upon the occasion of the said Religion, tumults and troubles since happening, as also the execution of the same judgements and decrees, from henceforth cancelled, revoked, and annulled.

70. The children of those that are retired out of our kingdom since the death of Henry II our father-in-law by reason of religion and troubles, though the said children are born out of the kingdom, shall be held for true French inhabitants: and we have declared and do declare, that it is lawful for such at any time within ten years after the publication of this present edict to come and dwell in this kingdom without being needful to take letters of naturalisation, or any other provision from us than this present edict notwithstanding all ordinances to the contrary touching children born in foreign countries.

82. Those of the said Religion shall depart and desist henceforth from all practices, negotiations and intelligences, as well within as without our kingdom. And the said assemblies and councils established within the provinces shall readily separate and also all the leagues and associations made or to be made under whatever pretext, to the prejudice of our present edict, shall be cancelled and annulled, as we do cancel and annul them; prohibiting most expressly to all our subjects to make henceforth any assessments or levy of money,

fortification, enrolments of men, congregations and assemblies of other than such as are permitted by our present edict, and without arms. And we do prohibit and forbid them to the contrary upon the penalty of being severely punished as contemners and breakers of our commands and ordinances.

Given at Nantes in the month of April in the year of grace 1598, and of our reign the ninth.

HENRY.

Secret articles

2. Those of the Reformed Religion shall not be obliged to contribute to the repair or building of churches, chapels or presbyteries, nor to the purchase of vestments, lights, the founding of bells, and consecrated bread, nor shall they contribute to religious brotherhoods or the renting of premises for housing priests or monks, and similar things, unless they are obliged to do so by endowments, foundation or other arrangements entered into by them, their ancestors or predecessors.

3. Nor will they be obliged to drape and decorate their house-fronts on the feast days when this is statutory: they will only be expected to allow the local authorities to do so, without having to make any contribution themselves.

6. Concerning the articles which mentions *bailliages*, the following declarations and concessions have been made: first, in order to establish the practice of the Reformed Religion in the two places granted in each *bailliage*, *sénéchaussée* and *gouvernement*, those of the Reformed Religion shall name two towns in the suburbs of which the said worship shall be established by the commissioners His Majesty deputes to carry out the edict. And if these proposals are not approved by the commissioners, those of the said Religion shall suggest two or three neighbouring towns or villages for each town, from which the commissioners will then choose one.

11. According to the terms of the edict made by His Majesty to obtain the submission of the Duke of Guise, the Reformed Religion shall not be practised or established in the towns and suburbs of Rheims, Rocroi, St Dizier, Guise, Joinville, Fîmes, and Moncornet in the Ardennes.

21. As a result of the edict issued on the surrender of the Duke of Joyeuse, the said Religion cannot be practised in the town of Tou-

louse, its suburbs, or a radius of four leagues, or any nearer than the towns of Villemur, Caraman, and l'Île-Jourdain.

25. The edict issued for the surrender of the town of Dijon shall be observed, and according to this edict there will be no other religion practised in this town and suburbs but the Catholic, Apostolic Roman faith, or for a radius of four leagues.

26. There will be similar observance of the edict made upon the surrender of the Duke of Mayenne, whereby there shall be no worship according to the Reformed Religion in the towns of Châlons, or for two leagues around Soissons, for a period of six years beginning from January 1596. After this period the edict of Nantes will be in force there as elsewhere in the kingdom.

33. A place shall be provided for those of the Reformed Religion to serve the town, *prévoté* and *vicomté* of Paris at not more than five leagues' distance from that town, in which they can worship publicly.

37. Those of the said Religion may not keep public schools except in the towns and places where they are allowed public worship. The provisions formerly granted them for the erection and upkeep of schools will if necessary be verified, and will operate completely and effectively.

43. His Majesty allows those of the said Religion to assemble in the presence of the judge royal, and on his authority to raise from among themselves the expenses of their synods, and the upkeep of those entrusted with the conduct of their worship.

Today, the last day of April 1598, the King is at Nantes and is desirous of giving all the pleasure he can to his subjects of the so-called Reformed Religion, in response to the demands and requests made by them, concerning matters they judge necessary to them both for their liberty of conscience and the safety of their persons, fortunes and property. And because His Majesty feels certain of their fidelity, and sincere commitment to their service ... His Majesty, in addition to what is contained in the edict he has recently drawn up, and which is to be published to regulate their affairs, has granted and promised them that all the fortified places, towns and châteaux which they held up to the end of last August, in which there will be garrisons, shall, by a statement which His Majesty will draw up and sign, remain in their hands under the authority and allegiance of His Majesty, for the space of eight years.

HENRY.

Source: Quick, *Synodicon* [F1], pp. lxi-xcv, and Roland Mousnier, *The Assassination of Henry IV* (London, 1973), pp. 316-63.

32 The Synod of Montpellier, 26 May 1598

M. Berault, chosen President, M. de Montigny, Assessor, and M. de Macifer and M. Cartau, Scribes.

The provinces of Normandy, Anjou and Vivarais were censured for not sending elders together with their ministers.

General matters

2. Forasmuch as it is the duty of all the faithful heartily to desire the reunion of all the subjects of this kingdom in the unity of faith, for the greater glory of God, the salvation of millions of souls, and the singular repose of the commonweal; yet because of our sins, this being rather a matter of our prayers, than of our hopes, and that under this pretext diverse profane persons attempt openly to blend and mingle both religions, all ministers shall seriously admonish their flocks, not in the least to hearken unto any such motions, it being utterly impossible that the temple of God should hold communion with idols; as also that such wretches design only by this trick to debauch easy credulous souls from the belief and profession of the Gospel. And whoever attempts such a reconciliation, either by word or by writing, shall be most severely censured.

14. M. Chamier and Brunier, having brought letters from the assembly of the churches at Châtellerault, together with the edict granted us by his Majesty, and understanding by them that had it not been for that good union and correspondence which is among us, we would never have obtained the liberty of our consciences in the public profession of the Gospel and service of our God, nor justice to be administered to us, nor other needful securities for our lives. This synod, considering former defects in this matter, doth now protest and resolve that for the future that union subscribed and sworn at Mantes shall be better and more strictly kept and observed than ever, that so the articles of this edict may be performed by us, and all other things needful to our preservation, in our obedience to His Majesty and his edicts. And we will also take care that all the provinces do the same, and that if any person should in the least transgress them, or prove disobedient to our remonstrances herein, they shall be prosecuted by all the censures of our Church.

26. This synod proceeding to distribute the 43,333 crowns, and of the one third granted by His Majesty to the relief of our churches, ordains that 3,333 crowns and one-third should be employed in the

erecting of two universities at Saumur and Montauban, and towards the maintenance of each of them it ordains 1,111 crowns, 6 sous and 8 deniers, and to the erecting of two academies in theology at Montpellier and Nîmes, for Montpellier 500 crowns, the rest to Nîmes. The remaining 40,000 crowns shall be distributed among the churches, as well those which are already as those which may hereafter be constituted. And a catalogue was read of the churches in being, whose number was found 760, to wit:

in the Île de France, Picardy, Champagne and Brie 88; Normandy 59. Brittany 14; Burgundy 12; Lyonnais 4. Forêt; Dauphiné, and Provence 94; Vivarais 32; Lower Languedoc 116; Upper Languedoc and Upper Guyenne 96; Lower Guyenne 83; Poitou 50; Saintonge 51; Anjou 21; Orléans 39; which is for each of them 52 crowns, 37 sous, and 10 deniers.

Source: Quick, Synodicon [F1], i. 190-9.

33 The implementation of the Edict of Nantes: some evidence from Dauphiné

The King's instructions to the commissioners, 6 August 1599

To make a start on the implementation the commissioners are to ask the clergy to inform them of any places in the province where the exercise of the Catholic, Apostolic and Roman Religion cannot be practised in full liberty, or any places where churches, houses, goods and revenues belonging to the clergy are occupied; in such cases the commissioners, before they proceed with any other implementation, are to secure the entire restitution of the aforementioned rights as the edict demands ... .

The commissioners are to urge the clergy to enter once more upon the exercise of their duties and to reclaim their dignities and benefices situated in towns and other places held by those of the Religion claimed as Reformed, and so that they cannot excuse themselves by saying that it is not safe to do so, they shall be offered by the commissioners special royal protection and safeguard, and also assured that they have the backing of the *sénéchaux* and of the town magistrates, consuls, town councils and so on, all of whom are responsible for seeing that the re-establishment of divine services is not impeded, and that clergymen are not insulted or attacked ... .

And where any resistance is encountered by the commissioners to the implementation ... they are given special power to declare anyone who impedes them, or his followers, to be rebels against the King, guilty of the criminal charge of *lèse-majesté* and to have incurred the pains and penalties set out in the said edict. The gentlemen and inhabitants of the towns, of both Religions are to accompany the governors and lieutenants-general of the King, and if need be to aid them with their persons and their goods, and are required to participate in the speedy putting-down of such disturbances and the punishment under the terms of the edict of those who perpetrated them ... .

Given at Blois, 6 August 1599. Signed: Henry.

The town of Die

On 6 November 1590 the clergy and other Catholics of the town of Die appeared before us, and declared that when they had been assembled before us in the hall of the bishop's palace to hear the publication of the edict and to witness the reception of the oaths for its observation, they had heard Master Charles Du Cros, advocate of the said town, speaking on behalf of those of the Religion claimed to be Reformed, insist that the oath which they were about to be asked to swear should not in any way damage or be prejudicial to the representations and memoranda that those of that Religion had submitted, which might later be taken into account by the King when amendments were made to the said edict, or when it underwent modification in the court of the *Parlement*. And because the aforesaid clergy and other Catholics do not know what is contained in the said representations and memoranda, they seek an assurance that these, which have been heard in their absence, can in no way damage or be prejudicial to them. In the light of this request we enacted the following provisions:

[*Concerning the use of church bells*]
After consideration of the disagreement which has arisen between those of the two Religions among the clergy, householders and inhabitants of the said town of Die about the respective claims they each have to possess and to use the bell which strikes in connection with the clock, that bell being at present in the tower of the church of Notre Dame, we have laid down that the said bell shall continue to serve as a clock as it has hitherto, as well as for the convocation of assemblies in the town hall, for the distribution of poor-relief and for

giving the alarm in cases of fire, all the inhabitants of the town being liable for a contribution towards the expense of the repair and upkeep of the said clock, without anyone being entitled to claim exemption; and to prevent all contentions it is laid down that the clergy and Catholics of the town shall purchase a bell, to be installed in their church belfry, and those of the Religion claimed to be Reformed[1] shall also purchase a bell, to be installed in their temple, or nearby, to summon them to their preachings, consistories, prayers and other meetings which they are permitted to hold according to the terms of the edict ...

[*Concerning Reformed worship*]
On the same day ... the inhabitants of the said town of Die and of its *bailliage* presented to us a written request ... [asking] us to lay down that the exercise of their religion be confirmed in Saint-Nazaire-le-Désert and in Glandage together with the areas under the jurisdiction of these places, just as it is to be confirmed elsewhere where it is already in existence, so that those places may enjoy the benefit of the provisions of the edict as it is to be enforced in the *bailliage* of Die ... .
[In response]: given that Die and its surrounding area count neither as a *bailliage* nor as a *sénéchausée*, we have declared that there is no warrant for according to Saint-Nazaire-le-Désert or to Glandage the right to the exercise of the Religion claimed to be Reformed, since neither of these places can enjoy the status of a *lieu de bailliage*.

Source: Elisabeth Rabut, *Le Roi, l'Eglise et le Temple* (Grenoble, s.d.), pp. 51-5, 70-2.

---

[1] *La Religion Prétendue Réformée*, often abbreviated *RPR*: the customary Catholic term when referring to the Reformed.

Section 3
THE NETHERLANDS

During the 1540s the Catholic Church appeared to recover the initiative in its struggle with the Reformation. Taking their cue from the Sorbonne, the theologians of Louvain published a succinct statement of Catholic doctrine in 1545. There followed in 1546 a list of forbidden works, in which Calvin's name featured for the first time, and the reorganisation of the inquisition. Following the defeat of the Schmalkaldic League, Charles V set about the reform of the Catholic Church in his hereditary Netherlands. In the same years the Emperor stifled the formation of a Protestant power-bloc in the Lower Rhine when he invaded Gelre in 1543 and forced the evangelical prince–bishop of Cologne to make way for a Catholic successor in 1547. In the Low Countries a vigorous campaign of repression eradicated the last remnants of Munsterite Anabaptism, compelled the Antwerp printers to refrain from the further publication of evangelical literature, and snuffed out the earliest attempts to organise Reformed congregations in the French-speaking towns. Though the influence of Menno Simons grew steadily after 1544, Anabaptism was restricted to the 'small people' in the towns of Holland, Brabant and Flanders, who had neither the clout nor indeed any stomach for a confrontation with the political establishment.

But the persecutions which obliged many evangelicals in the Low Countries to adopt a feigned conformity or to embrace a sectarian existence also forced others to flee abroad. These refugees, many of whom left with no specific confessional loyalties, gravitated to the stranger churches established at Wesel (1544) and London (1550) or sought membership of the local Reformed Protestant churches, of which Emden in East Friesland was by far the most important. A handful of evangelicals from Hainault and Tournai followed their French coreligionists to Geneva. These foreign churches played a crucial role in the revitalisation and confessionalisation of the Reformation in the Low Countries. The 'churches under the cross' could turn confidently to Emden for advice about a host of practical and doctrinal problems and, with less assurance, for experienced ministers [**documents 34, 35**]. From the safety of Emden Protestant printers, who had fled from Antwerp, could supply bibles, catechisms, metrical psalters and Dutch translations of Calvin's works, while *colporteurs* smuggled religious literature from Geneva into the francophone region.

The testimonies of Reformed martyrs, collected by Adriaan van Haemstede and first published in 1559, provided devotional literature and inspirational models for readers, who knew they too might be called to give an account of their faith [**document 35**]. The progress of Protestantism in England, Scotland and above all France in the wake of the peace of Cateau-Cambrésis encouraged the more reckless dissidents, especially in the industrialised countryside of Flanders, to defy the persecuting authorities. Here heretics were sprung from prison by their coreligionists and the earliest open-air services were held [**document 36**].

Since the middle of the century the political elites had been more critical of Habsburg religious policy. Though overwhelmingly Catholic, some at least began to count the cost of a policy which gave the highest priority to the preservation of Catholic uniformity. In the towns of Brabant and Flanders magistrates and merchants expressed concern that measures designed to ensure the orthodoxy of incomers might hinder commerce with their Protestant neighbours. Edicts intended to promote summary and exemplary justice for heretics were also resented, less on humanitarian grounds than because these overrode privileges which safeguarded judicial and property rights. In 1565 a small group of Calvinist minor nobility exploited these fears when they established a league to put an end to the repressive policy. The Compromise, as this league was known, presented its demands to a government, whose temporising policies only emboldened the Calvinists to take matters into their own hands. In the summer of 1566 their ministers, swollen by renegade clerics and lay preachers, began to preach in public in Flanders. Those in authority feared the worst, but were powerless to intervene [**document 37i**]. Evidently these preachers made a powerful impression on their curious auditors, few of whom had any previous knowledge of Calvinist doctrine [**document 37ii**]. In August that year the onslaught on the churches started in the Flemish Westkwartier from where it spread to Antwerp and Holland [**document 38**]. The responsibility of the hedge preachers for the destruction has remained a matter of debate ever since 1566; some at least doubted the legitimacy of deeds, no matter how well intentioned, which lacked the sanction of those in authority. In the event the image-breaking proved a turning-point. As a result the Calvinists forfeited the sympathy of the silent majority, and were exposed as a relatively small minority. By the spring of 1567 their hastily constructed churches [**document 39**] were being demolished, while those who had compromised themselves fled the country at the approach of Alva and his army. Retribution was inevitable and harsh and several thousand were cited before the Council of Troubles to answer for their part in the preachings, iconoclasm and local insurrections [**document 40**].

In exile the Reformed leadership elaborated the sketchy synodal church government, known in the southern Netherlands since 1563, into a full-blown presbyterian organisation. The synod held at Emden in 1571 [**document 41**] proposed the typical pyramidal hierarchy of ecclesiastical assemblies beginning with consistories and rising through *classes* and synods to the general (national) synod. When the revolt in Holland in the spring and summer of 1572 opened the way for a Calvinist reformation of the local church, the ministers were guided by the Emden church order. But that reformation was not easily achieved. In most cases the ministers began, as at Dordrecht, almost from scratch. They had to expel the Catholics from the churches, obtain control of the endowments, and introduce an unfamiliar system of church government and discipline [**documents 42,43**]. To make matters worse, there was an acute shortage of experienced ministers while the local authorities often showed little initial enthusiasm for the changes [**document 44**]. To a large extent the progress of the Reformed churches depended on the efficiency of the *classis*. This body provided the means to re-train the numerous ex-priests who now served as ministers and to bring persistent pressure to bear on the civil authorities [**document 52**]. In the province of Utrecht, where the mass was forbidden in 1580, the magistrates postponed the introduction of *classes* for forty years. No doubt this contributed to the unsatisfactory condition of the Reformed churches in that province as late as 1606 [**document 54**].

In Holland the Reformed churches and the civil powers reached a *modus vivendi*, but mistrust and misunderstanding sometimes strained relations. As a result there was no mutually acceptable church order until 1619, though this was not for want of trying on the part of either the synods or the States of Holland. The order framed at Emden in 1571 had not provided for a situation where the Reformed minister officially re-placed the Catholic priest in the parish church, as happened after 1573 when the mass was proscribed. Controversy chiefly arose concerning poor-relief and parochial institutions, discipline and admission to the Lord's Supper, and the powers of the ecclesiastical assemblies.

In the countryside especially the advance of Calvinism was hampered by Catholic patrons and by the unreformed character of the parish: until deep in the seventeenth century 'papists' continued to serve as church-wardens, sextons, schoolmasters and overseers of the poor [**documents 45, 46, 54**]. While the Calvinist ministers accepted that they should baptise the children 'of all and sundry' [**document 48**], they departed most drastically from the practice of the medieval Church when they restricted access to the Lord's Supper to the 'congregation of Jesus Christ', i.e. to those who had made profession of their faith [**documents 43, 44, 46, 48**]. Those who became members submitted themselves to the discipline of the consistory, which had no jurisdiction over those parishioners who merely attended the church services. Many magistrates (and some ministers) advocated a comprehensive church to which all inhabitants belonged by virtue of their baptism and residence and they therefore wanted parishioners to have unrestricted access both to baptism and to the Lord's Supper [**documents 47, 49**]. From this perspective independent ecclesiastical assemblies appeared unnecessary since 'godly magistrates' now governed the State. By 1583, however, the provincial states were prepared to give conditional recognition to consistories, *classes* and synods. The civil powers were, however, adamant that the ministers of the new religion were public office-holders [**document 47, 49**]. The Reformed synods for their part also understood the need for compromise and accepted the presence of 'political commissioners' at their assemblies, i.e. deputies from the civil authorities. Only with the assistance of the States could the Reformed synods hope for reform of the abuses of which they roundly complained [**document 50**].

In the wake of the Pacification of Ghent (1576) the Calvinists in the southern Netherlands began to stir again and open-air services began around Ghent in May 1577. Calvinist congregations emerged from their underground existence and, with the support of the magistrates, especially in Ghent, a Reformed church was organised with remarkable speed. By the summer of 1578 some fifty ministers were active in Flanders, which had a network of *classes* by 1579. In Antwerp and Brussels a greater degree of religious pluralism was permitted, to the chagrin of some ministers [**document 51i**]. Calvinism attracted considerable support in the southern cities, especially from among the well-to-do merchants, many of whom were prepared to go into exile rather than seek reconciliation with the Catholic Church when Farnese recaptured the Flemish and Brabant towns [**document 51ii**]. According to recent estimates as many as 150,000 people may have migrated northwards. Although by no means all of these were committed Calvinists, there can be little doubt that this influx consolidated the relatively small Reformed congregations in the towns of Holland.

(a) The beginnings of Dutch Calvinism

34 The first Calvinist congregation. Antwerp and Emden, 1555

The leader of the new Reformed congregation at Antwerp seeks the advice of the church at Emden, 1555

The grace and peace of God our Father and His Son Jesus Christ be with you all. Amen.

Dearest brothers in Our Lord Jesus Christ. I greet you all with respect from the bottom of my heart in the brotherly unity of the faith and of the Spirit so that I cannot forbear to write to you concerning my situation and that of our brethren, namely that we have begun in Christ the Lord through the Holy Spirit to gather a small tender bride or congregation (as I have told you in other letters to the brethren). Likewise I have also written concerning our ordinances, how we come together here every Sunday evening, further how the place of the meeting is only declared and made known to everyone on the day itself (by those charged with this task) so that everything is done with resolution and calculation, just as Christ commands us to use the cunning of serpents. For this reason and since ignorance is still very rampant in many people and moreover sects and heresies are so numerous, I have thought it good and profitable to require from each a confession of his faith so that consciences may be strengthened, all false teaching refuted and excluded and the Scriptures searched. Everyone has agreed and this [confession] therefore also follows. Firstly, concerning the will of God according to the Law, the power of the same and our own insufficiency. Secondly, concerning the grace and mercy of God in the Gospel of Our Lord Jesus Christ and our freedom through our trust in Him. Then everyone makes a brief and apt confession of each individual commandment in particular, likewise also of the articles of faith and of the [Lord's] Prayer as well as of the sacraments, as I hope you now understand. And when that is done (for it is taking a long time since there is so much discussion on every commandment and article of faith as a result of the attacks of the sects, because almost everyone is at a loss), we will then, with God's grace, start on the Catechism and the Acts of the Apostles. May He always urge us forward with the power of His Spirit, for the acquisition of which we desire the communion of your prayers, hoping also for our advancement with your good advice, for the little flock increases daily and would do so still more if we kept company with

[133]

those who yet sometimes partake of the Roman abominations and superstitions, such as the baptism of children, marriages, burials and so on.

You will know, my brothers, that my Lord Jan à Lasco, unaware that I was at Antwerp, has summoned me by letters and other messengers to come to him. I have now considered this and informed the brethren here, who do not readily consent to my going, as they fear that they will again be scattered. There are many zealous men here, and some Anabaptists have been converted to the true faith. Thus I am afflicted from two sides, as I wish neither to leave this little flock nor to stay with the congregation. For if I remain with them the burden, on top of my work, is more than I can bear, for every day they give me so much to do that I would eventually not be able to gain my livelihood, and that would also force me to depart. Besides I would learn much from my Lord [Jan à Lasco], which is my heart's desire, except that my Lord wanted me as his domestic servant, which will hardly profit and advance my craft. If he wanted me to do something else, such as reading, writing and so forth, I do not know what I would make of it, since I do not have the gift of Latin. Please give me your brotherly advice in this matter. If I were to leave, our brothers could not manage without a leader, therefore I also want you to come to their assistance so that they are not again dispersed. They have come to me with a proposal and asked me whether I would take on the burden of the ministry, giving up my work entirely, and that they would maintain me. I find it difficult to refuse them this and also difficult to accept, for you know how great is the burden of those who speak against all the nations. So I have replied telling them to write to you and Jan à Lasco for someone better suited than myself and to choose the best for this purpose since you are better acquainted with the mysteries of the faith than they. Even supposing that they desired no one other than myself, as they say, I will neither act myself, nor will I accept their election, but only yours so that we do not resemble the false prophets, who go about [preaching] of their own accord before they have been properly charged. In this matter, most dear brothers in Christ Jesus, consult diligently and faithfully with one another for the upbuilding of the congregation in conformity with God's Word and beseech this also from the Lord God by praying in the name of Christ and He will certainly not withhold from us His Holy Spirit, who may guide us in all truth, and write presently in reply to all things.

Further, I beg my brother Gerard tho Camp to send me the summary and epitome concerning alms on which our brother

Hermannus had begun to preach, while I was with you, namely on what possessions people should [base their] giving, in what way they should give and to whom and so forth. Secondly, a copy of the arguments concerning the objections of the Anabaptists, the reasons why children should not be baptised in the Christian congregation, which I think Hermannus read aloud in Latin before my departure. Not that I have any doubts in these matters, but I desire your help against our opponents, as I should in still other matters, if I remained with the brethren here in Antwerp. Thirdly, write to me also concerning the distinction of the right hand of God, where Christ sits, for the Lutherans take this to mean God's Omnipotence ... [Gaspar van der Heyden proceeds to list the theological arguments employed by the Lutherans in support of their doctrine of the ubiquity of Christ's body and asks the ministers at Emden how he should refute these] ... and still less can I persuade [the Lutherans] of the unity of Christ's body, ... which according to all the Scriptures can only be in one place and so forth. If they [the Lutherans] should ask me, I can give no clear answer to such questions without you.

You should know that the man who was in Emden about six weeks ago and there came to a knowledge of God, has visited me and he was filled with joy. I have visited his wife; I hope the Lord will also open her eyes in His time so that we may all serve Him in holiness and righteousness all the days of our life. Amen. Tell my beloved brother Jacob Michiels that I cannot yet send him the account for the books which he charged me to sell, but I know nevertheless that I have sold more than what he has received from me, for I still sell one or two from time to time and I have already paid out the money ... but I hope soon to settle accounts with him. I also occasionally sell one of my Lord Utenhove's Psalters[1] and I would also certainly sell more if they were not so expensive for there are those who would sometimes take a dozen copies together if they could have them for 3 daalders in order to make some profit. Some of the brethren will only pay 2 stivers a copy and reckon that for the number of the pages they are too dear: that is the reason why they have not sold.

I commend myself heartily to you and to all our dear brethren, especially to the ministers of the Word Gellius, Hermannus and Arnoldus,[2] and to Jacob Michiels, Joos de Rose, Anthonius Asch,

---

[1] Probably *Vyf-en-twintig Psalmen ende andere Ghesangen.* The only surviving edition which predates this letter was printed in London in 1551; this may well be an unknown Emden edition.

[2] Gellius Faber de Bouma, Hermannus Brassius, Arnoldus Veltman, the three ministers of the Emden church.

Gellis Veriaen, Hermanus Spormaker, Gerardus Mortaigne and all who sincerely seek Our Lord Jesus Christ.

Written from Antwerp, 17 December 1555, by me Gaspar vander Heyden, brother to you all in Our Lord.

Tell Martin Micronius that I have forwarded his letter, which he wrote from Frankfurt, to London.

Source: Meiners, *Oostvrieschlandts kerkelyke geschiedenisse* [D2], i. 365-370. Corrected against the original in Emden, Archiv der evangelische reformierten Gemeinde, Repertorium 320-A. 49.

35 The seed of the Church. Martyrs' testimonies

Carolus de Koninck was a former Carmelite monk from Ghent in Flanders. When through God's grace he received the knowledge of the evangelical truth, he bade the life of a monk farewell, and followed the community of Christ to England, where he found employment as a translator of books (for instance the Apocalypse,[1] and the terrible life and death of Francesco Spiera, who had renounced the true faith, [both of] which he translated into Dutch).

When the community of the Lord was driven out of England through the tyranny of the cruel Jezebel, namely Mary, Queen of England, he went with the brethren to Emden in East Friesland. After this he desired to visit the dispersed brethren in Brabant and Flanders, and in 1556 he journeyed there. As he was taking ship in Emden, he felt a sensation as if he were going into a fire, a feeling which came over him again in Groningen, at the house of the godly doctor Hieronymus.[2] When he told his host of this experience, the doctor appealed to him not to go into the papist lands, where the Christians were so cruelly murdered. But he said, 'I must make this journey, but then no more.'

After spending some time in the congregation of the Lord at Antwerp, where Gaspar van der Heyden was minister, he travelled to Ghent, where he taught and exhorted the brethren. And seeing that a severe persecution had broken out, which also cooled the love of many, he earnestly exhorted them unfeignedly to serve Christ, and to shun the popish superstition as poison; and he told them that the Lord could not abide those who inclined to both sides, and were

[1] A translation of John Bale's commentary on Revelation, *The Image of Both Churches* (1545). De Koninck's Dutch ed.: Emden, Gellius Ctematius, 1555.

[2] Hieronymus Frederici, rentmeester of Groningen, and a noted evangelical.

neither hot not cold. After this he travelled to Bruges, where immediately there gathered around him all those who loved the Lord, and, as a result of hearing his Word, hungered after the righteousness of God. He exhorted them to a right Christian belief and a godly life. But Satan, a murderer from the beginning, saw that his kingdom would fall through the shining forth of the Gospel, and stirred up his servants the priests, who by trickery discovered where the Christian congregation met. When Carolus left the meeting at the house in the Ezelstraat they took him prisoner, and threw him in prison. When his brother in Ghent heard of it, he asked two Carmelites to go with him, hoping that in this way, and because Carolus was under a vow of obedience to the superior of his monastery, that he might save him. So he came to his brother and exhorted him to return to his obedience and put on again his monk's habit. Carolus answered him very frankly, that he had renounced the habit and the sign of the beast; that through Christ he had received his freedom, and that therefore he had no wish to be a slave of any man. And he asked his brother to spare himself any further expense and trouble, for it would be in vain.

The monks and priests disputed with him long and hard, but they were not able to withstand the truth of Holy Scripture. He refused to speak with them except in the presence of the authorities, because he knew how they were accustomed to make good their proceedings with lies and obscure the truth. His opponents repeatedly cited the Church Fathers in order to justify their masses, purgatory and intercession to saints. But he cited other Fathers who rejected all this, and based his beliefs above all on the Holy Scripture, which they could not. Thus he rebuked the monks in the presence of the authorities, saying that they were like dumb asses who gathered out of the Fathers nothing but thistles and thorns, and that they did not touch upon what in these books was Christian and good and agreed with Scripture. The authorities and the Council saw that he possessed an invincible foundation in the Holy Scripture, and some were persuaded in their consciences that he spoke the truth. Nevertheless from fear and awe of the bloodthirsty clergy, they spoke very differently when the priests were present than when they were alone with Carolus. When one of them saw such a clear understanding and knowledge of the Scripture in Carolus, so that none of the priests or monks could withstand him but rather withdrew chastened, he promised to help him if he did not remain stubborn, and would ask permission of the Pope to give up the religious life which he so abhorred, and above all that he would provide him with a well-paid position. Carolus answered, 'My Lord, I thank you for your good favour, but you do not know what you are proposing. Why do you wish to give me a well-paid post, so that I can live in peace and tranquillity? But you know well that no riches can bring peace to the heart, when the conscience is burdened. Now you are doing your best to make me deny the truth of the Gospel and affirm lies. That would cause me great disquiet and be like a worm always gnawing in my heart, and what use would goods and riches be then? It is better for me to suffer death for the truth in the Lord, than deny him and die a living death.'

When the priests saw that they could do nothing with him he was condemned as a heretic, and after that, on 22 April degraded from the popish priesthood. Then the bishop delivered him into the hands of the secular judges, just as Christ was given over to the heathen by the priests and the scribes. The authorities condemned him to be burned alive, for which he thanked them, and called upon the Lord to forgive all of them who had through ignorance persecuted him to his death. And then he was led very quietly and meekly like a lamb to the slaughter. When he was bound to the stake, he cast up his eyes to the heavens and called upon the Lord. As the wood caught alight he bore the pain so patiently that they all marvelled at it, and thus he passed to the Lord. A few days after his death the Lord smote one of those who was the cause of his arrest so sorely in his conscience that he paid with his life. God is a just judge of the wicked. Thus Carolus de Koninck was offered up to the Lord in the fire, 27 April 1557.[3] ...

Gillis Verdickt from Elversele in Flanders was brought by his brother Antonius to the knowledge of the truth, after which he went to the congregation where the Word of God was purely preached, and the sacraments dispensed and administered according to the Lord's ordinance. He travelled to Emden and to Norden, where he studied with Micronius, and attended Gualter Delenus's Greek lessons. Eventually he journeyed to Zurich in Switzerland, where his knowledge of Greek greatly increased. After this he returned to Antwerp, where he served the congregation of the Lord. When, on 18 June [1558], the Lord's Supper was dispensed at night, he was also among those who broke bread with the brethren. After this the devil entered the heart of a traitress, who delivered some of the brethren over to the Margrave. First the house where the minister Gaspar van der Heyden lodged was raided, but he was providentially delivered, although the owner of the house was taken. There they found the book of the congregation, in which were written the names of the elders and deacons, among them Antonius the brother of Gillis Verdickt. The Margrave sent his

[3] In fact he was put to death on 26 March 1557.

men to the house of Pieter Vermaarts expecting to find Antonius there, and they seized Gillis thinking he was his brother. But when they discovered their mistake they let him go ... .

About this time the congregation in Brussels desired a minister who could lead them in the ministry of the Word and the distribution of the sacraments. A hypocritical and ambitious man offered himself for the task, and took the office upon himself. When this was made known to the ministers in Antwerp, they thought it best to intervene, in order that the brothers should not be deceived and the congregation fall into disrepute, and so they asked Gillis whether he would put the gifts which God had given him at the disposal of the congregation. When he refused, saying that he preferred to learn a trade, they reproved him sharply, saying that he should not bury in the ground that talent which the Lord had given him, or the Lord would take it away, and chastise him as a useless servant. Finally he agreed to put his gifts to the test, and journeyed there with Adriaan van Haemstede, who was to dispute with an Anabaptist. Adriaan exhorted the community to discharge the other minister, and to take Gillis for a time on probation to see whether he was fit for the task.

At this point the hypocrisy of the other was fully revealed. He declared himself wholly opposed to the congregation, and sought not only to lead the weaker brethren astray, but also treated the Lord's ordinances as if they were marionettes. Thus he prophesied to some brethren that before three days were gone by, several of them would meet their deaths, as indeed happened. Within three days the officer appeared in the house where Gillis was staying and arrested the owner of the house, his wife and Gillis, and put them in the Steenpoort prison under a strong guard.

Shortly after this the officer came to Gillis and began to question him about his ministry, teaching and beliefs. Gillis answered very courageously and skilfully that he had been invited to come in order to edify the brethren with the Word of God; that he taught no other doctrine than that of the Apostles and prophets; and that his beliefs were grounded on this teaching. He questioned him on the sacrament of the altar, to which Gillis replied that he recognised no such sacrament. 'So,' said the officer, 'you are a profaner of the sacraments.' 'No, My Lord,' replied Gillis, 'it is your priests and monks who profane the sacraments, who have kept us and our forefathers in blindness and error, and led us to mute idols and almost to damnation in Hell.' When the officer wished to speak further about the sacraments, Gillis said to him, 'Bring your teachers and priests here, and I shall prove to you how shamefully they have deceived you.'

One of the council members said, 'You have said, I think, that we will all be damned.' Gillis replied, 'No, My Lord, you can repent and live.' The officer asked him how long it was since he had received the Holy Sacrament. He answered, 'I received the sacrament of the Lord's Supper less than six months past in the congregation of the Lord in Antwerp.' Then the officer asked, 'Is it not true that some of your people sometimes come here from Antwerp to hear your preaching?' Gillis answered, 'My preaching is not to be compared with that which takes place in Antwerp. If you wish to hear preaching you must go there; there it is done in the open, so that everyone may judge what is taught.[4] I am sent by them.' The officer asked who preached there. He replied, 'Adrianus Haemstedius.' He questioned him further about who belonged in the congregation here. He answered, 'I do not yet know them, since I have only just arrived.' When the officer left, he said, 'Prepare yourself, I will send learned men to you.' Gillis answered, 'If I had my books, I would rejoice to debate with all the teachers of Louvain openly in the market-place! If only I were permitted to do this.' The officer said, 'You will have the books that you require', and left.

After that the priest of St Goedele came to him, and later many other priests and monks with whom he conversed at length, especially over the sacrifice of the mass, whereby they set at nought the unique sacrifice of Jesus Christ. He showed them that Christ cannot be offered up again for our sins or he must shed his blood again, for without the shedding of blood there is no forgiveness of sins. He also proved that Christ was sacrificed once only, through which He brought an eternal deliverance, as is clearly set forth in the epistle to the Hebrews. He questioned them for two days, bringing them into great confusion. He asked them first, by what command of Scripture they had the power to make oblations for the living and the dead. At this they fell silent and knew not what to say, at which many of those present marvelled. His other question was, what scriptural justification they had for withholding the cup from the people in the communion. Here they advanced many pretexts which were all without foundation, and could not stand against Christ's express command: 'Drink this, all of you.'

Meanwhile the rumour had now spread all over Brussels that a learned young man, only twenty-four years old, had been taken prisoner on account of his beliefs, and had silenced all the priests and monks. This greatly offended the priests, and they therefore preached

---

[4] During 1558 Adriaen van Haemstede had preached publicly in Antwerp, to the dismay and indignation of many Reformed Protestants there.

in all the churches against Gillis and these heretics and seducers, as they called the Christians, and spread scandalous lies about them. For since they could not maintain their kingdom by means of God's Word and the truth, they must oppress the faithful with lies and executions, as is Satan's practice.

Since the officer saw that Gillis only affirmed God's Word, and that the priests could not withstand him, he asked Gillis to submit a confession of his faith in writing. This he did, supporting all his articles with the authority of the ancient teachers ... . The officer's most serious charge was that he had taken part in secret gatherings, which was against the King's command. Gillis said, 'My Lord, am I not permitted to speak of God's word? To call the people to repentance?' The officer answered, 'Preaching should take place in the church, other sorts of preaching cause sedition.' To which Gillis replied that what was good to preach in the church could not be evil out of doors, and he could not believe that it was the King's intention to forbid God's Word, but only sedition, of which there was no suggestion in the congregations, which went about with bibles and testaments rather than with weapons and swords ... .

After he had been in prison for about six or seven weeks, and had suffered a great deal, he was brought before the tribunal on 22 December and condemned to be burned as a heretic. And because he was a quiet and composed man, endowed with great intelligence, he spoke up in a very courteous and skilful manner, thanking them for their judgement, and praying that God would forgive them what they did out of ignorance. Then he said, 'My Lords, do you truly imagine that you will stamp out these faithful Christians, whom you call heretics, with torture and executions? Oh, how you deceive yourselves! Believe rather, that the ashes of my body shall be scattered through the town, and from it many Christians will spring up, for the blood of the martyrs is the seed of the faithful.' Then he was led back to prison. On the way he boldly exhorted the people and instructed them with God's Word, so that they might turn from the popish idolatry. The people, who had gathered there in great numbers, were greatly moved by his exhortation ... .

On the following day, when Gillis should have been put to death, the obsequies of the Emperor Charles V, the father of King Philip, who was then in Brussels, were held. So as not to interfere with the customary splendid ceremonies the burning of Gillis was postponed to Christmas Eve, 24 December 1558. After the King had performed the obsequies Gillis was brought out to die, and he continued to exhort the people throughout the route he had to take to the stake.

He was not at all afraid and his countenance was unaltered, and he showed such cheerfulness and courage that everyone marvelled that such a young man showed no fear in the face of death, and championed the truth with such perseverance.

When he was tied to the stake he called fervently upon the name of the Lord. The executioner put the rope around his neck and strangled him; then he lit the wood and his corpse was consumed. I truly believe that the monks imagined that the blood of this martyr would comfort the Emperor's soul in purgatory. In the same way the heathen were accustomed to offer sacrifices and to perform executions at the funerals of famous princes; through which they demonstrated that those who were bloodthirsty in their lives, must go with bloody sacrifices to Hell.

Source: *Historie des Martelaren* [D5], pp. 530-2, 634-8.

36 The beginnings of armed resistance

Pieter Titelmans, Inquisitor, to Margaret of Parma, Kortrijk, 17 July 1562

Madame. As it was Monday I went to Ieper to deal with some business for our most reverend father in God, the bishop of the same, and having heard a rumour about some disorder and scandal, which had taken place in the village of Boeschepe, near Steenvoorde, I went there on Tuesday to discover the truth for myself. From my investigation I learned that on the previous Sunday, at the time of high mass, a certain uneducated layman, who comes from the place, called Gheleyn Damman, had climbed up to a particular spot in the churchyard of the same which was quite suitable for preaching. He had delivered a sermon attacking our holy mother, the Church, the authority of our holy father, the Pope, the holy sacrifice of the mass, the sacrament of the altar and other articles and mysteries of our holy Catholic faith causing great disquiet and scandal to good people and insulting Our Lord Jesus Christ and His Church. This went on for an hour or more. At the sermon there were according to the estimates of those who saw it between 150 and 200 people from nearby places and elsewhere. Some of these carried rusty rapiers and staves, and others pistols to protect and defend their preacher. It was also reported that there were others in the surrounding hills in attendance to give help if this were needed, but we have not been able to establish the truth of this, for we had to return quickly the same day to the aforesaid Ieper.

Some years ago the said preacher Damman was apprehended and did public penance in his shirt in the aforesaid place for his heretical beliefs. He is the brother of Willem Damman, who was recently delivered by force from the bishop's prison in Ieper by some of his followers.

Although I have notified my lords in the Council of Flanders of the above, it nevertheless seemed good and necessary for me to acquit myself by advising Your Highness to provide a remedy. For it is very necessary and high time that everybody applies himself to the best of his endeavours, as we find daily more and more, although for our part we do not have the means to do as much as we wish.

As for the ordinary forces of law and order, Your Highness will find that every remedy which has been taken until the present is inadequate, haing regard to the situation in the open country and villages and the great extent to which the poor, simple people have been misled by those who go to and fro daily to England and elsewhere; likewise, the Anabaptists, among whom those of Armentières play a part.

Madame, I pray God, Our Creator and Redeemer, to keep Your Highness in prosperity and to grant her always good counsel for the salvation of your good subjects and His Church. From Kortrijk, 17 July 1562.

Source: De Coussemaker, *Troubles religieux* [D6], ii. 61-62.

(b) The Wonderyear

37 The hedge-preaching. Two accounts

(i) Calvinist preaching in French Flanders, June 1566

Maximilien Vilain de Gand, baron de Rassenghien, governor of Lille, Douai and Orchies, to Margaret of Parma. Lille, 30 June 1566.

... I am bound, furthermore, to inform Your Highness that two more preachings took place last night, the chief of which, attended by some 4,000 people, was held about two leagues from this town on the road to Tournai by a preacher whose name, I understand, is Cornille de La Zenne, the son of a blacksmith from Roubaix, who has long been a fugitive from this country on account of the religion. According to the report, which some reliable persons have submitted to me, whom I know to have been at the said preaching, the said preacher exhorted his auditors, among other things, not to start any trouble or [commit] any seditious act, because in such a case no one would assist them, but if anyone arrested them or examined them for no other reason than their faith, or for having gone to the preachings, they might all be assured that they would be helped before any ill befell them, and in conclusion he spoke more or less as follows: we pray to God that He may grant the destruction of this papist idolatry; be of good heart for we are quite strong, but our time has not yet come. And we pray God that He may keep the people of Tournai and Armentières in their convictions and likewise confirm the good start we see among the inhabitants of Lille. And when the said sermon was over, the preacher disappeared so quickly through the crowd with the help of twenty hackbutters, who escorted him, that it was impossible to know whither he had retired.

And in another preaching which took place a few days ago near the border with Tournaisis, three leagues from here, some rabble among the auditors told the preacher at the conclusion that they had decided on returning home to invade a certain house, I do not know which, in the vicinity of Tournai. He strongly warned them against this, saying that the time was not yet ripe and that he would tell them when the hour had come and that he hoped that it would be quite soon. Your Highness may judge sufficiently from these remarks that when the time and opportunity are favourable, they will be very ready somewhere to play a trick on some unsuspecting monastery in the countryside or some undefended town. We are afraid that once the corn has been harvested and gathered into the barns, which will be in two or three weeks' time at the outside here, they will try to seize control of the countryside somewhere, before the towns have the means to obtain supplies, in order in this manner to starve the towns and to recruit by poverty a larger following, for which reason it would be expedient to give orders in good time and to find a way in advance of averting their assemblies. People have told me that many French gentlemen secretly hold themselves in readiness in order when sedition first occurs to offer their services, boasting that instead of the 4,000 Spanish soldiers whom the Catholic King sent to France, they could send 4,000 gentlemen to Flanders and that the Constable [Anne, duc de Montmorency] must have replied a few days ago to some Catholics in Paris, grumbling about the Huguenots, that it was time to importune the King there and that they waited first to see what measures the Catholic King would take in Flanders. I hope, however, that we may place our trust in the nobility of the Low Countries and that the members of the Request [Compromise] have no understanding with the assemblies of these rabble sectaries, and that we can yet find a means to undo the schemes of the people without violence, by some declaration from the said nobility. If Your Highness would find it expedient to enter into discussions with the leading members of the Request in order to ascertain their intentions in the matter of the assemblies (which are harmful to both the consideration and the publication of any provisional edict Your Highness might think good to make), for some of the leaders of their deputation are present in each quarter [of the country], I do not doubt but that this would be most beneficial, for it would both remove the mistaken impression held by the infected people and also greatly reassure the judges and officers of the good intentions of the said nobility. Nevertheless I leave everything to the noble discretion of Your Highness, for whom I would always do everything in my power to obey.

Madame, I pray that Our Lord may give Your Highness the fulfilment of her highest and most virtuous desires, after having most humbly kissed your hands. From Lille on the last day of June 1566.

Source: S. Deyon and A. Lottin, Les 'casseurs' de l'été 1566. L'iconoclasme dans le Nord de la France (Paris, 1981), pp. 215-16.

(ii) Hedge services at Ghent, June and July 1566

[Sunday 30 June 1566] ... then someone preached, dressed like the other [preacher] in lay attire, with an ermine-trimmed gown and a fine felt hat. [He was] short of stature and aged about thirty, and seemed, to judge from his speech, to hail from Kortrijk. Close to the chapel outside St Lievenspoort [he preached], bare-headed and with great modesty, on a small hill surrounded by copses and plantations. He sat on some hoods and cloaks, lent him by those who had come to listen, and he had in front of him a book, from which he read from time to time, before closing it again and continuing with his sermon. Before he preached, he knelt folding his hands together very devoutly. To avoid being arrested or surprised, he was led into the enclosure in a group of six people in such a way that no one knew who out of the six was the preacher until he made ready to speak. He expounded the Gospel of the day, reproved sins and prayed for the magistrates, the King and the Pope that God might enlighten their minds so that the Word of God (as they called their doctrine) might go forward peacefully. He had promised to preach at three o'clock in the afternoon, but he began at two o'clock.

Those present sat in three separate, closely-packed small companies made up of men, women and young girls; each of these had about as many members as the preacher had years. Each company had its teacher and the members had small books in their hands and from time to time sang the psalms; you could buy books there in which the psalms were printed in metrical form for a stiver. Many onlookers stood around; they had come to see what was going on there because it was for everyone a strange, unheard-of event, especially for those who lived in Flanders. I was told this by my washerwoman with whom I strongly remonstrated. I said to her that we were threatened by a great evil and danger, if it were not quickly stopped, but, like many simple folk, she thought it was quite innocent and even edifying ... .

On Sunday 7 July [1566] they preached again, in defiance of the authorities, at Stallendriesche at high noon. Thousands of people attended from the town and from the surrounding countryside, including many of the common people, who were not very well-versed in the Holy Scriptures and the Church Fathers. They [the Calvinists] gave these the impression that now for the first time the truth had been revealed and the Gospel preached aright because the preachers especially cited the Scriptures most valiantly and stoutly. They let the people check each passage in their testaments to see whether or not they preached faithfully, [when they said that] the New Testament contained the Word which the Lord had commanded all men to proclaim; not the human inventions and institutions, with which the papists (as they call them) had busied themselves; having raised these above God's Word or allowed these to obscure God's Word, it could not advance as it should and must [instead] be bent and give ground in order to accommodate human invention and contrivance; that it was much more proper that human laws should yield and make way for the sacred and blessed Word of God, for this, not rosaries, pilgrimages, voyages, and many suchlike superstitions, will prevail at the Last Judgement; that we are also under a far greater obligation (as the Apostles tell us) to obey the Word of God than men or magistrates, even though we are forbidden to hear this on pain of death, for the Lord says that we should not be afraid of those who would take the body captive, but only those who would cast the body and the soul into the everlasting fires of Hell; and that He shall be ashamed to confess before His heavenly Father and the angels of God those who are ashamed to confess Him in this world; that also Christ (who cannot lie) has prophesied that those who preach and hear His Word in its naked purity shall be oppressed and persecuted for as long as the world exists.

With these and other similar arguments they struck such a marvellous chord in the hearts of good and uneducated people that many of them declared that they were ready to forfeit both their property and their lives for the Word of God and Christ's name. This sprang, alas, more from a naïve fervour than from any judicious circumspection, for if they had heeded and properly understood the counter-arguments, they would have come to the opposite conclusion. Not everything that claims to be the Word of God is in fact the Word of God. You must search out what has been the judgement of the Holy Spirit of God, which lies hidden under the letter of God's Word. It was not without good cause that St Paul said that the letter kills but the Spirit brings life.

Source: Van Vaernewijck, *Van die beroerlicke tijden* [D10], i. 2-3, 13-14.

38 The image-breaking

(i) News of the image-breaking to the north of Lille

Maximilien Vilain de Gand, baron de Rassenghien, governor of Lille, Douai and Orchies to Margaret of Parma. Friday, 16 August 1566.

Madame, I have wanted to warn Your Highness in all haste because yesterday evening several sectaries arrived from the side of the Pays de l'Alleu, and travelling along the river Leie on the pretext of going to their preachings, suddenly entered Mesen, Quesnoy, Warneton, and Comines, where aided and abetted by their local accomplices, they sacked and smashed statues and sepulchres and ran riot in the churches, hospitals and monasteries without, as far as I have heard, having killed or injured anyone, because there has been no resistance. From here, as I hear, they have headed off towards Wervik and Menen to commit, presumably, the same intimidation there and to return via Wambrechies, a village in this castellany, which is much infected [by heresy], to continue their purpose, intending to do the same hereabouts and in the town [of Lille], if they are able. And as they have their informants everywhere, it is difficult to prevent them from taking by surprise some undefended place, the more so because, fearing the intelligence which they receive from this town, I dare not leave or part with the very few soldiers at my disposition in order to relieve the countryside. The only remedy, in my opinion, is for Your Highness to send post-haste and with all speed several companies of men-at-arms and to raise troops to oppose them. In the meantime one should make certain of the nobility of the Request, lest out of despair they join forces with this multitude of people. The country will be in less danger of ruin, if they can first be satisfied that the justice, authority and obedience of His Majesty and of Your Highness can be safeguarded, until we have some apter remedy. However, if we could have at least some loyal and reliable company of men-at-arms, I trust that, with the assistance of the well-disposed, we might prevent many of the disorders, which may befall the country, until we may have another means of help. We beseech Your Highness most humbly to give orders promptly. Otherwise, the confusion and terror of good men, seeing no sign of a solution, will become so great and widespread that they may be ready to abandon their lands and houses. Nor can I be certain of this town unless I have additional help quickly, not even of the castle, as I grow more and more afraid that I am not the master of the heavy ordnance. If I have some forces for this purpose, I can at least seize the authority. If it comes to the worst, I shall not abandon the town or the castle as long as there is any opportunity of serving His Majesty. I beseech Your Highness urgently to provide a remedy as the necessity demands in order to prevent still worse danger so that I at least have the means to guard and supply the town of Douai, if I am forced to quit here. I assure Your Highness that I would not hesitate to risk my life and my fortune as often as she commands me for the service of God and His Majesty. But the confusion which I witness daily without being able to find a remedy grieves me for I do not know how to discharge the responsibility which Your Highness has entrusted to me.

I pray, Madame, that Our Lord may grant Your Highness the fulfilment of her highest and most virtuous desires, after having most humbly commended myself to her good grace.

Lille, 16 August 1566.

Source: S. Deyon and A. Lottin, *Les 'casseurs' de l'été 1566. L'iconoclasme dans le Nord de la France* (Paris, 1981), pp. 217-18.

(ii) The image-breaking in Antwerp, August 1566

The magistrates of Antwerp feared that in the absence of the Prince of Orange, who had been summoned to Brussels on the morning of 19 August by the Regent, the storm against images might blow likewise that way, the more because it was the fair, and the town was full of strangers. They therefore caused the image of the Virgin Mary (which otherwise used to be exposed for a week together on that occasion) to be removed in the afternoon from the body of the church into the choir that it might give no offence. But their good intentions produced bad effects ... for the mob, observing the fears of the magistrates, began to grow insolent; and some of them, in a sarcastic way, asked the image whether her fright had driven her so far from her post and whether she would join in crying, 'Vive les Gueux', and other mockeries. A bunch of young lads was playing about the pulpit, and one of them went into it and began to mimic the preaching [of the monks and priests]. Some were for hearing, others for pulling him down, but he defended himself with his feet against them, until at last a young shipmaster climbed above him on the other side and threw him down headlong. The men espoused the boy's quarrel, and daggers were drawn against the shipmaster, who, though wounded, escaped out of the church ... .

The magistrates ... neglected to feel the pulse of the *schutterijen* and guilds, whether they were disposed to stand by them against these insolences, which threatened the common weal. However, they were not slow to signify the importance of this affair to their Governor the Prince of Orange ... . They also informed him how Herman Modet, and other teachers, had upon the same day inveighed against idols, saying that 'they ought to be removed from our sight, as well as from our hearts'.

The next day, when the mob gathered in and about the aforesaid church, the contentions relating to Our Lady began afresh. An old woman sitting before the choir to sell wax tapers, and to receive oblations, began to scold the people, and to throw ashes and filth at the boys, provoked, perhaps, at their telling her that her wares were out of fashion and that it was high time she shut up shop. The officers of the church, seeing that as the mob increased so also did their insolence, endeavoured to clear the church of them, and to shut it up, but nobody heeded them. When the *Schout* and the magistrates ... at the town hall were informed of these disorders, they repaired to the said church, and admonished the people to leave it, as some did; but others pretended that they had a mind to hear the 'Salve Regina' after vespers; these were told that there would be none that evening. Whereupon they replied that they would then sing it themselves; and accordingly one was heard to begin a psalm or hymn in one corner of the church, which was at once taken up by the others. Some of the young fellows played with balls and kicked stones about the church others threw them about the church and yet others threw them at the altars.

This was the prelude to the mischief. Some thought that if the magistrates left the church, they might draw or carry away the mob after them. Therefore the burgomasters repaired to the Council Chamber and eventually they resolved to arm the *schutters* and to summon them to the town hall. They also urged the crowd which stood outside to disperse. In the meantime they caused the church doors to be shut, save for one wicket, to let out the remainder of the people. The *Schout*, having laboured with his men to dismiss those that stayed outside, went again into the church, and endeavoured ... to clear the remnant. These included the most obstinate, who ... refused with stern countenance and rebellious language. In the meanwhile, a great mob rushed in at the little gate, and the *Schout* was forced to give up and quit the church. The moment he was gone, they began to sing psalms lustily. The treasurer, and other officers of the church, having secured the holy relics and other valuables, fled out by the north door. The rabble that were outside forced their way in, and broke open all the doors. Hearing this, the *Schout* and other magistrates went there again, but being terrified at the countless mass of people, and the shouts and noise that echoed from the church, they thought they would have enough to do to secure the town hall, which did not remain unthreatened. In the meanwhile the rabble locked up, closed the doors and, as the sun declined, set about the breaking, robbing and plundering.

The Virgin's image, that had been carried about in procession only two days before, was the first to suffer. The chapel in which it stood was entered by force, and the idol thrown down and dashed to pieces, all the people roaring, 'Vive les Gueux'. They then attacked the other statues, pictures and altars as well as the organ, heedless of their antiquity, beauty or value. They cast down or plundered these with such vehemence and headlong insolence that before midnight they had reduced one of the largest, most glorious and splendidly adorned churches in Europe with its seventy altars to an empty and ghastly hulk. No locks were strong enough to protect the treasures entrusted to them. Yet there was no quarrelling about the booty: indeed, no less strange, in the confused commotion of this raging mob, which perpetrated so many excesses, there was such unity and orderliness that it seemed as if each person had been allotted his task beforehand. Remarkably, while they vied with one another to climb the ladders, laboured to cast down the great marble-stones and heavy pieces of copper, and eagerly plundered the choicest pieces, not one out of this entire multitude hurt himself by falling and no one was injured in the slightest by the descent of objects as they crashed down and fragments flew in all directions, or by colliding and knocking into those who, wielding their instruments of destruction, pressed on to break everything. In the eyes of some this appeared so strange that they attributed a role to the hellish spirits in this transaction, scarcely believing that it could be the work of men. When they had finished in the principal church, they ran through the streets, carrying lighted candles and stolen tapers, like men possessed and escaped lunatics, roaring 'Vive les Gueux' and demolishing all the crosses and images in sight. Driven on by the same fury, and reinforced by fresh numbers, they flew to other churches, chapels and monasteries, where they not only mishandled stocks and stones, but living creatures too, among whom the Franciscans fared the worst. They broke open chambers and cellars; stove in all the barrels, and set the floor awash with beer and wine.

Strada[1] adds that they laid hands on the sacrament or mass wafers, trampling them under their feet. The consecrated chalices they filled with the wine they found in the churches, and drank to one another's health. They smeared their shoes with the holy oil, defiled the church vestments with ordure, and, daubing the books with butter, threw them into the fire. Some of the images were kicked up and down; others they thrust through with swords, or chopped off their heads with axes; they put others in armour, and then tilted against them with spears out of wantonness, until the images fell down, and then they mocked and jeered at them ... .

At daybreak, these destroyers of images sallied out of the town, and fell to plundering the Abbey of St Bernard, and other religious houses roundabout, sparing none that were in their way or sight. The rest of their gang that stayed within the town made an end of all that remained there. This rage, which grew unchecked through the perplexity of the magistrates, lasted for three days. In addition the mob grew yet more bold because some people of quality and means, armed with pistols and daggers under their clothes, mixing with them and lurking in corners and side streets, terrified all that were inclined to oppose them, to such an extent that some watches of burghers, who sought to protect these, were filled and overcome by fear. The burghers dared not exert themselves, for the Papists, suspecting that the Reformed had unanimously plotted their ruin, did not dare to oppose the violence for fear of being fallen upon, and the Reformed, fearing these disorders would be revenged upon them, thought they did enough in keeping a watchful eye on the Romanists. In one thing

[1] For his account of events at Antwerp Brandt relied on the Jesuit historian Famiano Strada's *De bello belgico decades duo*, first published in 1632.

[151]

F

however they all agreed, viz. in keeping the rabble out of their houses and from their coffers ... .

Herman Modet, one of the most zealous preachers, declares in his *Apologie ofte Verantwoordinghe* [Apology] which he published soon after these disorders, 'That neither he, nor any of the consistory, had any more knowledge of this design of destroying images when it was first contrived, than of the hour of their death ... .'

Next day [23 August] no church or monastery was open, except the Grote Kerk. In the meantime, a great part of the most valuable goods, which had been missing ever since the tumult, was voluntarily delivered either to the magistrates or their owners, but a great quantity of still greater value was kept back. This occasioned an ordinance, published the same day, requiring the restoration of all stolen goods to the owners within twenty-four hours, and an end to violence on pain of the gallows, which was set up immediately in the Grote Markt, and defended by armed men. But to prevent fresh troubles arising from such a proclamation, it was agreed to inform those of the Religion, both Dutch and Walloons, and that the pensionary van Wesenbeke should prevail upon the ministers by arguments and promises, to censure the insolence and plundering of the people in their sermons, to persuade them to restore the stolen goods, to exhort them to live quietly for the future, and to submit to their magistrates, and lastly, to make them acquainted with the ordinances lately made. But whilst the ministers were preparing an answer to these propositions, in the consistory, there were further disorders that afternoon in the Grote Kerk. They went on plundering and defaced the royal coat of arms and those of the Knights of the Golden Fleece, that were finely painted in the choir, though some say they were broken by a crucifix, which fell upon them accidentally from a great height. This was looked upon as a violation of the civil authority, and the magistrates were sensibly affected at it. Hereupon the *Markgraaf* (who was likewise the *Schout*) with some of the magistrates, sergeants and guilds marched there, and the mob retired as fast as they could but ten or twelve of them were seized. By this one could appreciate what loss had occurred through their not acting with such zeal at the outset.

Source: Brandt, *History of the Reformation* [D9], i. 192-6, revised according to Brandt's original text, *Historie der Reformatie*, i. 342-50.

39 Church-building. A description of the Calvinist church at Ghent

... Because I had begun to give an account of all these changes which had never been witnessed since Ghent had become Ghent and Flanders Flanders, I ventured to go this *temple* of the Beggars, not in order to hear the doctrines taught there but to view its interior design, as I thought it would not long survive, and therefore to leave a record for posterity. Certainly I never heard a single word of the sermons nor did I once permit anyone in my household to attend.

This *temple* was then octagonal and surrounded by a gallery, so that it was much broader at its base than at the top. It was largely built of wood, like the churches of Muscovy, except that the spaces between the posts had been filled with brickwork set in tanner's mortar. Both the lower and upper storeys of the building were lit by numerous windows. These were all glazed with plain glass, except for the lower windows which bore inscriptions from the Ten Commandments of God and from other passages of Scripture. Looked at from both the outside and inside, the *temple* resembled a lantern or riding school, only much larger. As I remarked in Book iv, chapter 3 the building measured 150 feet in length and 130 feet in width. The master-carpenter Willem de Somer, who had worked very industriously on the building with his brother Lievin, told me this.[1] Inside there was an enclosure, a good twenty feet wide, where men could stand or sit around. The women all sat in the middle separated by a partition or parapet against which they had put benches for the men to sit on and those outside, in the said enclosure, could use it as a balustrade on which to lean. The interior of the *temple* was supported by roof timbers, the work of some master craftsman. The pulpit, recently made of fir in the ancient style, stood at the far end. In the middle before the pulpit was the great wide enclosure, mentioned above, where the women and girls sat. The entrance to this was some fifty feet wide so that it would not be too congested. A large number of fixed benches stood behind and on either side of the pulpit and these extended at the back to two small separate rooms, with hearths, built on to the *temple*. The children and youth received their instruction in their sort of confession or catechism sitting on these benches; they were asked questions and had to reply. They worked so cheerfully that many a heart would have rejoiced and many would have been moved to pious tears, if only the doctrine had been sound. On working days they used,

[1] Marcus van Vaernewijck had visited the site where the *temple* was being built on 23 November 1566. It was situated just outside the town, by the gate leading to Bruges.

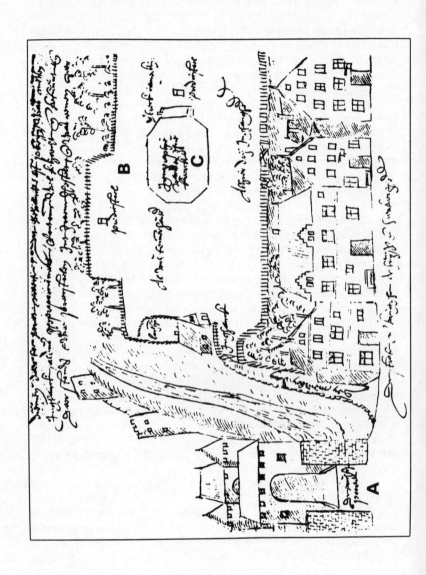

moreover, to teach one another the psalms in the evening, which fostered a truly godly exhilaration, the more so because each understood the fine words of the Holy Scriptures which he sang. This *temple* had a very fine thatch while the roof of the surrounding covered way below (which we call the gallery or storey) was covered with planks from Magdeburg, the joints and seams of which were packed with linen cloth and pitch to prevent the rain from seeping through.

Source: Van Vaernewijck, *Van die beroerlicke tijden* [D10], ii. 108-9.

40 Retribution. Investigations in a Holland town

The troubles at Den Briel, 1566-67

[On 20 October 1568 eighty-three men from Den Briel and the surrounding region were banished and their estates confiscated. The sentences summarised the charges laid against those who had been convicted.]

Willem van Treslong, having been a gentleman in the household of the *Heer* van Brederode, a member of the Compromise of the Nobility, having been a signatory to their pernicious and seditious league and for this reason present at the presentation of the Request,[1] as is notorious, and also at the meeting at St Truiden, having seduced his eldest brother Jan van Treslong also to appear and to sign the said Compromise and in January 1567 to have presented the last Request of the *Heer* van Brederode to Her Highness, according to which they demanded complete freedom to exercise the new religion in return for laying down their arms ...; *Nicolaas van Sandijck*,[2] having also been a member of the said Compromise, and having been a signatory to their seditious league and having maintained two horses in the service of the *Heer* van Brederode, and who gave refuge and advice to

[1] 3 April 1566.
[2] Former bailiff of Den Briel.

[facing] Marcus van Vaernewijck sketched the site of the Calvinist church at Ghent in November 1566. The church was located just outside the town by the Bruges gate [A]. Hedges surrounded the grassy enclosure on which stood two outdoor pulpits, used while the church was under construction [B]. The octagonal outline of the building with the adjoining small rooms at the rear can be clearly seen [C].

From *Van die beroerlicke tijden in die Nederlanden*, Manuscript in the Library of Ghent University, Handschrift 2469. fo. 103v°.
Reproduced by kind permission.

the image-breakers of the town of Den Brielle. *Hugo Quirynsz.* was present in the chamber of the Rhetoricians in the town hall on Ash Wednesday 1567 and there with other brother rhetoricians to have mocked the mass by drinking from the chalice belonging to the altar of the same fraternity. On this occasion the missal, the canon of the mass and the statue of St Rochus were put on trial, and, after psalms had been sung by way of a refrain, they sentenced the said missal, canon of the mass and the statue of St Rochus to be burnt; this was carried out and the whole lot thrown on the fire. *Corvinck Thonisse* and *Jan Thysse*, deans of the rhetoricians, were present during the said blasphemies and abominations, when four statues from the altar of St Rochus (which had been removed from the parish church and taken to the said chamber to keep them from being broken) were likewise condemned to be burnt, and indeed thrown into the fire, together with the ornaments and furnishings belonging to the said altar. *Dierick de Nayer* also drank from the said chalice. *Aert Daniels, Pieter Michielsz., Jan Commersz.* and *Jan Lenartsz.* were very thoroughly involved in the new preachings, and had carried messages for the members of the consistory, and had shown great favour to the image-breakers and had been commissioned by the sectaries to go the Prince of Orange and the *Heer* van Brederode; and the said *Pieter Michielsz.* had been present during the image-breaking in the convent of the Poor Clares, instructing the iconoclasts what they ought to smash, [and] when a Catholic asked him 'if the Gospel commanded the breaking [of images]' he replied that 'it was necessary and that the Whore of Babylon must be overthrown'. The said *Hugo Pietersz., Jacob Cornelisz., Mr. Pieter van der Heyde* and *Andries de Wever* had been deacons; and the said *Jan Commersz., Mr Pieter* and *Andries de Wever* had broken in the parish church of Maerlant; and the said *Hugo Pietersz.* held the consistory in his house; and the said *Mr. Pieter*, besides having one of his children baptised in the Calvinist way, had been the ringleader and one of the chiefest of the said breakers. *Jacob Jacobsz. Coster*, having been detained on account of the past troubles, had broken prison and escaped; [he] was charged with having led his pupils to the burial of someone of the new religion and there made them sing psalms. *Eeuwout Cornelisz.*, until recently the *schout* of the said town, and *Willem Willemsz. Apotheker* had been foremost in promoting and encouraging the iconoclasm there and had themselves broken [images]. The said *Eeuwout Cornelisz.* had been commissioned by the sectaries and put in charge of the ordnance drawn up on the town fortifications and in front of the gates of the same to defend them and to have worn the badge of the Beggars. *Boudewyn*

Jansse [was] also a member of the Compromise and had been a signatory to their seditious league under the *Heer* van Brederode and to have worn their badge and dress. *Mathys Andriesse* and *Jacob* his son had also broken in the convent of the Poor Clares as have also broken … [54 names follow], all of whom have been convicted of having broken images. The said *Simon Jansse Sleeper* has been a member of the said Compromise of the nobility, having been a signatory to their seditious league and had one of his children baptised in the new way and having broken statues. *Jan van Delft* also broke [images] and attended the aforementioned abominable insolence perpetrated against the service of the mass. *Adriaen de Kleermaeker* had been a messenger for the consistory and broken images in the convent of the Poor Clares. *Cornelis Heyndricxz.*, a burgomaster in 1566, had lodged a minister of the sectaries. *Mr Cornelis Rutgersz.* had shown great favour towards the image-breakers and was alleged to have hired some of them to break the said statues and to have expressed several blasphemous remarks against the Catholic religion and the venerable Sacrament [of the altar]. *Pieter Jansz. Coninck* [was charged with being] thoroughly involved in the new religion and their preachings, [with] having made several journeys on behalf of the consistory, received the sums collected on behalf of the *Heer* van Brederode and [with having] held the consistory at his house. *Lenaert Benoyt alias de Wael* [was charged with being] deeply involved in the said new religion and preachings, having been a member of the said Compromise and a signatory to their league; also [with having] received money for the said *Heer* van Brederode. *Mr Dirck Cock*, rector and schoolmaster, is one of the foremost authors of the alteration of the old religion and of the introduction of the sects and new preachings, having infected all his pupils with his false and erroneous doctrines and having instructed them in Calvin's catechism and taught them to sing the psalms, no longer leading them to mass on feast-days and Sundays or to any other church service, yet taking them to the graveside of those buried in the new way to sing the psalms there, in these ways alienating them completely from the ancient Catholic and Roman religion so that most of the youth of the town are infected by the said false doctrines; and when he was summoned before the magistrates and asked whether he would not instruct his said pupils in the old way, he roundly replied that he would not, but that he wanted to teach what he had recently learned; having also ripped up the missal and other books in the convent of St Catherine; and the said *Jan Smeet de Borst* having gone into hiding because he had married a nun who had fled from the convent of St. Catherine.

Having also seen the evidence shown by the said *procureur-generaal* in support of the facts set out above ... His Excellence [the Duke of Alva] banishes all those who have been cited.

Done in Antwerp 20 October 1568.

Source: Marcus, *Sententien* [D8], pp. 155-64.

(c) The establishment of the Reformed churches

41 Organisation in exile. The Synod of Emden, 1571

Acts of the synod of the Netherlands churches both under the cross and scattered through Germany and East Friesland, held at Emden, 4 October 1571

1. No church shall have dominion over another church, no minister of the Word, or elder or deacon shall exercise dominion over another. Rather shall they be vigilant lest they should give cause to be suspected of desiring dominion.

2. In order to bear witness to the doctrinal harmony between the Netherlands Churches, the brethren thought it good that they should subscribe to the Confession of Faith of the Netherlands churches and also to sign the Confession of the churches in France to attest their common faith and consensus with the same French churches, surely trusting that the ministers of the same French churches shall, for their part, in like manner subscribe to the Confession of the Netherlands churches in order to demonstrate their agreement.[1]

6. Each church shall have assemblies or consistories, composed of the ministers of the Word, the elders and deacons. These shall meet at least once a week at a time and place which each congregation finds most convenient and suitable.

7. Besides these consistories, classical meetings of neighbouring churches shall take place every three or six months, as seems expedient and necessary.

8. In addition separate annual meetings shall be held each year for all the churches scattered through Germany and East Friesland, for all the churches in England and for all those under the cross.

9. Furthermore, a general assembly of all the Netherlands churches shall be held every two years.

[1] See below, doc. 57.

The classes *of the Netherlands churches scattered through Germany and East Friesland*

10. One *classis* shall be composed of: the two congregations at Frankfurt, the congregations at Schönau, the French congregation at Heidelberg and the congregations at Frankenthal and St Lambert [Lambrecht]. Another shall be composed of: the two congregations at Cologne and Aachen, the congregations at Maastricht, Limburg, Neuss and those in the duchy of Jülich. Another *classis* shall be composed of: the congregations at Wesel, Emmerich, Goch, Rees, Gennep and those in the duchy of Cleves. Another *classis* shall be composed of: the church at Emden, with the fugitive ministers and elders from Brabant, Holland and Friesland.

The classes *of the churches under the Cross*

11. One *classis* shall be formed from the two congregations at Antwerp and the congregations at 's-Hertogenbosch, Breda, Brussels and any others there may be in Brabant. Another *classis* shall be formed from the congregations at Ghent, Ronse, Oudenaarde, Wervik, Comines and any others situated in East and West Flanders. Another *classis* shall be formed from the congregations at Tournai, Lilles, Arras, Douai, Armentières, Valenciennes and other French-speaking churches. A further *classis* shall be formed from the congregations at Amsterdam, Delft and the other churches in Holland, Overijssel and Friesland.

12. The brethren in England shall be exhorted to divide their churches into *classes*.[2]

13. Ministers of the Word shall be chosen by the consistory with the counsel and approval of the classical assembly, or of two or three ministers from neighbouring churches. Once chosen, they shall be presented to the congregation which may give its silent consent or, in the event of the congregation refusing to endorse the election, the objections should be declared within a fortnight. However those churches which prefer the ministers to be chosen by the congregation may continue to do so until the general synod decides otherwise.

14. Elders and deacons shall be chosen in the same manner, though there is no obligation to seek the opinion of the *classis* or the local ministers.

[2] The English exile churches were not represented at the synod. Although they had met to elect representatives, they were prevented from attending by the English authorities, who objected to their recognising the authority of a synod abroad.

Adiaphora at the Lord's Supper

21. In the churches where we are at liberty to arrange matters as we desire ordinary bread should be used and the same should be broken in the administration of the Lord's Supper. But we consider it a matter of indifference whether the Lord's Supper is taken standing or sitting. Congregations should use the form which seems most apt to them. Churches are free to sing psalms or to read from the Holy Scriptures while the Lord's Supper is administered. Likewise, the churches are free to use the words of Christ or Paul during the distribution of the bread and the wine. But care should be taken to avoid giving the impression that any consecration has occurred because these words are spoken.

Ecclesiastical discipline

25. We believe that ecclesiastical or Christian discipline should be kept in each congregation. Therefore the office of the minister of the Word shall not only be to preach publicly, to exhort and to censure, but also privately to remind everyone of his obligation. The elders should also see their work here.

30. Anyone who obstinately rejects the admonitions of the consistory shall be suspended from the Lord's Supper. If he shows no sign of repentance despite repeated admonitions, he shall be excommunicated.

31. The minister shall admonish the obstinate sinner from the pulpit, publicly declaring his offence and informing (the congregation) what endeavours have been made to censure and to suspend him from the Lord's Supper. He shall exhort the congregation to pray fervently for this unrepentant sinner before the congregation is compelled to proceed to the final remedy of excommunication. Three such admonitions shall take place. On the first occasion the sinner shall not be named so that he may to some extent be spared; on the second occasion he shall be named and on the third occasion the congregation shall be told that he shall be excommunicated unless he repents. If he remains obstinate, he shall be excommunicated with the tacit consent of the congregation. The interval between one admonition and the next shall be left to the discretion of the consistory. If, despite the diligence of the ministers, he cannot be brought to repentance, the congregation shall be told that the obstinate individual has been banned and excommunicated from the

Body of Christ. The minister shall explain at length the practice and purpose of excommunication and he shall admonish the congregation not to have close and unnecessary dealings with the excommunicant: they should avoid his company in order that the excommunicant may thereby be brought to a sense of shame and so to repentance.

41. Where the ministry of the Word cannot be established the ministers of the *classis* should appoint readers, elders and deacons so that congregations may be gathered together.

48. The *Heer van* St Aldegonde [Marnix van Sinte Aldegonde] shall be asked on behalf of this synod to write an account of recent events in the Low Countries and chiefly of those matters which pertain to the establishment of the churches and their persecutions, the overthrow and the restoration of images, the constancy of the martyrs and God's terrible judgements against the persecutors and the mutability of states.

49. All ministers as well as all others who can advance this purpose should diligently search out anything pertinent to such a history. These [documents] should be sent under seal to those appointed to receive them and they shall then faithfully transcribe these for the *Heer van* St Aldegonde.

53. These articles regarding the constitution and due order of the churches have been agreed unanimously. But they can, and should, be changed, increased or diminished, if the good of the Church requires. Nevertheless, individual churches are not at liberty to make changes: all churches should endeavour to maintain these articles until a synod decides otherwise.

Emden 12 October 1571

Gaspar vander Heyden, *praeses*

Johannes Polyander, *scriba*

[Then follow the signatures of the 29 ministers and elders in attendance at Emden.]

Source: Rutgers, *Acta* [D14], pp. 55-119.

42 In the wake of the revolt. The planting of churches in Holland, 1572

Bartholdus Wilhelmi to the Dutch church in London, 29 August 1572

... Most dear brethren and fellow ministers in the Lord. You will be pleased to know that I arrived at Dordrecht on 27 August in good health and without meeting any danger from the enemy of God, for

which I cordially beseech you to praise the Lord for this Grace ....
Further that you will, as you promised, inform the congregation why
I travelled here without taking my leave, namely for no other reason
than to prevent the danger that was consequently to be expected and
not out of any contempt or negligence, and therefore ask the congregation not to take it amiss ... .

Further, because those of Dordrecht ask for still more ministers,
since the harvest grows but the workers are very few, I beseech you
(on behalf of the notables of this town, who have also desired the
same from me), that you will show in this matter the love which you
owe to both God and his Holy Congregation and send at least four or
five of our ministers of the Word as quickly as possible. There are not
only still some deficiencies in Dordrecht, but in addition there are
some ten or twelve places in the neighbourhood, both towns and
villages, with neither ministers nor services. The inhabitants of these
same places daily complain and cry out, 'alas, we are like sheep
without shepherds, we live without religion and hear nothing of
God'. In one place you will find eight unbaptised children, in others
six or four, and it is impossible to improve matters and to assist them
in their great need unless we have more ministers, for much depends
on Dordrecht and therefore this place in particular must be provided.
All the ministers whom you send across shall be well received and
looked after. The town governor himself[1] was so delighted by my
arrival that he did not know how he could sufficiently thank the
congregation and consistory of London for the love they had shown
by sending one of their ministers. Should this not move us, my dear
brethren, more and more to help advance the preaching of the Gospel
which has begun? Should we not consider how many sheep who have
strayed may in this way be brought, by God's grace, to the sheepfold?
Likewise, how precious they stand in the sight of Christ, for did He
not also shed His blood for the same on the wooden cross? Oh, what
fruits there shall be if they can be won for Christ. Ought we not to
ponder on this and still other matters, too long to enter into here?

And since almost no one in Dordrecht and thereabouts has ever
heard anything about the reformation of worship or has been in
Reformed congregations, you will readily appreciate that we need
ministers with some knowledge of the government of the Church, who
can set matters in good order. And who is more apt in this respect than
our brother [Godfried] van Winghen, who has long experience with
the congregation, or Silvanus [Joris Wybo], if he be fit, or [Pieter]
Carpentier, or [Jan] Lamoot, [Johannes] Cubus, etc. Therefore do your

---

[1] Johan de Hornes, baron of Boxtel.

best in this matter so that the Lord's dilapidated house may again by the Lord's grace be built up. I do not doubt that as you have begun well you shall likewise continue ... . I would have written more, but as the shipmaster wants to sail I have not been able to complete everything as I would have wished. Therefore you shall take it in good part on this occasion. Farewell. From Dordrecht, 29 August 1572.

Greet my wife and continue to comfort her in my absence ... and take good care, dear brethren, of the flock that God has acquired by his blood, for there will be a time of reckoning so that you may always have a good conscience before God ... .

Your fellow brother and servant, so far as I am able, Bartholdus Wilhelmi.

Any letters you want to send me should be addressed: to Cornelis Franssen Wittesz. on the Nieuwe Haven.

Source: Hessels, *Archivum* [D1], iii. 174-6 (no. 206).

43 Extracts from the Consistory Book of Dordrecht, 1572-74

Anno 1572. In July 1572 Master Johannes Lippius came from Wesel to begin his ministry in Dordrecht. In August 1572 Master Bartholdus Wilhelmi came from London to begin his ministry at Dordrecht. In September these two ministers summoned those whom they considered well disposed to the Gospel into the consistory and had some of these chosen to hold provisionally the office of elder and deacon: and this was done. But since most of these disdained this service, the aforesaid two ministers of the Word had many times to choose provisionally others until elders and deacons were chosen in the proper fashion.

Anno 1573. On 14 June 1573 there took place the first public confession of faith of those who professed the Holy Gospel. And on the following Thursday a public fast and day of prayer was held for the election of the elders, which election took place in the following way.

We two ministers of the Word and some of the magistrates who had made profession of their faith proposed twelve brethren whom we thought the most suitable to the congregation and exhorted them to choose from the twelve and to write down [the names] in the consistory of those whom they considered best qualified.

The names of those brethren proposed were as follows:

1. Jan Adriaenssen,
   cloth merchant
2. Cornelis Evertzen
3. ...
4. Jan Canin, printer
5. ...
6. Claes Janssen Jager, skipper

7. Cornelis Jacobzen,
   bowyer
8. Jan Aertzen, hatter
9. Jan Anthonissen
10. Simon Franssen
11. Meuwes Janssen
12. Bouwen Aertzen

... the members of the congregation were exhorted to register in the consistory any objections about the doctrine and conduct of the chosen elders between Thursday [25 June 1573] and ... ; and those who were chosen by the most votes from the twelve were these:

1. Jan Adriaenssen
2. Jan Canin
3. Cornelis Evertzen

4. Jan Thonissen
5. Meuwes Janssen
6. Claes Janssen

On 28 June the aforesaid brethren, who had been proposed, were confirmed in their ministry in the Grote Kerk before midday after the sermon, since nothing had been said against any of them which might prevent their confirmation.

On the same day the elders gathered with the two aforesaid ministers for the first time and discussed the Lord's Supper and the administration of the Lord's Supper, which was to be administered to the congregation next Sunday. [It was] decided by common consent that Bartholdus should administer on the first occasion and Lippius, our fellow minister, should read for as long as the proceedings took. Also decided that Jan Canin and Jan Thonissen should serve at the Table.

First Lord's Supper

On 5 July the Lord's Supper was held for the first time in this town of Dordrecht and the number of communicants was 368.

9 July in the consistory. The brethren of the consistory, being assembled, discussed the election of the deacons and it was decided to hold a fast-day on 14 July and on that occasion to propose certain men to the congregation so that they should choose the best qualified for the office of deacon from these. [The same procedure was employed and the congregation chose 8 from the 16 men nominated.]

21 July in the consistory. [The case of] a certain Jan Hendrickzen, pinmaker, was discussed by the brethren in the consistory. He had remained for several years with his wife without being married because

his conscience, as he said, did not permit him to be married by the priests. Nevertheless this was known to none save some confidential friends although they were held and regarded by all burghers as properly married persons. After the consistory had diligently considered all the circumstances and reflected what would be most edifying, the brethren resolved that they should both be exhorted in the consistory to confess their sin and to repent and to marry privately in the consistory. This also took place on 23 [July] on the conditions set down in writing.

26 August [1573] in the consistory. The Calling of Jacobi. Jacobus Michael, minister of the Word, appeared in the consistory. He was informed that he had been called as minister to this congregation by the consistory, which desired him to accept his calling. But we told him in advance that the salaries of the two ministers of the Word were badly in arrears on account of the defective payments, which happened there. And if he also suffered the same, he should not say that he had not been warned. Jacobus replied that he was not worried about payment and he also doubted not that all should be well, not least because Monsieur Nieuvelt[1] had been appointed *schout*. Jacobus said that on the matter of the calling, he wished to obey it on condition that if at some time the door opened at 's-Hertogenbosch,[2] he wanted to go there without hindrance, because he had made, as he said, a promise to them. He was told that his call by the congregation at Dordrecht took precedence over the promise, which he had made to them. Jacobus however refused to accept this. So it was later agreed that if those of 's-Hertogenbosch [i.e. the Reformed congregation there] could at some time demonstrate to the *classis* that they had a better claim to Jacobus than the congregation at Dordrecht and the *classis* upheld this claim, then Jacobus should go there; if the congregation of Dordrecht had a better title, then he should remain with it.

I Jacobus Michael acknowledge the foregoing.

Second Lord's Supper

On 13 December the Lord's Supper was again administered to the congregation by Joannes Lippius and the number of communicants was 436. On the same day Janneken Gerardts, the wife of Jan Nordthoudt, and Lijntgen, her sister, both from Ghent, did public

[1] Willem van Zuylen van Nyevelt, one of the leaders of the noble Confederation in 1566, and subsequently a dedicated supporter of the Reformed congregations.
[2] I.e. when a Reformed congregation could be established there.

penance and both were reconciled with the congregation of Christ and received publicly with much edification with the kiss of peace.

Third Lord's Supper, anno 1574

On 21 March 1574 the Holy Communion was administered again to the congregation by Jacobus Michael and the number of communicants was then 536. On the same day His Princely Excellence broke bread with us.

Source: *Uw Rijk Kome* [D11], Jensma, pp. 1-8.

44 Spreading the word in the countryside. Naaldwijk, 1572-75[1]

(i) The Consistory register

On 1 April 1572 the Count vander Marck, lord of Lumey, entered the Maas with some ships and captured Den Briel in Holland. Immediately thereafter the Almighty and Wonderfully Wise God began to deliver his poor Christians from the tyrannical Spanish Inquisition and from the Kingdom of the Antichrist.

Shortly afterwards the Spaniards retreated from Holland with great dishonour and the towns of Holland everywhere received the aforesaid Count vander Marck, acting for the Prince of Orange as *stadhouder* of Holland, Zeeland, Westfriesland and Utrecht. They also began everywhere in Holland about this time to purge all the churches, religious houses and other foundations of all idols and to root out the papist superstitions and to preach the Word of God and the Gospel of Jesus Christ purely.

On 9 August 1572 the first public service took place in the church at Naaldwijk in conformity with God's Word. And shortly afterwards, in the same month, the church at Naaldwijk was completely purged of all idols and all images made of wood and stone and its altars were cast down and destroyed. The brethren of Naaldwijk would have preferred to have carried this out with the agreement and consent, indeed also with the help of their magistrate, namely Willem van Hooff, castellan of the House of Honsholredijk, in accordance with God's Word, but he (the same magistrate) violently opposed [this] and would on no account give his consent, declaring, 'Remember

[1] Naaldwijk lies in the Westland of Holland, a little to the south of The Hague.

that what you do you must sooner or later answer for.'

On 15 October 1572 Adam van Malsen, who had been a canon of Naaldwijk in popish times, forsook and abjured popery with all its idols in the public service and, having embraced the true religion with his wife, they married in the presence of the whole congregation and thereby placed themselves under the obedience of God's Word.

On 25 November 1572 the minister, by name Thomas Gerardus Morus alias Dockum, with the brethren of the Reformed congregation of Naaldwijk chose, following the example of the Apostles in the first Church (Acts 6), their elders and deacons from the same congregation. The elders are Matthijs Jacobsz. and Pieter Matthijsz. The deacons are Adam van Malsen, Philips Thomisz., Lambrecht Jansz., and Claes Huijgensz.

On 24 May 1573 the Holy Supper of Our Lord Jesus Christ was administered for the first time in the congregation at Naaldwijk and the same Supper was administered to these following persons after making confession of their faith and undergoing examination of themselves by the minister of Naaldwijk, who also has received the same. These are they who have been on the aforesaid day at the Holy Supper of our dear Lord Jesus Christ. [A list with 38 names follows.]

On 25 September 1573 the Supper of Jesus Christ was held in the congregation at Naaldwijk for the second time and the congregation of God grew with these following persons, who also went to the Supper. [A list with 19 names follows.]

On 27 September 1573, following the decision taken by the consistory of Delft with our brethren, it was decided in our consistory that henceforth the bell shall, for the time being, not be rung at the burial of the dead in order to remove from men's hearts the abominable superstition of the Papists, who believe and teach that the ringing confers benefit on the dead.

On 23 May 1574 the brethren of the consistory of Naaldwijk ordained that henceforth if anyone shall present any children for baptism, the parents of the same children shall be obliged first to speak to the minister and allow the names of the children to be registered; children shall only be baptised on Sunday afternoon or during the week when there is usually a sermon.

On the same day the consistory also decided that any persons who desire to enter into the matrimonial state, if they have parents, or, in the event of their parents having died, if they have guardians, the same persons, each with their parents, guardians or friends, shall come to the minister before they make known their [betrothal] and show that it has taken place with the consent of their parents;

marriages shall now take place on Sunday afternoon.

On 4 July 1574 Franciscus Franckenssen, the minister of the Word, and the brethren of the consistory with some other brethren of the congregation of Naaldwijk, having fled to Delft on account of the enemy's invasion,[2] held their consistorial meeting there. The maintenance of the poor and sick both in Delft and in Naaldwijk was discussed and it was decided and agreed that the aforesaid poor shall be maintained from the property of the Holy Spirit[3] and that the bailiff, Matthijs Jacobsz., shall enter what he has lent in his accounts.

At the same time it was decided that the deacons shall go to the houses of the benevolent brethren of Naaldwijk then living in Delft once every two weeks for the maintenance of the poor and if that brought in too little, thereafter they shall go around once a week. The deacons shall diligently record everything they have received, from whom and how much and likewise also what they pay out to whom, how much and when, and to render an account every month before the consistory and the brethren.

On the same day the brethren also decided that the expenses incurred at the synod of Dordrecht, where Franciscus appeared with Matthijs Jacobsz. and lodged for about two weeks,[4] shall be claimed against the manor of Naaldwijk because the same expenses were incurred for the common good of the entire community.

1575. After the scattering of the congregation which had occurred in 1574 [and] in which scattering many brethren died and after the relief of Leiden, the enemy withdrew from the surrounding region in the beginning of February. And after the second former minister died the usual preaching of God's Word started again at Naaldwijk.

27 March [1575]. Item, that the examination of faith should take place in accordance with the ordinance of the synod, in the minister's house in the presence of one or two elders, on Wednesday and Friday.

Source: Archief van de Nederlandse Hervormde Gemeente te Naaldwijk, Consistory Book, 1, pp. 1-12.

---

[2] During the second siege of Leiden, the Spanish troops remained in The Hague and the Westland (including Naaldwijk) from the end of May 1574 until February 1575.

[3] The charitable institution created for the relief of the parochial poor was often called, as here, the Holy Spirit [*heilige geest*], and those who administered poor-relief were therefore known as Masters of the Holy Spirit.

[4] The synod of Dordrecht opened on 15 June and ended on 28 June 1574.

(ii) The castellan's view

... shortly afterwards [i.e. after 19 July 1572] a Matthijs Jacobsz., carpenter at Naaldwijk, who had fled to Emden on account of the troubles of the past years[5] ..., appeared at the House at Honsholredijk. He requested consent and leave from me, as castellan and steward, for the opening of the said collegiate church in order to practise and to use there God's Word and his religion (as he said): the mass-priests (as he called them) had abandoned and deserted the said church and the community had to be served. Whereupon I replied that I had no commission to consent to what he was requesting and desiring, but that he must address his request to my mistress, the Countess of Arenberg, in her capacity as Lady of Naaldwijk and patron and collator of the said collegiate church and of the estates belonging thereto. Howbeit I also believed that the same, in my opinion (as I said), would neither consent nor allow any other religion than the old Catholic and Roman and permitted religion to be practised and used within her said church and manor ... .

But shortly afterwards, on 18 October 1572, he returned to the same house and castle at Honsholredijk, attended and accompanied with yet another carpenter from Naaldwijk, called Peter Matthijs (both being strangers, being neither born nor related to Naaldwijk but having come through marriage). He too had been banished and had been a fugitive abroad on account of the first troubles.[6] Together they persisted and stuck by the said request concerning the church and, what is more, also proposed and desired that I, in the said capacity, should release all such ecclesiastical incomes due to and belonging to the chapter of Naaldwijk, as well also as the ecclesiastical and spiritual property at Naaldwijk, in order thereby to maintain their minister, schoolmaster, grave-digger and sexton. [Following a negative reply] the said two carpenters went to the sexton of the said church and fetched the keys to the said church (without his leave) from his house and opened the same church. They and their accomplices broke the images and altars of the said church, hacking and chopping them in pieces, burning quite indiscriminately the books from the library of the same church, for they not only burnt and destroyed books concerning the said Catholic

[5] Both Matthijs Jacobsz. and his companion Peter Matthijs had been active in the Calvinist movement in Naaldwijk in 1566-67. In November 1572 they were chosen as the first elders of the Reformed congregation and in April 1573 William of Orange appointed Matthijs Jacobsz. to the office of bailiff and *schout* of Naaldwijk.

[6] I.e. 1566-67.

religion, but also those which treated of the imperial written law, medicine, philosophy and other histories, which had nothing to do with religion. They also broke some certain portraits and paintings of those who have been lords and ladies of Naaldwijk during the past 265 years as well, also, of the deans during the same period, which were very fine ancient works. ... They also conducted services in the same collegiate church after their way of doing, notwithstanding my protest and prohibition to the contrary. ...

On the last day of January 1573 ... there appeared before me at the said house ... the said minister of Naaldwijk, accompanied by Matthijs Jacobsz. and Peter Matthijs, the said carpenters, and the same minister put it to me, in effect, that I should consider the salvation of my soul and also of those of the inhabitants ... over whom I had been sufficiently charged and placed in authority, and how, on account of my absence and my staying away from the church and from the hearing of God's Word, the chief men, magistrates and the community of Naaldwijk also did not appear in church and in the services, with the result that he could not build up God's Word so fruitfully as otherwise he would have expected. If I came to church and to the services with my household and used the talent that the Almighty Lord had bestowed on me, as he said, and since he was the one who should take heed for the salvation of my soul and of the subjects, he therefore wanted me, indeed, to come to church and to the services. Whereupon I asked him who had agreed and appointed him as a judge and overseer of my conscience and who had given him the authority and order to take possession at Naaldwijk of the church and the office of preaching, seeing that the Countess of Arenberg was Lady of Naaldwijk and patron and collator of the said church ... .

Source: P. J. Goetschalkx, 'Invoering van de hervorming te Naaldwijk, Honsholredijk en andere plaatsen rond de stad Delft', *Bijdragen tot de geschiedenis van het bisdom Haarlem* 27 (1903), pp. 343-60.

45 State of the Reformed churches in the villages around Dordrecht, 1582

The ministers [at the *classis*] were asked in turn about the condition of their church and from the ministers' reply is found respectively:

that at Ridderkerk there are as yet no deacons, but the collection for the poor is carried out by others from the village;

that at Westmaas the Catechism [of Heidelberg] is not preached

[and] that the consistory there even disapproved of it;

that at Zwijndrecht there are two deacons, one from the congregation and one from the village; that the Catechism is not always preached there because he [the minister] often deputises at the morning sermon in the town [Dordrecht];

that at Rijsoord and Hendrik-Ido Ambacht there is as yet no congregation and that no collection for the poor takes place at Hendrik-Ido Ambacht;

that at Bleskensgraaf and Molenaarsgraaf there is neither congregation, school, nor diaconate;

that at Mijnsheerenland there is as yet no congregation, but that there are hopes of holding the Lord's Supper by Whitsun, that two of the inhabitants collect alms, that there is a school and the Catechism is preached;

that at Heinenoord there is as yet no congregation, but there is hope; that the Catechism is not preached, [but] that there is a school and collection for the poor takes place;

that at Barendrecht there is a congregation, that the *schout* collects alms, that there is a school;

that at Sliedrecht and Wijngaarden there is no congregation, that alms are collected at Wijngaarden, but not as yet at Sliedrecht, that neither place has a school.

Source: Van Dooren, *Classicale Acta* [D12], pp. 112-13.

(d) Church and State

46 The Synod of Dordrecht, 1574

5. The ministers and elders shall see that in the consistories, *classes* and synods they only discuss ecclesiastical matters. But in those matters which belong both to the ecclesiastical and to the political spheres (for example, many matrimonial matters belong there), they should seek the judgement and authority of the civil magistrate, if any difficulty should arise.

22. (i) On the matter of schools it has been decided that the ministers of all the *classes* shall consider where there should be schools.

(ii) [They should ask] whether the schoolmaster of the place in question previously received a public and regular stipend.

(iii) They should ask the magistrates for leave to appoint a schoolmaster and [they should also ask] that the magistrates give instruction that he be paid the stipend which he used to receive.

(iv) The ministers shall see that the schoolmasters subscribe to the Confession of Faith, submit to the discipline and also instruct the youth in the Catechism and other useful things.

(v) If there are any schoolmasters who refuse to comply, the minister shall ask their magistrates to exclude or to dismiss these.

(vi) If the ministers fail to obtain any of the above mentioned things from their magistrates, they shall petition the superior magistrates for satisfaction and press on with the matter.

29. In those places where the Christian congregation does not derive any benefit from the income of the hospitals, the endowments administered by the Holy Spirit and other foundations for the relief of the poor, but only collects and distributes alms given in church or elsewhere, the procedure for the proper election of deacons already agreed[1] shall remain in force. But where the magistrate permits [the Church] to share in endowments already mentioned, the consistory shall choose two men for each single vacancy and then present these to the congregation. If the congregation approves all these candidates, they shall present the said men to the magistrates, who shall select from this number one half: these shall then be elected [as deacons]. But where the former electoral procedure is equally acceptable, the same shall be followed as the most suitable.

36. It has been decided that where the deacons have only alms to gather, they shall present their accounts every month to the consistory. But where they receive a share of the income from the Holy Spirit and the other foundations for the relief of the poor, they shall present their accounts to those whom the magistrates, together with some members of the consistory, shall appoint. And this shall be laid before the congregation on each occasion so that everyone who wishes to be present for the accounts may attend.

[The *classis* of Walcheren asked] whether it were good and expedient to make a request to His Excellency for a warrant to all officers to the end that the people be obliged on Sundays to attend the Word of God or incur some penalty; and likewise that public sales, taverns, commerce and manual work should close or cease on weekdays during the sermon, it being understood that the same would not extend beyond one hour.

47. The *classes* should ask their magistrates to forbid buying, selling, drinking, working and strolling during the sermon, especially on Sunday. If any magistrate should show reluctance in this matter, they should petition my lord the Prince [of Orange] that he admonish

[1] Articles 13-14 of the Synod of Emden, see above, doc. 41.

the magistrates to look to their office and to conduct themselves after the manner of those who had already put such [ordinances] into practice.

48. The ministers shall ask the magistrates to do away with profane and secular proclamations concerning buying, selling and lost property in the church.

68. The Lord's Supper shall not be administered where there is no formal congregation, i.e. where there are no elders and deacons to supervise the receiving and regulation of those admitted [to the Table] ... .

[The *classis* of Voorne and Putten] asked how one should treat the receiving of those who enter the congregation of God for the first time. Whether they should be publicly questioned in church about their faith, or whether this should be done in the consistory with a 'yes', because we see that many do not enter the congregation for fear of being questioned at length, though they are otherwise well-disposed to the same.

70. It has been decided that the receiving and examination of those who enter the congregation shall take place before a minister and two elders, or simply two ministers, who shall appoint a convenient time to visit these. And the profession of faith and submission to the discipline shall take place in public, either in the consistory or in the church, where everyone may attend, and the names of those who have been received shall be solemnly read out there.

72. It has been decided that, while the Church is yet young, those who have already been examined shall profess their faith by answering 'yes'.

88. Since the officials of the Antichrist annexed the authority and jurisdiction of the civil powers in the matter of divorce in papist times, the magistrates shall be entreated and exhorted by the ministers from God's Word to assist those who need and desire their help in such matters, according to the tenor of God's Word and other laws.

[The *classis* of Voorne and Putten] sought advice as to the best means of combating the sect of the Anabaptists, for they do not attend the preaching of the Word nor can they be persuaded to enter into debates. In the meanwhile their false doctrine spreads like a cancer: besides it spreads out from the village of Zwartewaal, where the majority are inclined to the sect, to infect the whole of Voorne, including the chief villages, such as Heenvliet, Zuidland and Abbenbroek, etc., and in some villages no children at all are baptised.

Art. Qu.3. To the question raised by the [*classis*] of Walcheren how to combat the Anabaptists or to bring them back to the right path, it

[173]

has been decided that the ministers should entreat the magistrates only to accept or allow those who take a valid oath to obey the authorities. And to exhort those who already live there to hearken to God's Word and to bring their children to baptism. If they refuse to do so, they should be summoned into the presence of the ministers and obliged to declare and to justify their opinions. Furthermore, it would also be good if the ministers seek to enter their secret meetings and to indicate and demonstrate that their conduct is wrong.

Art.Qu.3. [To] the question raised by [the church of] Delft, whether a moneylender may be admitted to the Lord's Supper, is replied in the negative. Although such a trade is permitted by the magistrates, it is nevertheless permitted more on account of the hardness and wickedness of man's heart, than on account of God's will. Besides, many hundreds of people would be offended if such a person were admitted.

Organisation of poor relief at Den Briel

5. Hitherto we have ministered through the deacons to all the poor in our town without distinction, both to the members of our own congregation and to those outside, according to our ability. But henceforth we need only minister to our fellow-members, for the following reasons.

(i) Those who are called the masters of the Holy Spirit receive the revenues from the foundations for the relief of the poor by custom and since the revenues and the administration of these should be kept together, we think it proper to send all poor people, who are not known to us as fellow members, to the masters of the Holy Spirit, as they have a claim on the revenues of the Holy Spirit, and not to minister to these any longer.

(ii) Because we see that the Holy Spirit allows us to minister each week to the poor who are their concern, but when these die, they lay claim to the estates which the poor have left and directly after their death, they take it away in wheelbarrows.

(iii) As our deacons are ordinary craftsmen, they must gain their livelihood by working and they cannot abandon their families and enter the service of the whole town, for which purpose the masters of Holy Spirit have been appointed.

6. The members cannot be relieved in accordance with their needs unless we have other means than we have at present.

7. The ministers of the poor [i.e. deacons] complain about the great influx from all sides because they are situated on the frontier, and

they declare that henceforth they shall assist no strangers unless they receive help in this respect from other churches, for the poor are sent to us from all sides contrary to article 45.[2]

Source: Rutgers, *Acta* [D14], pp. 131-217.

47 Ecclesiastical ordinances drafted for the States of Holland, 1576

We William, Prince of Orange ... by the authority of the most invincible King, Philip of Spain, ... Governor of Holland, Zeeland, [West] Friesland and of the province of Utrecht, and we the States of Holland and Zeeland ... having nothing more at heart ... than that the doctrine of the Holy Gospel may be propagated most purely and that the churches too may be best governed, in our towns ... have thought fit, after mature deliberation, to make these ordinances, which we will also require to be observed inviolate. And we have thought it necessary that the same [ordinances] should chiefly relate to the administration of the ecclesiastical government, of which four principal offices are to be found in the Holy Scriptures, namely [that] of pastors, who are also called in the Holy Scriptures bishops, elders and ministers, whose office chiefly consists in the teaching of the Word of God and the administration of the sacraments; [that] of doctors, whose place has now been taken by the professors of theology; [that] of elders, whose principal office was formerly to watch over morals and to set transgressors once more on the right path by friendly admonitions; [that] of deacons, who care for the poor and the sick.

Concerning the ministers: first their appointment

1. The magistrates of every chief town shall, on the information and with the advice of their ministers, choose ministers for their town and all the places under their jurisdiction.

5. Every minister chosen for a town shall be examined by the elders whether he be endowed with learning and eloquence, and with an upright and pious conversation for the office.

6. The person found to be qualified shall present himself to the magistrates so that they may give their approval to the aforesaid declaration that he be shown to the people from the pulpit.

[2] Of the synod of Emden.

Oath to be taken by the ministers

I swear by Almighty God and Our Lord Jesus Christ that I shall be a faithful subject of the King of Spain, his *stadhouder* in these provinces the Prince of Orange, ... and likewise of this magistracy in all things which are not contrary to the will of God and my office; and that I shall also strive, to the best of my endeavour, so that the people may likewise obey the same as peaceably and submissively as possible; moreover, I swear that I shall treat the Word of God after the purest manner and I shall proclaim the same diligently so that it may bring forth the most fruit in the congregation committed to my charge, and that I shall not accommodate the same to suit my fancy, nor alter it to please someone else, but that I shall expound the same in all good faith, seeking only the honour of God and the good of this congregation ... .

Concerning the meeting of ministers

10. The ministers of every chief town and of the places belonging thereto shall come together every two weeks in the chief town to which they are attached in order to confer about doctrine so that they may keep the same pure and uniform.

Concerning the settlement of controversies among ministers

13. If any dispute on a matter of doctrine arise, the ministers shall compose the same among themselves, and, if the matter requires it, the elders shall be called in; but if no agreement can then be reached, the matter shall be laid before the magistrates, whose responsibility it is duly to settle the same.

Concerning the correction of misdemeanours among the ministers

16. As for those misdemeanours committed by ministers, for which there is no punishment in law, but which nevertheless cause offence, as, for instance, unaccustomed and unwarranted expositions of the Holy Scriptures; curious enquiries into vain questions; the introduction of any novelty in the congregation ... the elders shall ... inform the magistrates, and at the same time declare their opinion

thereon, though in all cases the final judgement concerning the punishment shall always rest with the magistrates.

Concerning the visitation of parishes

19. Two elders from each chief town and one or two ministers shall make a circuit each year through the country [districts] which fall under the same chief town and they shall investigate how the ministers in each place behave, and if they discover anything amiss, they shall inform the magistrates of the chief town concerning the same so that these may promptly remedy it as the occasion requires.

Concerning the Lord's Supper

27. The Lord's Supper shall be held four times each year at Easter and Whit Sunday, on the first Sunday in September and on the Sunday nearest to Christmas Day.

28. On the Sunday preceding the administration of the Lord's Supper, the ministers shall make known the day so that children who will be admitted for the first time to the Lord's Supper may in the meantime come to them in order to give an account, based on the [Heidelberg] Catechism, of the Confession of Faith. At the same time the ministers shall issue a general exhortation that all who may perhaps desire to be more fully instructed should appear before them and they shall earnestly urge everyone to examine and try himself so that no one comes unworthily to the Lord's Table, nor eats and drinks to his own judgement because of his failure to discern the Lord's Body.

Professors of Divinity or Doctors

36. Since Professors of Divinity now stand in the place of Doctors [or Teachers], we have likewise instituted such in our new university of Leiden, after the same manner as the Professors of other arts and sciences; and we shall take care that they raise up learned and worthy pastors, by expounding the Holy Scriptures purely and truly, according to the rules prescribed to them, which it is not necessary here to rehearse.

37. But the magistrates of every town shall take care to provide godly schoolmasters for their youth, whose business it shall be to

instil both the true religion, as well as learning, and to teach them to sing the psalms in the accustomed way.

38. Those schoolmasters that are not inclined to the Reformed religion, shall by no means be allowed to instruct children.

Elders

39. The magistrates of every place shall choose from among themselves more or fewer persons, according to their numbers, good men, and such as are not inexperienced in the business of religion, who shall assist the pastors in church affairs, and to be present at their meetings, to the end that if anything should be transacted there, of which the government ought to be informed, they may give an account of it, and do what belongs to their office as has been set down in many places in these laws.

The justification for these ecclesiastical laws drafted on behalf of the States of Holland

That godly rulers have always appropriated to themselves a right of making laws about religion, is beyond dispute; and accordingly God was pleased to give such laws, not by the hands of Aaron, but of Moses; and so it always continued a custom among the people of Israel, that the supreme authority, and power of those laws, should be vested in their judges, kings and finally princes ... . But at the time of the writing the books of the New Testament, the magistrates and rulers were not only strangers to the true religion, but indeed implacable enemies of it; insomuch that men of piety were obliged to keep themselves apart or separate, and in case any regulation were wanting in matters of religion, they made them of their own private authority; and in this state they remained for some hundreds of years; but when the chief Monarch of the world, Constantine, had embraced the [Christian] religion, he himself ordained and appointed everything that was necessary for the propagation, relief and support of the same, as also his successors have since done for many hundreds of years ... . Meanwhile in the West the Bishop of Rome assumed by degrees the same [legislative] authority, as well as usurping the Empire, and consequently became the reverse of what he was, and ought to be. For this reason the godly found themselves reduced to the same straits in which they had been during the reigns of the pagan emperors, so that they were forced to return to their secret assemblies ... . Therefore since God has given us the grace to throw off the slavery of superstition and and the courage to profess the pure religion, we have thought it our bounden duty to frame laws for the government of the Church, agreeable to the minds of our people. In so doing we have followed the foregoing examples as well as those powers which have openly embraced the true religion in this age, all of whom have prescribed a rule and order for the government of their churches. Now our pastors or ministers at [the synod of] Dordrecht [1574] have prescribed such regulations as seemed to them most convenient in church matters ... . But weighty reasons, which shall be disclosed when we explain why we have framed our laws concerning the religion, have persuaded us not to adopt the same.

Now the reason why we have committed to the civil magistrate the authority to choose ministers (by which we make the office of pastor subordinate to them, as are all other offices) is, because the office of pastor is like all those offices that receive their stipends or wages out of the public income of those places where they are discharged. If anyone else should have a right of appointing them, he would in that respect assume the authority of the civil government, and so there would be two sorts of magistracies in each city or place. We do not need to employ many arguments to demonstrate how dangerous that is ... . But some will say that there be few among the magistrates that are well affected to the [Reformed] religion. Whether there be few, or whether there be many, it makes no difference, for they have all of them solemnly sworn to defend it ... .

But the reasons why we have decreed that the magistrates of every chief town shall provide all the places under their jurisdiction with ministers, are these; first, to secure to them their ancient privileges; and, secondly, [to ensure] that no unworthy minister may be imposed on them from outside ... . We have not thought it fit to consider the *classes* in the distribution [of offices], since that cannot be practised without the confusion of jurisdiction. This is so obvious that it needs no explanation ... .

Those of Geneva have chiefly had regard in their ecclesiastical laws to the churches which had their own magistrates in the districts to which they belonged, and we have justly copied these, so that there is not much in which we do not agree both apparently and in reality with each other. There are some other matters, which our circumstances will not yet allow: neither did they at first make absolute decrees concerning the government of churches ... .

The seventh article appeared so necessary to the ministers of the city of Geneva (who have no equal either for learning or piety), that when the practice of the same had for some time been discontinued, they themselves petitioned the magistrates, in the year 1560, that it might be re-established. They protested that they did not in any way seek their own advantage, but rather that they and their successors might be better kept in check and this matter is also mentioned in the ecclesiastical laws of the said city ... .

And why should not the magistrates help to compose the differences and quarrels among the ministers in case of need? Though they may not be all favourers of the [Reformed] religion, they are all bound on oath to maintain it. If there should be anything which they do not understand, they may lay the same before us [the States of Holland]. This is the purport of the thirteenth article.

Such is the nature of our government that even the Papists, who on account of the common cause have embraced our side, are faithful to us by virtue of solemn promises. For that reason we ought also to have permitted the public exercise of the Papist religion, were it not that the priests and monks, our sworn enemies, had endeavoured to incite them to sedition. Indeed we even tolerate the Anabaptists themselves, being convinced that [knowledge of] the true religion is a gift of God, and that men ought not to be forced into it through the fear of banishment, or other punishments, but invited with charitable exhortations from the Word of God.

Given the variety of religions, we were bound to order some things differently than perhaps would have been suffered in a country where there was uniformity in religious matters. We would have it understood that it is for this reason that we will not allow baptism to be refused to anyone and our defence is Christ's commandment that the little children should not be kept from Him. We have therefore ordained that [the religion of] the parents should not be an obstacle to baptism. Those who are stubborn on this point will cause the Papists to have their children privately baptised by mass priests summoned from abroad for this purpose and at the same time will estrange them from us. The office of the pastor, amid these confusions is, after Paul's example, to become all things to all men, that he may gain many ... .

Christ was pleased to let Judas, whom He knew would betray Him, to participate in His secret Supper: He did this, as He Himself testifies, that the saying of the Prophet David might be fulfilled ... . But we should not take this as our pattern, because Christ elsewhere forbids us to give what is holy to dogs, or to cast pearls before swine. As this now was His concern, neither can our towns and many of our villages permit too strict an order in the holding of the Lord's Supper such as the examination of all those who desired to partake of the Supper, obliging these to make confession of faith ... . How many there are among such a great number of people that fall short in these matters! Paul seems rather to insist upon self-examination, when he says, 'Let a man examine himself, and so let him eat of that bread, and drink of that cup.' If this be not done, the rest are only hypocritical actions and gestures, which have nothing to do with the true preparation for the Lord's Supper ... .

The numerous labours and preoccupations that rightly belong to the office of the ministers demand the whole man. We have therefore deemed it right to relieve them of all those tasks which might be discharged by others. On that account we have reserved cognizance of all matrimonial matters, which would have caused the ministers a great deal of trouble, whereas the same will add but little to the general business of magistrates. But so that there might be convenient rules, by which to judge those matters, we have prescribed certain laws, which we have based (as far as our age and customs permit) on divine and imperial laws. So much for the articles relating to matrimonial affairs [articles 30-31] ... .

Just as magistrates are responsible for making appointments to all other offices, so too the institution of elders belongs to them. It is not possible for others to choose them without giving the appearance that there are two sorts of magistrates. Because these [elders] are appointed by the civil magistrates, their authority will be greater and they will treated with more respect. But the religious turmoil and unstable condition of our state do not allow us at present to annex any other powers to their office than are contained in our laws. The authority which they customarily exercise over every particular person with respect to his morals shall be entrusted to them in general by the magistrates so that, as far as is possible, they may restrain all licentiousness, and restore the commonwealth to its ancient lustre [article 39] ... .

Source: Brandt, *History of the Reformation* [D9], i. 318-25; *Historie der Reformatie*, i. 567-78.

48 The Synod of Dordrecht, 1578

Ch. 1 The ministers of the Word, the elders and deacons

4. The nomination of ministers shall be made by the consistory, assisted by the deacons and the ruling of the *classis*, if the same can meet; if not, with [the ruling] of two or three of the closest ministers of the same. The examination shall be conducted by those responsible for calling [the minister]. However in the case of those adjudged fit by the university of Leiden or any other university subscribing to our religion there shall be no re-examination concerning doctrine. When the ministers have been tried and chosen, the Reformed civil authority shall be informed and then they shall be presented to the congregation for a period of fourteen days so that if anyone has any objection, he may without hindrance disclose the same. He shall do this in good time in the consistory so that the same, with some members of the *classis*, may carefully consider the matter. If no one presents any objection silence shall be taken as consent.

11. In those places where a congregation must first be gathered and order established, the minister who is sent there shall use some of the most pious to advise him, to govern the church and to dispense alms; then he shall exhort his hearers to prepare themselves for the exercise of the [Lord's] Supper by making confession of their faith. Once the congregation has grown somewhat in size, he shall appoint some as elders and deacons in the proper way from among those who have been to the [Lord's] Supper.

Ch.4 Doctrines, sacraments and ceremonies

53. In order to bear witness to their doctrinal unanimity we recommend that all the churches in the Low Countries should subscribe to the Confession of Faith contained in the thirty-seven articles, which was reprinted in this year 1578 and which was presented to the King Philip many years ago. And this should also be done by the elders as it is done by the ministers of the Word and professors of theology.

64. No one shall be received into the congregation until he has been examined by the consistory or at least by one minister and elder touching the chief heads of the Christian doctrine. And before they go to the Lord's Supper, they shall publicly affirm in the consistory room or in the church after the sermon which immediately precedes the administration of the Supper that they approve the doctrine

received by the congregation, which shall be briefly explained by the minister, and that they wish to persevere in the same with the Lord's help and that they submit themselves to the Christian admonition.

67. Before the [Lord's] Supper the ministers and elders shall visit the members of the church, especially the weakest and those most in need so that to the best of their ability they may properly prepare the congregation for this most worthy act by giving instructions admonition and consolation and by settling objections, which have arisen.

73. Likewise, the Lord's Supper shall not be administered where no church order has yet been established, but in the best ordered churches it should be administered, as far as possible, every two months. But the churches shall be free to hold it as frequently as they deem fit, especially the secret congregations and those which live under the cross.

Ch.6. Ecclesiastical admonition and discipline

92. Since the Lord Christ, besides the service of the Word and the sacraments, also instituted the ecclesiastical admonition and discipline, the ministers shall not only publicly teach, censure, exhort and refute, but they shall also especially exhort everyone to do his duty. But as Christian discipline is spiritual and exempts no one from the civil punishment, so the ecclesiastical censure is of necessity required, over and above the civil censure, in order to reconcile the sinner with God and his neighbours and to remove the offence from the congregation of Christ.

96. The stiff-necked [sinner] who rejects the admonition of the consistory shall be suspended from the [Lord's] Supper; but if, after suspension, he shows no sign of repentance, despite several admonitions, it [the consistory] shall proceed to excommunicate him.

Particular questions

2. Whether it is necessary for the civil authority to confirm the synodal articles. It is replied that the civil authority shall be asked to confirm with their authority those articles, where the authority of the same is necessary for these to be put into effect. And to that end two persons shall be appointed to request the same from the States [of Holland].

27. Whether the children of all and sundry, including those of fornicators, excommunicants, Papists and such like should be bap-

G

tised without distinction. Answer: since baptism pertains to children who stand in the covenant of God and it is certain that these children are not outside the covenant, they shall not be turned away. Nevertheless they shall be baptised in a proper manner: they shall be represented by someone who can reply with understanding to the questions in the ceremony of baptism and who accepts the doctrine.

35. Whether one may admit to the Lord's Supper persons who acknowledge the Bible alone as the Word of God but who refuse to answer the customary questions put to those who wish to go to the Supper and will not consent to these. Answer: the churches shall maintain their usual practice of requiring the Confession of Faith. Everyone is bound to give an account of his faith after the teaching of Peter [1 Peter 4: 5]. For it is moreover unseemly to change the common practice of the congregation for the sake of some special persons.

55. Whether it is seemly for the ministers in their sermons to cite from the ancient Fathers [Church Fathers] and to refer listeners to the works of recent writers like Luther, Calvin and such like. Answer: the articles of the Christian doctrine should only be confirmed in sermons with the testimony of the Holy Scriptures. But the testimonies of the Fathers may be used in moderation, chiefly in order to convict Papists of their stubbornness. But the names of the recent authors should be omitted entirely from sermons.

Source: W. van 't Spijker, 'Acta synode van Dordrecht (1578)', in *De nationale synode van Dordrecht 1578* (ed. D. Nauta *et al.*, Amsterdam, 1978), pp. 142-84.

49 Ecclesiastical ordinances drafted by order of the states of Holland (1583)

William by the Grace of God etc.,

Forasmuch as it is proper for the Christian magistrate everywhere to ensure that the doctrines of the Holy Gospel of Our Lord, Jesus Christ, are presented to the people in all purity and that good order and government are maintained in the Christian Church ... having meanwhile paid special regard to the present circumstances and to whatever else shall be found pertinent, and without nevertheless rejecting [the example] of any foreign churches, although these may adhere to or may have ordained and enacted some other customs in indifferent matters, we hereby ordain and enact that throughout the lands and counties of Holland the following heads and articles concerning the ministry of God's Word and other ecclesiastical matters, or such as may appertain thereunto, shall be observed and followed.

1 The election and appointment of ministers in the towns

When a minister of the Word is required in the towns, the four burgomasters ... together with the minister or ministers of the same town or the most senior elder in service who together should make up four in number shall proceed, after holding prayers and carrying out an examination among themselves, to choose such a person or persons as they consider necessary, useful and qualified for the said ministry. The same shall present their choice to the college of burgomasters and schepenen of the aforesaid town. If the same choice is acceptable to the magistracy, the chosen person shall be examined in the following manner and in so far as he is found to be competent and sufficiently endued by God, he shall be presented to the congregation of the church and, if within fourteen days, no one gives any reason why they should not accept him, he shall be admitted to the aforesaid ministry, either with the laying on of hands or in accordance with the practice of each church and instituted in the ministry of the aforesaid charge. But in so far as the burgomasters and schepenen object to the aforesaid elec-tion, the aforesaid deputies shall proceed to elect a new candidate as before.

2 [The election and appointment of ministers] in the countryside

And whenever a minister of the Word is required in the villages, the chief officer with the schout and two or three of the most senior magistrates in the village, as well as the elders, if there be any, and four of the neighbouring ministers from the classis shall proceed to the election of a competent minister of the church. They shall examine the same properly and then present him to the congregation in the church so that the minister-elect may be admitted to his charge in the manner described above and instituted in the ministry ... .

4 Oath to be taken by ministers of the church concerning their obligation as teachers

All ministers of the church shall on admission to their charge be bound to take an oath at the hands of the magistrates in the presence of the people: first that he shall teach and preach God's Word and Gospel sincerely and faithfully for the edification of the church to which he has bound himself, that he shall not bring before the people any new doctrine, which has not previously been accepted by the Church, and that he shall not misuse his learning for his own inclinations or thereby to please someone, but that he shall apply the same with an upright conscience for the glory of God and the most edification of the church.

7 His duty of obedience to the magistrate

And finally he shall submit himself to all civil laws and ordinances of the province and to set everyone in this matter a good example; to obey the magistrates in all things so far as his ministry permits, that is without thereby diminishing his liberty to proclaim boldly the Word of God.

19 Administration of the Lord's Supper

Anyone who wishes to attend the Lord's Supper for the first time shall approach one of the ministers in good time to confer with him about the faith and then, on the day before the Lord's Supper is held, he shall come to the church to make with the others a general confession of faith after the minister. After he has done this he shall be admitted to the Lord's Table, unless he has been told at the aforesaid meeting or subsequently by the minister that he should continue to stay away on account of some public scandal or other hindrance.

Ecclesiastical assemblies

43. The ... consistory shall take place each week with the minister or ministers of the Word and the elders of each church, though where the number of elders is small, the deacons may attend; the magistrates or regents of the towns and villages respectively shall also be permitted to send one of their number to keep an eye on everything done there, though he shall not have a vote, so that all the business of the church may be conducted in good order and in the most edifying way and all scandals which may arise or have arisen in the congregation may be removed or prevented.

48 Purity of doctrine

And in order that the ecclesiastical discipline (which notwithstanding exempts no one from the punishments laid down by the criminal law) may be properly applied in the province of Holland, it is enacted that whenever any person commits an offence against the purity of the doctrine and pious conduct, and that offence is private and no public offence has been given, the rule prescribed by Christ [Matthew 18: 15-18] shall be observed ... . And in so far as he obstinately rejects the admonition of the consistory and refuses to make a declaration of repentance before the consistory, he shall be suspended from the Lord's Supper, and if, after suspension and several [further] admonitions, he refuses to make a declaration of repentance, the consistory shall report the same to the civil authorities, i.e. the burgomasters and *schepenen* in the towns or the chief officer and local judges in the country districts, and having obtained their consent to proceed to the final remedy, to wit public excommunication of the sinner, who shall be named. But if the magistrates shall object to the aforesaid public excommunication, and the members of the consistory still consider that the same [i.e. excommunication] should be followed for the sake of the church, the same shall be brought before the next provincial synod and there resolved and the sentence shall be pronounced by the synod, which shall be attended by as many deputies as the superior magistrate and the provincial states think appropriate for the matter in hand.

Source: C. Hooijer, *Oude kerkordeningen der nederlandsche hervormde gemeenten (1563-1638)* (Zaltbommel, 1865), pp. 233-46.

50 The Synod of The Hague, 1586

The ministries

4. In both the towns and villages the valid calling of those who have not previously served [as ministers] requires: first, the *election*, which shall be made by the consistory and deacons with the opinion of the *classis* or of two or three of the nearest ministers, and in those places without a consistory, by the *classis*, with prayers and fasting; secondly, the *examination* or investigation of both doctrine and conduct, on the basis of which they shall be chosen, it being however understood that novices, mass-priests, monks and those who have other-

wise left some sect shall not be admitted until they have been tried for a period of time; thirdly, the *approbation* and approval of the local magistrates (who shall be informed to see whether they have any legitimate cause to object on account of his behaviour and civil conversation) and of the whole congregation, once the name of the minister has been made known in the churches for a period of fourteen days and no objections arisen; finally the public *confirmation* before congregation, which shall take place with proper conditions, examination, exhortations, prayer and the laying-on of hands by the minister responsible for the confirmation (or by some others where there are several ministers) in conformity with the order on this matter. It is understood that the laying-on of hands may, in the case of newly-ordained ministers who are to be sent to churches under the cross, take place in the meeting of the *classis*.

Instructions of the deputies in attendance at the synod

27. An urgent demand shall be made that the manifold and appalling profanations which occur on Sunday and other days when there are pious assemblies, and about which almost every church complains greatly, should be abolished.

The deputies of the general synod shall also recount how grievously Sundays, festivals, fast-days and days of prayer are profaned. This comes from shops which stay open for trade [and] markets held on such days; from public dances, dancing schools, plays, fencing masters, rhetoricians, drinking-bouts in taverns. Tennis and sports are played about the church during the services; the country folk stand gossiping before the church door and on the dykes; the dyke-reeves, dyke-overseers, courts, guilds and such like meet at these times; writ-servers, sergeants and other officials lease lands, collect debts and meet to transact the business of the world. Something must be done because the authorities do little or nothing about it and the common people drink themselves silly, even on fast days, and sometimes fights break out.

The *schouten*, secretaries and other officials are themselves also largely responsible for this state of affairs because they often keep taverns or come to taverns at such times to collect fines and connive at all the disorders committed by the people, indeed they compound with the people for their disorders, and have themselves no concern for godliness and the Word of God. Devout people, who are well-disposed towards the Religion should therefore be appointed as officers, in order to prevent the subjects from following all [these] evil examples.

Source: Rutgers, *Acta* [D14], pp. 487-643.

(e) Retrenchment and consolidation

51 Collapse in the south. Two letters from southern churches

(i) Daniel de Dieu to the London Stranger Church, 9 August 1582

Honourable brethren, since an opportunity has arisen to write to England, I have not wanted to delay greeting all the brethren any longer ... . As for the state of our oppressed fatherland, we may well compare it, as the prophet Isaiah [1: 5-6] does his Jewish people, to a wretched man, whose whole head is sick and his whole heart has grown weary and in whom nothing wholesome can be found; from the soles of his feet to his head there are only wounds, stiffness and ulcers, which can neither be closed, bound up nor soothed with oil. For the Lord does lay aside His wrath, but His hand remains stretched forth and the land is still filled with idolatry, injustice, treachery and every kind of infamy. God's Holy Word is received by few and read by still fewer. Everywhere you find multitudes of atheists and libertines, some of whom openly scoff at religion and call it a fable and invention, saying that it is nothing more than a matter of policy, devised by crafty and cunning rulers to keep simple folk in fear and obedience. These therefore regard those who do, and suffer, so much for the sake of religion as mad. Others who wish to conceal their contempt for God say that such a variety of contending beliefs has arisen in our fatherland that they neither know which is true nor what they should believe. Some set their cap to the wind and outwardly conform with all sorts of religion. Others extol the peace and prosperity of everything under popery and make out that God's Word is the cause of all this misfortune and strife. It is therefore not surprising that the wrath of God is still kindled against the country. We on the other side too, who should have been all the more godly as the world grows more godless, have by our sins also increased the fire. Instead of bringing water, we together carry oil to it so that it burns more fiercely than ever. For this reason we see that the Lord gives advancement to the enemy and sets us back. He makes his horses sturdy and his soldiers strong and bold and by contrast He makes ours fearful and timid.

Thus God has also allowed our fellow brethren at Lier to be treacherously surprised and wretchedly treated.[1] Some of these escaped naked and many others, having no money to buy their ransom, were miserably murdered, among whom one of the ministers, a virtuous god-fearing man (by name Jan Schijve: he had earlier served at Mechelen) was according to reports most cruelly put to death. The chief men and leaders of the country are not exempt from all sorts of assaults on their person, as was quite recently planned and about which you will have certainly heard.[2] What then should anyone think? Shall we allow ourselves to become discouraged and bereft of all comfort? Our answer is no, certainly not. For we know that, although we shall have tribulation in the world (John 16), we nevertheless have peace in Christ. Recently we had here a great mutiny of our garrison; they seized the court, grievously threatened the burghers and forcibly removed some officers, both from the magistracy and from the council of war, from their houses. Whereupon some burghers, both Papists and others, were given arms to protect the market, the town hall and magistrates from any insolence, though not to fight the soldiers, for that would have been the height of folly. Nevertheless the situation was as a result far worse because the servants of the mass and malcontented spirits strove thereby to incite the soldiers against us by spreading many slanders and threats so that it seemed as though the soldiers and our people would have fallen on one another with their swords. But the affair has been settled and entirely made up so that our pro-Spanish party has not yet achieved their boast. Soon afterwards we were warned from all sides that the enemy was coming to besiege us and great preparations were laid, but this cloud also seems to have passed over. Our mass-enticers have now been pressing the Duke [of Anjou] for several months on end to be allowed to take possession of the church on the Koudenberg close by the Court (which is used by the Walloon congregation) and openly to celebrate mass. But so far they have failed and only time will tell what they shall obtain hereafter once the Duke comes. God will meanwhile keep away all idolatrous services from us. Brussels, 9 August 1582.

Source: Hessels, Archivum [D1], iii. 679-81 (no. 804).

[1] A Scottish captain in the service of the States betrayed Lier to Farnese on 2 August 1582. The Walloon troops sacked the town.
[2] On 18 March 1582 Jean Jaureguy made an attempt on William of Orange's life in Antwerp.

(ii) The ministers in Antwerp to the church in Emden, August 1585

[An attestation for a Calvinist family leaving Antwerp shortly before the city capitulates to Farnese.]

We, the ministers of the Word and elders of the Reformed church of Christ at Antwerp, testify that Gilles Huyge and Johanna his wife are not only members of our congregation, but that the said Gillis Huyge is also an elder of this our church in the service of which he has acquitted himself well and faithfully. We would have liked (had it pleased the Lord) to have continued to make use of his service, help and assistance in the government of this church. But since it has pleased the Lord to put his congregation to the test by granting our adversaries the victory, and the said Gillis Huyge with his wife and family are therefore minded to depart elsewhere so that they may better serve the Lord in accordance with his Word, so it is that we the above mentioned pray in the name of the Lord Christ that each and every brother, whatever their condition and state, might recognise the said persons forasmuch and therefore to render due Christian assistance and help, whensoever they might seek or have need of the same. Each and every one of us shall always acknowledge our debt and stand ready [to help] according to our ability and wherever it may be fitting. In witness thereof we have below subscribed this in all our names and sealed it with our usual church seal. Antwerp, 13 August 1585.[1]

IJsebrandus Trabius Frisius	Andries de Meester
Gaspar van der Heyden	Libertus Fraxinus
Thomas van Tielt	Philippus Lansbergius
Jeremias Bastingius	Assuerus van Reghenmortel
Petrus Hardenberg	Joannes Becius

Source: Janssen and van Toorenenbergen, Brieven [D3], pp. 26-7 (no. 11) (incorrectly dated 1 August).

52 Visitation of Reformed congregations around Dordrecht, 1589

[Westmaas]: After prayers had been offered the elders and deacons were asked about the condition of the minister, how he conducted

[1] On the fall of Antwerp six of the ten Calvinist ministers went directly to churches in Holland, and two others after a brief interval abroad. Only two took positions in the exile congregations.

himself in his ministry, whether they know anything concerning his doctrine and personal life which he should be told to reform, whereupon they answered together that they could only testify to his piety and that they could find nothing to say against his doctrine and life, for which they thank God the Lord.

Next asked whether they hold their church meeting [i.e. consistory], they replied that they held it as far as possible every fortnight, unless something exceptional prevented it.

Concerning the diaconate there is also no problem and it is looked after by the congregation who maintain the poor in general and to the best of their ability.

Next concerning the church services and everything related to these; and there is no difficulty except that they want Frans Jansz. [the minister] to be relieved of the service at Klaaswaal so that the Catechism might be preached at Westmaas on Sunday afternoon and the congregation, as a result, might be better edified.

Some discussion also arose concerning the choice of elders. Among other matters it was said that Frans Jansz. visited the members [of the church] at home with the list of candidates presented to the congregation to have their vote for whom they wanted to elect as elders. Although this was done with the agreement of the consistory, some were suspicious. The consistory has therefore been admonished not to do this any more, but to act in accordance with the church order to prevent any suspicion.

[Alblasserdam]: The elders and deacons were first, in the absence of the minister, asked about the doctrine and conduct of the same and whether he carried out his ministry as he should, whereupon they answered that they can only speak well of him, thanking and praising God for the grace shown to him, although they wished that he also taught on Thursday so that the people therefore might be better instructed. When informed of this, he said that he was prepared to do as much, if the consistory would agree.

Secondly, asked whether they hold church assemblies, they replied that they do not have a set day, but come together if they have a problem. Hereupon they have been admonished to set a certain day, which they have promised to do.

In addition they were also admonished (since the marriages and the baptisms of the children were as yet not recorded) henceforth to record the same most diligently, which they have promised to do. [They] have also been admonished to keep good order in the election of elders and deacons in accordance with the church order (since the procedure followed until now is somewhat confused and might cause still more confusion), which they have promised to do.

[*Puttershoek*]: Two brothers, members of the congregation, appeared there and [were] asked about the doctrine and conduct of the minister. They have nothing but good to testify concerning his doctrine and conduct, [for which] they thank and praise God.

As yet there are no elders or deacons on account of the small size of the congregation, and they therefore been exhorted to work in order to put the same in hand when God shall grant more growth.

Further, baptisms and marriages are conducted as they should be and in accordance with the church order.

Baptised children and marriages are recorded as they ought to be.

[*Heinenoord*]: Four members of the church appeared as well as the *schout* and some of the dyke board, who were asked about the doctrine and conduct of the minister, how he behaves. They answered together that they can only speak well of him [and they] give thanks and praise for his gifts and ministry. There is as yet only one service on Sunday.

We also asked about poor-relief, how it is administered. It was found that it is still administered by the masters of the Holy Spirit[1] and the local officer and the dyke board have promised next time, if it pleases God to spare their lives for so long, that they will then speak with the minister about this and reach an agreement and [they] have nothing against this.

[*Oud-Beijerland*]: The elders and deacons being assembled, they were asked about the doctrine and conduct of the minister; they answered that they know of nothing at all against either his doctrine and conduct, but they thank and praise God for his grace and for the gifts which he gave him and wished that it was so everywhere.

The minister was asked in private about the condition of the elders and deacons, how they conduct themselves in their service. Whereupon he replied that he can only speak well of them, but wants them to be exhorted to diligence in their service. Done.

There are three services a week, one during the week and two on Sunday, but only every second Sunday since he [preaches] at Nieuw-Beijerland on the other Sunday.

Further, marriages are recorded as they should be and both parties appear before the minister.

Poor-relief is still administered by the masters of the Holy Spirit, yet there are also deacons, but they do not have a collection. They have been exhorted to work so that the collection might be done by

---

[1] These overseers of the poor were appointed by the parish and therefore not accountable to the Reformed consistory.

the deacons, whereupon they replied that they will work to this end, [that they] have worked for this already for a considerable time using many means. And they shall persevere, hoping that eventually they shall accomplish the same, if God now grants [His] grace so that they acquire in the congregation persons of better substance for this purpose.

The brethren have also told of a man, who has stayed away for a considerable time from the Lord's Supper and has adhered to several heresies and, despite being admonished, he does not repent, but goes so far that he will acknowledge no visible Church; they desire advice as to how they should proceed in this matter, because the Church ought to exercise her office in this. We have therefore recommended to them that the minister should visit him with an elder and admonish him once again and, if he gives no answer, that they shall deal with him in accordance with Christ's commandment.[2]

As for the school, there is no difficulty here, thanks be to God, but the schoolmaster has been exhorted to let the children sing the psalms at school; if they also [sing] these repeatedly they might in time sing the same in church.

[Klundert]: Some of the elders and deacons as well as a few members came together and, being asked about the doctrine and conduct of the minister, replied that they can only speak well of his doctrine, and they thank God for his gifts, yet they do wish that he sometimes studied rather better. As for his conduct they testify that they would have preferred if his way of life had been an adornment to his doctrine. And at bottom that he is a bit headstrong and he is also given on occasion to visiting the watches.[3] When we admonished him in this matter, he paid little heed to our warning; on the contrary he says that he will not stop.

As for baptisms, marriages and election of elders and deacons everything is done in conformity with the church order.

As for his absence from the *classis* he made some excuse about the danger and the expense, and although we thought this unsatisfactory, we have left the next *classis* to call him to account for this as well as other matters such as visiting the watches and suchlike.

Source: Van Dooren, *Classicale Acta* [D12], pp. 265-9.

[2] Matthew 18:15-18.
[3] The minister, Johannes Blocquius, subsequently served for a time as an army chaplain.

53 Dilemma of a Calvinist minister with a rural charge, 1602

To the Reverend and Most Renowned Master Franciscus Junius, Doctor of Sacred Theology and Professor at the university of Leiden. (I will pay the boatman who brings your reply.)

Greeting many times over, most Reverend, Renowned and Esteemed Doctor, Pardon my boldness, that I should interrupt you so boldly, involved as you are in the concerns of the university of Leiden and of the Church and immersed in the controversies with the Jesuits: necessity compels me and the care for my church to which my God has destined me. It is now two months since I undertook the ministry of the Word of God in this village of Aarlanderveen. I have quite shocked the rustics, simple souls, who can scarcely tell A from B. This is not surprising for they have been without a minister for a good two years and they are all devoted either to Lutheranism or to the Papists. The church consists of only six men and seven women; there are no elders and only a single deacon. In general the village is quite populous and many here would wish to join the church, but they fear the mocking laughter of the Lutherans (of whom there is here a huge number). Hear, most renowned master, the state of the church and entertain briefly the reason for my writing. Whitsuntide is at hand when the Lord's Supper is administered in all the villages. When therefore I now summon even those who are outside the church and invite these with more kindly words to Holy Communion, I cause offence to many. These say that they are indeed convinced in their hearts of the truth of our religion, but are, however, too little advanced in the fundamentals of religion and cannot advance sufficiently on account of their agricultural pursuits. Nevertheless they seek to be received into the church, saying that they believe in Christ crucified, that they renounce their works except [those performed] by the sole merit of Christ. I ask whether this profession is adequate and whether I am allowed to admit such to the church, when their outward life is coincides with this confession. I ask you, Reverend Doctor, in the name of Jesus Christ to the increase of whose Church I devote myself, to reply to me at once, if you are able, for they press me greatly. Once I have admitted them, the Lutherans will say that they too can profess the same [things] and are similarly not be excluded in future from the service or else (for they are embittered) they will say sarcastically, 'behold, these are the Reformed'. On the other hand, if I exclude these (since the people here are simple souls), no one, who is conscious of his ignorance, will ever join the church. As I am beset on all sides I eagerly await your judgement. I ask you urgently to free me from my difficulties with a few words, or else, if you are unable to do so because you are busy, to prevail on Master Gomarus or Master Trelcatius to write me. For those who wish to join the church press for an answer. May the perfect and almighty God keep you safe for a long time for the sake of the churches of Holland, the University and the Commonwealth to the glory of His name. 3 May 1602.

Most humble servant of Christ and admirer of your learning, Johannes Lydius, minister of the Word of God in Aarlanderveen.

Source: W. Cuno, *Franciscus Junius der Ältere, Professor der Theologie und Pastor (1545-1602). Sein Leben und Wirken, seine Schriften und Briefe* (Amsterdam, 1891), pp. 391-2.

54 State of the churches in Utrecht, 1606

Rhenen. The minister there reported the reasonable condition of his church, though he complained that the services on Sunday were impeded by the buying and selling at the market, which was held then. Many of the children were not baptised in the church and since no one afterwards had any knowledge of the same baptism, great confusion might arise later. He also complained that some sort of private school was held in the monastery to the detriment of the Christian religion. He declared that he had not presented these complaints in order to invoke the help of their noble lordships, the States, but only to demonstrate the present condition of the church there, since he intended to seek such [assistance] from his own magistracy, who had also given him an undertaking to remedy [matters] (which has also happened with other towns).

Wijk bij Duurstede. The minister of the church declared that the condition of his church was good and to that intent he showed a certain document which set forth the government of the church by six elders besides the minister, the administration and care of poor-relief by two deacons and also that the Holy Supper was held three times a year and that on each occasion [the members] were visited or examined at home and a preparatory sermon delivered, that newcomers were catechised in the presence of two elders in the articles of faith and then admitted to the Supper; that three services were held each week, two on Sunday and one on Thursday, with the Sunday morning sermon on the Sunday Gospels and the afternoon sermon on the Heidelberg Catechism (when the [school] rector also instructed the schoolchildren in the psalms) and the Thursday sermon on the first epistle to the Corinthians. He also exhibited another document in which the consistory of Wijk bij Duurstede, having given thanks to their noble lordships, the States, who had been pleased to summon the synod, petitioned for the continuation of synodal and classical meetings in Utrecht. The aforesaid consistory also complained in the same that several papist conventicles occurred in the town of Wijk (in contravention of the edicts of their noble lordships the States) at which mass was celebrated, children baptised and marriages confirmed. This was done by the *Heer* Steven at Overlangbroek and by others. Also petitioned that the rector's salary, (being only 145 guilders) should be supplemented from the monastic properties administered by their noble lordships the States.

Montfoort. The minister reported the sorry state of the church there as a result of the manifold activities conducted by the Roman Church there; that there is still no organised church; that he administers the Supper twice a year, has few communicants, to wit only thirty in number; that previously 300 would attend (sometimes 500 or 600 on feast-days), but now only 100 because a certain priest, called *Heer* Hinderick, coming there from Utrecht, impedes the progress of the Gospel by holding mass, preaching, baptising etc.; that the magistrate looks after poor relief, the school is middling: though the school-master is of the Reformed religion, he uses books of all sorts.

Amerongen. The minister reported that his church was in a dismal state because (although a fair number attended, often between 100 and 150) there are few, indeed no communicants; that the church also, as regards its external condition, suffered from having been very badly ruined as a result of destruction inflicted by soldiers who had marched through. [He] complained that the congregation also leaves the church when baptism is administered before the public prayer and general blessing; that the superstitions associated with St Cunerus's Day are very detrimental to the religion; that the sexton only comes to church now and then; that he cannot lead the singing and also refuses to give any undertaking to do so; also believes that the schoolmaster teaches from books of all sorts, whatever comes to hand.

Zeist. The minister reported that his church is in a fair state, but he complained about two hindrances; in the first place, since there is no bell, there is much heavy drinking during the service; the tavern-keepers say that they do not know the time and the taverns remain open during the services. Secondly, [he] also complained about a certain priest from Wijk, who did great disservice hereabouts. Reported further that he had three communicants at Christmas and forty at Easter and hoped to choose elders; that he himself taught there at the request of the inhabitants; that also certain endowments, belonging to the school, are kept back by a knight; for this reason a letter might be written to his grace van Beverwijk in order to obtain in this way a schoolmaster of their own.

Houten. The minister reported the dismal state of his church; few attended [church] because of a former priest, called *heer* Jan van Houten, who keeps watch on the inhabitants from the Tolsteegpoort and threatens them with damnation if they want to go to church to hear the sermon, also inducing some inhabitants to stand by the church and to jeer at those who enter the church. [He] also showed certain sheep, etc., made of wax which the inhabitants even offered in church during the service. [He] also reported that the *maarschalk*[1] only comes on Whit Monday; complained that the local officer resides in Utrecht and does not appear in church; consequently the inhabitants act very insolently.

Abcoude. The minister reported the reasonable state of his church, having a reasonable attendance, also holding the Supper with twenty-eight communicants and everything in accordance with the Reformed churches; relating that he has a suitable sexton and schoolmaster, employing Reformed textbooks, but adding thereby that he resorts to the taverns rather too often and he [the minister] certainly wished that he might be admonished by apt measures. [He] complained about some assembly of Anabaptists. Also complained that the inhabitants of Abcoude often went into Holland to take part in papist exercises held in certain houses belonging to Holland, whither the Jesuits and other young students training for the priesthood, maintained by merchants from Amsterdam, came to hold services. Said that he usually only preached once and in Lent also on Wednesday in order to draw the Papists, but he cannot accomplish much here because they [the Catholics] have bound them not to go to the [Reformed] services, threatening otherwise to take away their means of existence.

Mijdrecht. The minister reported the good state of his church so that he, despite many having died from the plague, still has 120 communicants. Said that he holds the Supper every ten weeks, not only on feast-days. Related also that he also preaches the catechism on Sunday afternoon, except during the harvest, that he also preaches during the week on Wednesday during the winter. Also said that he sometimes gives three sermons on Sunday, in the early morning at Mijdrecht, at nine o' clock at Thamen and in the afternoon the

[1] The name given in Utrecht to a superior officer who discharged administrative and judicial functions in the countryside (closely resembling a bailiff in Holland).

Catechism in the school mid-way between the two [villages] … . Also complained that the school is not well endowed and that there is some guild of pot-companions, from whose income the school-master's pay could certainly be increased.

Source: Reitsma and Van Veen, *Acta der Provinciale Synoden* [D13], vi. 298-307.

Section 4
INTERNATIONAL CALVINISM

All over Europe adherents of the Reformed religion spoke of the 'republic of Christ'. They held that this community, to which they felt themselves to belong, was the true Christian Church, recognisable in their own day wherever the Gospel was proclaimed and where the sacraments were administered according to God's Word.

The 'internationality', or rather the universality, of this idea had powerful imaginative force. It came, after all, right out of the heart of the Christian tradition. A sense of brotherhood transcending time and place was neither new in that tradition nor unique in the sixteenth century to the followers of the Reform. What gave the godly cause its special voice, however, was a certain view of history more or less peculiar to itself. In this scriptural and providential perspective the Pope was cast as Antichrist and the long centuries of papal ascendancy, now ending, were seen as an aberration in the history of the Church. Men committed to the cause of the Reformed religion believed that they were fulfilling God's providential plan when they sought actively to promote the cause of true religion within and beyond the area of jurisdiction of their own domestic civil power. They exhorted princes to act likewise, holding that no frontiers, no boundaries, no limits should confine the zeal of pious princes in the matter of God's glory and of the reign of Christ. They held that the Scriptures taught that although in general the civil powers were to be obeyed, subjects finding themselves commanded to ungodly actions by ungodly rulers were faced with two choices only, disobedience (in ways specifically laid down), or flight. Acceptance of this teaching made its followers potentially subversive, and filled the sanctuaries of Protestant Europe with self-righteous migrants whom 'ungodly' princes suspected of plotting from afar to change the religious power-balance in their native land.

Were such suspicions well-founded? Beyond the rhetoric of godly preachers, did an international Calvinist conspiracy to overthrow the citadels of Antichrist ever actually exist? And whether or not it did, can we dismiss the rhetoric as insignificant? It has recently been suggested that even if 'for a full half-century there was more of fantasy and nostalgia than substance in the protestant cause', we should be careful not to underestimate 'the negative importance of the impossible dream'.[1] Its language became familiar to the Roman Catholics, the Lutherans, the Anabaptists, the anti-Trinitarians, and the sceptics upon whom it had declared war, and affected, as it was intended to, their perception of the danger presented to them by zealous upholders of the Calvinist cause.

In any case, the protagonists of the Reformed religion were engaged in a great deal more than a war of words. Convinced of their calling, they were indefatigably active. Some of this activity, naturally enough, took place within the confines of their own local community. But for the intellectuals, printers, booksellers, soldiers and diplomats who (with many different degrees of ideological commitment, and from many different motives) associated their efforts with the cause, the scene was as wide as Christendom. Manuscript and printed material of all kinds circulated along the routes of trade, finding a ready market and apparently stimulating an appetite for more. Translation flourished and many works were repeatedly reprinted. The material included psalters, bibles, sermons, and treatises denouncing false doctrine or discussing fundamental issues of political thought. It included also sensational accounts of executions or massacres, printed singly or more elaborately edited and presented in the form of martyrologies, works of propaganda and histories of the Church and of the world. A deliberate effort was made to raise public consciousness about religious and political issues, and to internationalise and indeed to universalise the episodes involved. Material of this kind was produced and distributed in many cities including Frankfurt, Heidelberg, Strasburg, even London and La Rochelle. But Geneva, in the scale and direction of its effort, outclassed them all. No description of the international efforts of the Reform can omit to mention the contributions of the printer and scholar Robert Estienne, the printer and martyrologist Jean Crespin, the pastor and historical propagandist Simon Goulart, or for that matter the lifelong and deliberate use of publication as a weapon on the part of Calvin and of Théodore de Bèze.

Fraternal relations between the Reformed churches were also fostered by the mutual recognition of confessions of faith [**documents 41, 57**], proclamation of fast-days and of days of special prayer [**document 59**], the training, transmission and interchange of pastors and professors and students [**documents 63, 64, 65**], collections towards poor-relief [**document 60**], and the raising of public subscriptions for the defence of the godly cause [**document 66**]. This carefully cultivated solidarity strengthened hearts and minds; it distributed resources [**documents 59, 60, 61, 62**], and it helped bring about, if not uniformity in doctrine and church

[1] By Patrick Collinson in Menna Prestwich (ed.), *International Calvinism* (Oxford, 1985), p. 203.

discipline, then at least some co-ordination and a declared harmony of confessions, and the explicit condemnation of doctrines perceived to be false. But it was not in itself sufficient, without the self-interested co-operation of calculating statesmen, to ensure the more than local survival of the congregations of the Word. If this survival, even locally, was not to be haphazard, semi-private, sectarian and clandestine, it depended in the end not merely upon the prayers and labours of the faithful, but upon the establishment of synodical discipline and ideally also the legal backing of the civil power. If beleaguered congregations suffering persecution and oppression were to be helped by those in other countries, co-operative efforts of a diplomatic and military kind would need to be made. The Scottish Kirk showed a clear realisation of this in 1572, when it spoke of the need for 'a league and confederacy to be made with our neighbours of England and other countries reformed ...' [document 55], as did Bèze and the Geneva pastors when they saw that security for their threatened brethren in the Empire could not be obtained through the intercession of other godly congregations unless this was backed up by the secular governments concerned [document 56].

The development of this political and diplomatic international Calvin-ism may best be understood if the period between 1555 and 1610 is treated as falling into five phases. The first may be said to run up to the death of Calvin in 1564, the second to the massacre of St Bartholomew in 1572, the third to the assassination of William of Orange in 1584, the fourth to the promulgation of the Edict of Nantes in 1598 and the fifth to the aftermath of the assassination of Henry IV of France.

Before 1556 Protestants, already deeply divided among themselves, were still engaged in desperate struggles against hostile monarchs and entrenched ecclesiastical authorities. In 1555 however, Lutherans in the Empire secured the religious Peace of Augsburg, and for a time extended the hand of friendship to those of their fellow-Protestants who would accept its terms. Between 1558 and 1563 non-Catholic religious settle-ments were adopted in England, Scotland and Sedan, the enemies of Calvin were routed in Geneva, the Rhenish Palatinate adopted a version of Protes-tantism closer in doctrine and in discipline to the Swiss than to the Lutheran Reform. Far and wide 'Calvinists' began to prevail over everybody else among the heterogeneous religious sects and congregations of France, the Netherlands, Poland, Transylvania and Hungary. Their success was uneven, but greatest where an ascendancy of disciplinarian ministers backed up by *classes* and synods managed to restrict the vagaries of religious enthusi-asts, wayward intellectuals, arrogant noble patrons and insubordinate congregations. Only in such areas could pastors and elders organise their churches in such a way as to hound dissenters into flight or into silence.

In retrospect the years 1556 to 1564 could be seen to have been the golden and expansive years of the Protestant Reform. Already its religious teachers were up to their necks in politics, and their perspectives were European. Calvin from an early date had cultivated all the potentially godly princes he could find, urging them in frequent letters to heed God's call to found their church upon Scripture rather than upon the 'merely human' teachings and traditions of the Roman Church; he ostentatiously targeted specific rulers in the dedications of his printed works. In Edinburgh and in Heidelberg, in Emden and in Debrecen (Hungary), indeed everywhere where congregations were growing, it was obvious to all that religion and foreign politics were inextricably intertwined.

Between 1564 and 1572 the tangles grew tighter and more confused. Under the tutelage of his Calvinist counsellors the Elector Frederick III began to see a universal danger and the need therefore for a co-ordinated response. In 1568-70 he was prominent in diplomatic activity on an unprecedented scale, the aim of which was to build a Protestant (or at any rate an anti-Habsburg) coalition. The papal excommunication of the Queen of England raised hopes that she would join, and for a time in 1571 the ascendancy of the Huguenot princely party at the court of Charles IX made real the prospect of a grand alliance of the kind of which the godly zealots dreamed. It was precisely this which prompted the botched attempt to assassinate Coligny, which in turn precipitated the massacre of St Bartholomew's Day. The Crown of France was revealed as the enemy not the ally of the Reform and all hopes collapsed of combining in a grand coalition the Calvinist and the anti-Habsburg cause.

Between 1572 and 1584 Calvinists had repeatedly to adapt to changing fortunes at local level. In 1576 the conflict in the Netherlands seemed for a moment to be resolved in the Pacification of Ghent, only to break out again more bitterly and with a greater admixture of religious intransigence than before. Between 1576 and 1584 the House of Orange–Nassau was a dominant force; at this time the Palatinate was ruled by the Lutheran Elector Ludwig, so the initiative in Germany passed increasingly to his brother Duke John Casimir, who disposed of a sizeable army and who persuaded Queen Elizabeth, among others, to foot his military bills, only to lose all support from England and from Orange when publicity was given in 1578 to his irresponsible partnership with the extremist Calvinists of Ghent [**document 67**]. This disclosure once more put an end to a scheme for a godly coalition. More indicative of the priorities of Protestant princes were the marriage of William of Orange to Louise de Coligny in 1581, and the elaborate political manoeuvres conducted by various members of the House of Valois over the succession to the English Crown. The Genevan agent Jean Maillet succeeded in collecting a great deal of money from well-wishers in England in 1582-83, but his success was almost entirely among individual members of the puritan party; the Crown remained aloof.

The whole pattern shifted in 1584, after the assassination of William of Orange and the death of the Duke of Anjou. The new Elector Palatine, Frederick IV, was a child, his foreign policy in the hands of his uncle John Casimir, who remained until his death in 1592 a dangerous and incalculable player on the international stage. Throughout 1585 efforts were made by the political puritans in England (prominent among them the Earl of Leicester and his retainers and associates, together with Throckmorton and Sir Francis Walsingham) to engage Elizabeth in a Protestant alliance, and to send a military expedition to support the States-General of the United Provinces. Despite the Queen's reluctance Leicester was despatched. The advocates of a godly crusade were jubilant; this looked like the moment for which they had longed; a European monarch had espoused their cause. But they were soon to be disappointed; indeed the more wary and *politique* of their number had been sceptical all along. Elizabeth proved unwilling to assume the role of Deborah, and Leicester became bogged down in the political complexities of the Low Countries, where the Holland oligarchs who had once welcomed him soon cooled. There was no grand Protestant alliance in 1586; the moment passed. In 1587 the Catholics dispersed a Huguenot–Palatinate force under the Duke of Bouillon, and Leicester's presence in the Netherlands came to an ignominious end; he died the following year, and with his death, and that of Walsingham and Warwick in 1591, came the collapse of the internationalist puritan interest at the English court. Not even the disclosures of treason and plot which had led to the execution of Mary Stuart, and not even the Armada itself persuaded Elizabeth that defending the kingdom against Spain entailed full-scale commitment to the international Protestant cause. In 1591-92, however, she was persuaded to take part in a military enterprise despite the fact that the motives and interests of the other parties were different from her own. Yet another attempt was being made to construct a Protestant coalition. This was in part the brainchild of the dangerously visionary Christian of Anhalt, but more importantly it had the backing, for the moment, of Henry IV who employed as his spokesman and agent in the Netherlands and in England the militantly Calvinist second Duke of Bouillon (Henry de la Tour d'Auvergne). Bouillon secured the promise of English troops for Brittany and their active presence at the siege of Rouen. This disastrous episode (and the wars in Ireland) made Elizabeth more reluctant than ever to send soldiers to the Continent for the sake of any cause. As always the very credibility of a grand Protestant coalition (without the Lutheran princes) rested upon the calculations of a King of France. Predictably, Henry at this stage saw no future in it; the pragmatic course demanded accommodation with the Catholics, and a realistic acceptance by the Huguenots that the best they could hope for would be some form of limited safeguard and guarantee.

Negotiation on this issue was to be a central feature of the 1590s. Hard-liners everywhere encountered co-religionists arguing for compromise. Huguenots were divided, some still hankering, Bouillon among them, for an independent godly republic in south-western France. But the French pastors based in Geneva did not take this line; abandoning the internationalism and the radicalism which had once been a feature of their political thought, they advocated negotiation with and subsequent obedience to the civil power. Faced with the serious possibility of limited recognition of the Reformed religion in the kingdom, their writings show a noticeable shift in tone. In Germany, on the other hand, the nerves of Calvinists were kept on edge by the ceaseless ingenuity of Christian of Anhalt and the strident campaign of alarmist propaganda in which the scholar Camerarius played a leading part. A superficial appearance of internationality was given to the Palatinate–Anhalt alliance made in 1598 by the presence among its signatories of the Duke of Bouillon and the Dutch. Despite this, however, the alliance was not a genuine Protestant coalition; the Lutheran princes did not join it, nor did the King of Denmark, nor the Queen of England, nor (significantly) did the King of France. Sensitive to the dangers of an independent Huguenot presence in international relations, the *Parlement* of Paris forbade the French Protestant Church to designate official representatives of its own to send abroad. Between 1600 and 1604 Christian of Anhalt was courting the United Provinces, arguing that their defence of their liberties against the Habsburgs necessarily involved them in a universal defence of the Gospel in the Empire and beyond. His enlistment of Brandenburg strengthened his hand. In 1608 his efforts met with some success when the Evangelical Union was formed, sworn to prevent the loss of Jülich to the forces of Antichrist. A simultaneous campaign was conducted by Christian to win over to his way of thinking the noble leaders of the Calvinist Bohemian Reform.

James VI and I of Scotland and England proved more difficult to frighten or to cajole, but the real prize of 1609 was the Machiavellian adherence to the coalition of Henry IV of France. An extensive conspiracy was afoot to set limits (by military means if necessary) to Habsburg power; deeply involved, naturally enough, were those who still took literally the old theory of the papal Antichrist, or who believed in the imminence of the last days, an even more dangerous sentiment which Calvin himself had most scrupulously eschewed. But all the threads which were being plaited together unravelled once more on the news of the assassination of Henry

IV. Without the active participation of the Crown of France there could be no grand concert of the powers. In 1609-10 there was a pause: the last apocalyptic confrontation had been, for the time being, postponed.

(a) Doctrinal solidarity. Solidarity of confessions

55 Reacting to the St Bartholomew's Day massacre: The Scottish General Assembly

The Heads and articles which are to be proposed in the name of the ministers, barons and commissioners of Kirks, to the Regent's Grace, nobility and Council.

The assembly of the Kirk convened at Edinburgh, 22 October 1572, according to the proclamation, first having thought expedient, so far as present convention is instituted, to provide remedy against the treasonable cruelty of the Papists, and to resist the same. To mitigate the wrath and indignation of God whereby they are stirred up against us for our sins, there shall be a public humiliation of them that fear God, throughout the whole realm, to begin 23 November next coming, and to end the last day of the same ... .

And first, it is thought necessary that all superintendents and commissioners of counties take diligent inquisition of the behaviour of all ministers, exhorters and readers, and what fail should be found, severe correction to follow thereupon ... .

Secondly, as concerning the Papists that be within this country yet remaining, that they, without all exception of persons, great or small, be charged, as well by the Council as ministry, to appear at certain days, as shall be appointed, ... to give confession of their faith ... .

Thirdly, for resisting of Papists of foreign countries, as well within as without, that my Lord Regent's grace and nobility shall take such order that a league and confederacy be made with our neighbours of England, and other countries Reformed, and professing the true religion, that we and they be joined together in mutual amity and society to support every one another, wheresoever time and occasion shall serve, for maintaining religion and resisting the enemies thereof. Likewise, that a solemn band and acts may be made by all them that be professors of the true religion within this realm, to join themselves together, and be ready on all occasions for resisting the enemies aforesaid. And if any be found negligent, he shall be holden a false brother, and excommunication to proceed against him.

Source: Calderwood, *History of the Kirk of Scotland* [S7], iii. 227-30.

56 The Reformed churches combine to defend their confession in Germany. Extracts from the register of the Company of Pastors in Geneva

Calvin hanged in effigy by the Saxons at the entry of the Emperor

On the last day of May [1575] M. de Bèze informed the Company that the people of Saxony on the entry of the Emperor had made a spectacle in painting of Hercules overcoming the Hydra, and, on the other side, had erected a gibbet with an hanged effigy of the late Monsieur Calvin on it, with the words, 'This is how the Elector of Saxony will exterminate all the Calvinists.' He also said that in view of the fact that at the end of July the Estates of the Holy Roman Empire were to meet at Frankfurt to elect the King of the Romans, we had to fear that some sort of decree would be issued there against those of our confession, given that it was clear that the Saxons at least were in favour of something of the kind. Monsieur Ursinus has written from Heidelberg that the Company of Pastors there thinks it desirable that magistrates of our confession should be present at those Estates to urge that despite the difference between us and the Lutherans on the matter of the Lord's Supper, nevertheless we all profess the true Communion of the body of Jesus Christ together with the other principal points of the faith, and that the diversity on the Supper should not divide us, nor prevent those of our confession from being included in the comprehensive peace settlement. The Queen of England and others – even some who were not of our religion – were prepared to help us in this.

It was decided that Monsieur de Bèze should reply to Monsieur Ursinus that we would thoroughly approve if their Company wrote to the Swiss Churches asking them to co-operate in this matter, and if the civil powers [in the Palatinate] agreed to join with them in making this point to the Estates of the Empire and that if all this were done, that our own Magistrates would associate themselves with it in whatever way they saw fit.

The Church at Strasburg in danger from the other ministers of that city

Monsieur de Bèze also produced letters from Monsieur Grenon, minister of the French Church in Strasburg, in which it was reported that the German ministers of the place, following the example of those of Saxony, are trying by all means in their power to break up the French

Church. The said Grenon entreats us to pray for them all, and asks Monsieur de Bèze to prepare some of the rulers of the City of Berne for a future request to use their good offices to persuade the rulers of Strasburg, with whom they enjoy some credit, to be more moderate, so that the Church may be preserved.

Decision to present a supplication for the churches of our Confession at the assembly of Estates of the Empire

Our brother ministers of Zurich, having been advised by those of Heidelberg that it would be good to provide against what we have to fear from our enemies, who have already shown in Saxony and elsewhere that they intend to exterminate the Churches of our confession, by securing at the assembly of the Empire due to be held in Regensburg in September a decree condemning us and the books of our teaching and even banning us from the Empire, have agreed that it is indeed necessary to provide for this eventuality, and have drawn up a supplication which they have sent with covering letters to our brethren in Berne, to seek their view on whether, in the first place, it would be advisable to send a supplication to that assembly, and, in the second place, whether the proposed text is good, and also asking them to communicate the whole of this to us. This our brother ministers in Berne have done, and our Company, given that it had already instructed those of Heidelberg to follow that route, has given its approval both to the decision to present a supplication, and to the proposed text, adding that it ought to be presented not by the ministers but by the magistrates of the churches, and not to the Elector Palatine, as the Zurichers suggest, but to the Protestant princes, for the reasons set out in the reply drawn up by M. de Bèze on behalf of the whole Company.

Source: Registre de la Compagnie des Pasteurs [G2], iv. 23-5, 30.

57 Mutual recognition of doctrine and church order. The French national synod and the Dutch Confession

The Twelfth French National Synod, Vitré, 1583

[*General matters*]

1. Our brethren of the Low Countries having requested that some good course might be taken, and means used that the deputies of their churches might for some time to come be present at our national synods, and ours at theirs. This assembly doth now ordain, that as often as the synods of the said Low Countries shall be convened, two provinces of this kingdom shall be obliged to send their deputies, to wit, two ministers and one elder, who shall be expressly named by those two provinces in every national synod, and their charges borne by all the provinces of this kingdom, and for this present approaching synod of the Low Countries the provinces of the Île de France and Normandy are appointed to send the deputies.

2. And whereas the brethren their deputies have tendered unto this synod the Confession of Faith, and body of church discipline owned and embraced by the said churches of the Low Countries, this assembly having humbly and heartily blessed God for that sweet union and agreement both in doctrine and discipline, between the churches of this kingdom and of that state, did judge meet to subscribe them both.[1] And it did also request those our brethren their deputies reciprocally to subscribe our Confession of Faith and body of church discipline, which in obedience to the commission given them they did accordingly; thereby testifying that mutual harmony and concord in the doctrine and discipline of all the churches in both nations.

3. Moreover this assembly having to its great grief understood the miserable condition of the greater part of the churches in the Low Countries, how they be exceedingly pestered with diverse sects and heresies, as of David Jorists, Anabaptist, Libertines, and other errors contrary to the purity of God's word, and against which they cannot use those remedies which are most desired; and yet on the other hand this synod did greatly rejoice at the glad tidings of their care and diligence in opposing and refuting those anti-scriptural heresies, subversive of divine doctrine, order and discipline, and it did most earnestly entreat them to persevere in the confutation and condemnation of them, as it would also on its part cordially join with them in so doing, and would give, as it now gives an unquestionable proof thereof, by

[1] The churches of the Low Countries had urged mutual recognition of confessions synod of Emden (1571), see above p. 158.

subscribing their Confession of Faith and Church Discipline.

4. And forasmuch as this holy union and concord established between the churches of France and those of the Low Countries seems necessarily to demand their mutual loves and assistance, this assembly judges meet that the churches of both the nations shall lend and borrow their ministers reciprocally, according as their respective necessities shall require.

Source: Quick, *Synodicon* [F1], i. 143-4.

58 Defending purity of doctrine in France

The Colloquy of Montbéliard, 1586

[*M. de Bèze required by Mle Comte de Montbéliard to attend the conference with Jacobus Andreae*]

On the Monday M. de Bèze demanded a ruling on a point required of him by the Comte de Montbéliard, who urged him most strongly to transport himself to the said Montbéliard to confer with Jacobus Andreae who would be there, and who had been warned to conduct himself with modesty at the said conference. M. de Bèze added that, since the opportunity had presented itself, he had written on the same day to the ministers of Berne and of Zurich asking their advice. It was agreed that the Company would wait for the replies from Berne and Zurich before coming to a decision, and that meanwhile M. de Bèze should write to the Comte de Montbeliard saying that he was not at all keen on attending such a conference, but that in any case he could not do so without leave from the rulers of Geneva and the advice of the churches of Switzerland. He will keep a copy of the reply.

Source: Registre de la Compagnie des Pasteurs [G2], v.97.

From the acts of the synod of Montpellier, May 1598

[*General matters*]

4. The churches of Geneva, Béarn, Basle, the Palatinate and many others from diverse parts of this kingdom, complaining of several writings published on the design of reuniting the two religions in one doctrine, to the apparent prejudice of God's truth, and in particular, of a certain book, intitled *Apparatus ad fidem Catholicum*, and another bearing this inscription, *Avis pour la paix de l'Eglise & Royaume de*

France. This synod, having read and examined those aforesaid writings, and received the judgement of the colloquy of Nîmes, as also the censures of the above-mentioned churches, doth condemn them as containing diverse erroneous propositions; to wit, that the true doctrine was kept entire and found among all that are called Christians; that those of the Church of Rome having the same articles of faith with us, the same commandments of God, forms of prayer, baptism, and the same means and ordinances to obtain everlasting salvation as we have, are consequently the True Church, and the difference between us is only verbal, not real. That they would have the ancient councils and writings of the Fathers to be judges of the points in controversy between us, and that because they quote the canons of Gratian under the name of the Catholic Church, therefore we are made the authors of that schism and of those civil wars which have happened in this kingdom, and several other suchlike matters. And all the churches are enjoined to beware of them.

Source: Quick, *Synodicon*, i. 196-7.

(b) Fast-days, collections and donations

59 Fast-days

Minutes of the Consistory in Emden

7 September 1562. It is decided that we will hold a day of prayer and fasting for affairs in France, where the community of God is in great peril and danger. And we will write to her Grace [Countess Anna of East Friesland] to ask her to publish a mandate for a day of prayer throughout the land on St Matthew's day [21 September].

10 May 1566. We will hold a day of prayer on Ascension Day, for the following causes:

The progress of the Gospel in the western lands, that it may not be impeded in this change for the better;[1]

The great power of the Turk against the Christians;

The beginning of the new year;

That our gracious Lords may rule wisely and well, and stamp out all disorderly houses, whore-houses and inns, etc.

Source: Schilling and Schreiber, *Kirchenratsprotokolle* [Gy7], i. 151, 249.

[1] A reference to circumstances in the Netherlands in the early months of the *Wonderjaar.*

Register of the French–Walloon church at Southampton

1. 3 September 1568, a fast was celebrated, to mark the descent of the Prince of Orange on the Low Countries from Germany, attempting with God's assistance to deliver the poor churches out of their affliction. A fast celebrated to pray to the Lord more ardently for the deliverance of his people.

2. 6 May 1570, a fast celebrated because Monsieur the Prince of Condé and other princes of France, at war to maintain the true religion which the King wishes to abolish, have lost a great battle. By which all the churches are desolated, and in danger of great calamity. A fast to pray for them.

3. 25 September 1572, a public fast celebrated because the Prince of Orange has returned to the Low Countries with a new army, to attempt to deliver the lands and the poor churches out of the hand of the Duke of Alva, that cruel tyrant, and also mainly because the churches of France face a terrible and horrible calamity because of this terrible massacre perpetrated in Paris on 24 August. Whereby a great number of nobles and the faithful have been killed, around twelve or thirteen thousand in all, preaching forbidden throughout the kingdom, and all the goods of the faithful pillaged. This solemn fast is celebrated for their consolation, and for that of the Low Countries, and to pray God to deliver them.

Source: Registre de l'Eglise Wallonne de Southampton, ed. H.M. Godfray (Huguenot Society Publications, 4, 1890), p. 125.

Minutes of the French church in London

Thursday 8 September 1575. The decision of the the three foreign churches here for a day of public prayers and fasting, will be announced on Sunday, to be celebrated on the 18th. The reason, the afflictions of the churches in France and the Netherlands, and the plague with which we are afflicted.

Thursday 11 November 1576. The decision of the three churches for a public fast-day will be announced on Sunday, to be celebrated in fifteen days' time, and to pray especially for the churches of France and affairs in the Low Countries. The other foreign churches in the country should be advised of it.

Source: Actes du Consistoire de l'Eglise Française de Threadneedle Street,

Londres, vol. 2, 1571-1577, ed. Anne Oakley (Huguenot Society, 48, 1969), pp. 169, 184.

Colloquies of the French churches in England

[*The Ninth colloquy, Canterbury, 1590*]

8. A solemn public fast, with extraordinary prayers, will be celebrated in our churches, as many as can: the fixing of the appropriate day will be left to the church of London, so that we may be more informed concerning the necessities of the churches of France and the Low Countries.

[*The Tenth colloquy, Norwich, 1593*]

14. A solemn public fast will shortly be celebrated in our churches, both for our present calamities, and for those which threaten in France and the Low Countries. The determination of the day, and making it known, is left to our brothers of London.

Source: Les Actes des Colloques des Eglises Françaises et des Synodes des Eglises Estrangères réfugiées en Angleterre, 1581-1654, ed. A. C. Chamier (Huguenot Society Publications, 2, Lymington, 1890), pp. 20, 22.

Register of the Company of Pastors of Geneva

[*8 December 1587.* Dark times]
And since at the moment these times are very dark because of the scattering of the German army, which had gone into France to assist the churches and particularly the King of Navarre, it was decided that the people should be prepared through the churches to make ready for a fast as soon as possible.

[*29 September 1598.* Public prayers for the churches of the Low Countries and for our brother of Thonon.]
We will expressly mention in the public prayers the churches of the Low Countries, for we hear that the enemies are gathering new and very large human forces against them. The same will be done for our brothers of Thonon.

Source: Registre de la Compagnie des Pasteurs [G2], v. 173, vii. 113.

60 Collections

Minutes of the French church in London

Sunday 21 October 1571. This same day the deacons informed the Company that the poor chest of our church is in arrears, for this month and last, to the extent of £30 sterling. This is on account of the necessities of the many poor families newly arrived here as refugees from the churches in Germany, France and the Low Countries. Also to advise us of the extreme necessity of the large number of poor people, refugees at Wesel, as we have been informed by letters from the church of Wesel. The large part of the poor people there are poor artisans, who lack the means to make their bombazine cloth,[1] and the great dearness of corn, and ask our help to get through next winter. These collections should be made by the refugee Walloon churches here in England.

Source: Actes du Consistoire de l'Eglise Française de Threadneedle Street, Londres, vol 2, 1571-1577, ed. Anne Oakley (Huguenot Society, 48, 1969), p. 28.

Register of the Company of Pastors of Geneva

14 October 1577. Collection and gift from Messieurs for the brothers exiled from the Palatinate.

Messieurs were also told of the large number of poor ministers and school teachers, up to 800 families, who have been exiled from the Palatinate by the new Elector because they hold our confession. May they be pleased to give something for these people, and to find it good that we too gather a collection from them from among the prominent and well-off, as we have been requested by letters from prominent people from that area. Messieurs gave 100 talers from the public purse. The Company taxing itself, each according to what God had given him, and also gathered the aforementioned collection approved by Messieurs, and received from the well-off French as well as from the Italians up to 200 écus, as well as the 100 talers from the Seigneurie, and the whole amount was sent to our brothers whom God will bless through his grace.

Source: Registre de la Compagnie des Pasteurs [G2], iv. 98-9.

[1] A mixed cloth made of silk and worsted, or cotton and linen.

Register of the St Andrews Kirk Session

20 December 1587. The same day it was concluded that the minister with the four bailies, Mr Martin Geddy, Alexander Carstairs, James Robertson, Patrick Guthrie and Charles Watson, collect the charity within the town for the poor French Church, banished for the cause of religion, in England. And that supplication pass to the eight quartermasters upon the land, to wit, Alexander Wood of Stravithie, Martin Corstorphine in Boarhills, for the east quarter; Mr Andrew Aytoun of Kinaldy and James Wemys of Lathoker for the south quarter; George Ramsay of Largo Law, and John Traill feuar of Blebo, for the west quarter; John Inglis of Strathtyrum and Patrick Dudingston of Kincaple for the north quarter. And this to be done with all diligence.

Source: Hay Fleming, *Register of the Congregation of St Andrews* [S3], ii. 610. According to a note, the collections in Scotland at this time raised 10,000 marks.

61 Religious charity

Donations from the legacy of Robert Nowell of London

[fos. 52-3] Money given to the Italian, French and Dutch churches, as hereafter appeareth. Anno 1569. And to certain persons of strangers also.

1. 14 February given to Jeronimus Jerlitus, Italian minister, as appeareth by his acquittance.   54s 4d
2. 12 [February] given to Jean Tawsin,[1] minister of the French Church   54s 4d
3. 17 [February] given to Rodolphus Chevalier, minister of Caen in Normandy, and now in exile and reader of the Hebrew lecture in St Paul's, over and above his gown before entered   20s
4. 14 February to Godfray Wingye,[2] the Dutch preacher   54s 4d
5. 14 February paid to Anthonius Coranus, Spanish preacher, over and above his gown   25s
6. 17 February, to Vincen Basse, a French minister   20s
7. 17 February, to Ciprian Valera, a poor learned Spaniard   20s
8. 25 February, to the seniors and deacons of the French church in

[1] Jean Cousin, minister 1564-72 or possibly Jean Taffin.
[2] Godfried van Winghen.

[215]

H

London, to be distributed among their poor £40

9. 27 February, given to the seniors and deacons of the Italian congregation In London, to be distributed among the poor of their company £10

...

1. 25 February, to the seniors and deacons of the Dutch Church in London, to be distributed among their poor £40

2. 25 February, to Barthelmy Willelmi, minister of the Dutch Church £26 8*d*

3. 8 March, to Jacobe Baelden and others, to be distributed among the poor of the Dutch Church in Sandwich £20

To Adrianus de Lano, a learned Brabanter 20*s*

4. To the poor of the strangers of the Church of Southampton, 20 March £10

5. To the poor of the strangers of the French and Dutch church in Norwich, 17 March 1569 £5

6. To the church of strangers in Maidstone, 29 March 1569 £5

...

2. To certain poor strangers, dispersed for religion, Frenchmen, 20 November 1571. Given by the hand of Mr Henry Knowles, who is one of the collectors of the same 20*s*

Source: The Spending of the Money of Robert Nowell, ed. A. B. Grosart (Manchester, 1877), pp. 100-4.

(c) Pastors and professors. Printing, intellectual contacts and Calvinist higher education

62 The Geneva Bible, 1588

Announcement made by the Company of Pastors to Booksellers and Printers in Geneva, 1 March 1588

The financing of this work, printed in three different formats at the same time for the convenience of different kinds of person, has been generously provided by a number of men of substance, who have not sought their own particular profit, but merely to serve God and his Church, with the intention that if, when all the costs have been deducted and met, there is any small sum left over, this shall be subscribed and donated, as they now subscribe and donate it, to the common fund of the poor refugees of various countries and nations in this Church. We have judged it necessary to notify everyone of this, so that, in addition to reminding you of God's commandment which forbids all illicit and dishonest gain, and of the praiseworthy custom observed by men of honour in the bookselling trade not to compete against one another, nor to poach each other's labours, we may remind you of charity, which commands all Christians to have pity on an infinity of poor persons, the sick, the old, the disabled, widows, orphans, vagrants, and others of all sorts receiving support from the aforesaid common fund, and we may also warn you not to put yourselves in the wrong, nor to cause damage to any man, by the sacrilege of reaping where you have not sown, nor to harm the aforesaid poor people, by depriving them unjustly of what little the Lord has given them for their relief. You are, accordingly, exhorted and entreated to attempt nothing in the way of printing this work, but, on the contrary, to ratify, in effect, for your own part, the privilege granted by various princes and magistrates and legitimately due to those who, in all simplicity, have employed themselves in this endeavour, to the end that the poor may gather up a little temporal benefit from this spiritual labour. If you do not comply you will have against you all men of good-will and especially He who is the guardian of the poor, to whom we hope you are favourable in all your good and Christian enterprises so that you may receive His holy blessing, to His glory and to your salvation.

Source: Registre de la Compagnie des Pasteurs [G2], v. 331.

From the acts of the synod of Montauban, 1594

[*General Matters*]

3. Reserving liberty unto the Church for a more exact translation of the Holy Bible, our churches imitating the primitive Church, are exhorted to receive and use in their public assemblies the late translation revised by the pastors and professors of the Church of Geneva. And thanks shall be presently given to Monsieur Rotan, and by letters unto our brethren of Geneva, who have at the desire of our churches so happily undertaken and accomplished this great and good work. And they shall be further entreated to amplify their notes for the clearer and better understanding of the remaining dark places in the sacred text.

4. A resolution being taken in the last national synod of Vitré, at the desire of the deputies of Saintonge, that they should consider

whether M. Calvin's catechism ought to be changed; it is now decreed, that it shall be retained, and ministers shall not be permitted to expound any other.

Source: Quick, *Synodicon* [F1], i. 161.

63 The Geneva Academy.

(i) Extract from the statutes of the Geneva Academy, 1559

Concerning the Professors

The three public Readers, in Hebrew, Greek and Arts, shall be chosen and confirmed in the same way as the others.[1]

On Mondays, Tuesdays and Thursdays they shall each lecture for two hours, once in the morning and once in the afternoon. On Wednesdays and Fridays they shall each lecture for one hour in the afternoon. On Saturdays, there shall be no lessons. Sundays will be employed in listening to the sermons.

On Fridays the Professors will attend, whenever possible, the Congregation and the Colloquy of the Ministers.

In the morning directly after the sermon the Professor of Hebrew shall teach some book of the Old Testament using Hebrew commentaries. In the afternoon (in winter from noon to one o'clock, in summer from one o'clock to two) he shall give lessons in Hebrew grammar.

The Professor of Greek shall follow the Professor of Hebrew in the morning, and shall expound some book of moral philosophy, by Aristotle or Plato or Plutarch or some Christian philosopher. In the afternoon (in winter from one o'clock to two, in summer from three o'clock to four) he shall lecture upon a Greek poet, or orator or historiographer, taking these turn and turn about. And he shall choose authors who are the most pure.

The Professor of Arts shall follow the Professor of Greek in the morning, and shall lecture for half-an-hour on some text in natural philosophy. In the afternoon (in winter from three o'clock to four, in summer from four o'clock to five) he shall expound learnedly the *Rhetoric* of Aristotle, or some of the most celebrated of Cicero's speeches, or Cicero *On the Orator*.

The two Professors of Theology shall expound the Books of Holy

[1] The others being the schoolmasters in the college for younger pupils.

Scripture on Mondays, Tuesdays and Wednesdays from two o'clock in the afternoon until three, taking it in turns to do this in alternate weeks.

Concerning the Students

The students in the public schools [2] shall report to the Rector to have their names inscribed and to sign with their own hand the confession of their faith.[3] They shall comport themselves modestly and with respect towards God.

Those students who wish to engage in formal exercises upon the Holy Scriptures shall enter their names in a register, and on Saturdays between two o'clock and three they shall expound some passage of Scripture publicly before some of the Ministers who will conduct the proceedings. Then they will listen to a critical response from the mouth of the presiding Minister. In the course of this critical debate any of those present are to be permitted to put forward their own opinion modestly and in the fear of the Lord. Each of these aspirants in turn must, every month, draw up in writing certain propositions, which must not be frivolous nor sophistical, and which must not contain false doctrine. They must hand these in in good time to the Professor of Theology. Then they must argue publicly in support of them against those who want to debate the issues. Everyone is to be permitted to speak. All sophistry, impudent cleverness and audacity in twisting the sense of the Word of God is forbidden, as is contentiousness and sticking obstinately to one's own opinion. Points of doctrine are to be treated reverently and religiously by disputants on both sides. The Professor of Theology, who is to preside over the disputations shall conduct them according to his discretion and shall resolve any difficulties which arise by reference to the Word of God.

Source: Charles Borgeaud, *Histoire de l'Université de Genève.* Tome I: *L'Académie de Calvin 1559-1798* (Geneva, 1900), p. 626.

(ii) The first 100 students

On 11 December 1559, we subscribed to the established laws of the Geneva Academy and by name to the Confession of the Genevan

[2] The Academy.

[3] According to the 1559 statutes the students were required to subscribe to a very long and detailed confession of faith in which they solemnly abjured the Manichaean heresy, the errors of Servetus and many other teachings which Calvin held in abhorrence. In 1576 a very much shorter and simpler declaration was substituted.

Church:[1]

Charles Berger from Tours
Lancelot Dolbeau from Jarzé in Anjou (M)
Jean Blanchard from St Julien in Dauphiné
Pierre Colladon from Bourges
Jean Colladon from Bourges
Jean Chartin from Orléans
Sans Tartas from Sorhueta
Claude Clavel from Oulens
Jean Trochereau from Beaulon
Michel Hortin from Lucens[2]
Giovani Battista Aurelius from Calabria[3]
Antoine Pellicier from Mauguio
Vincent Textor from Mâcon
Urbain Chauveton from La Châtre
Peter Young from Dundee[4]
Jean des Gallars from Geneva[5]
Daniel Bermond from Pragela in Dauphiné
Barthélemy Perrot from Pragela in Dauphiné
Antonius Olevianus from Trier[6]
Job Veyrat from Geneva

Odet de Nort from Agen
Gerald Goer from Cologne
Theodore Weyer from Cleves[7]
Heinrich Weyer from Cleves
Gerard Weshemius from Gelderland
Johannes Stralen from Cologne
Raymond Regis from Limousin
François Guarin from Dronero in Piedmont

---

[1] In fact the names listed here subscribed during 1559 and 1560. Those in italics later served as ministers (mainly back in France); those marked (M) were also martyred.
[2] Later professor of Hebrew at Lausanne.
[3] Subsequently pastor in Saintonge and of the Italian church in London.
[4] Later tutor of James VI of Scotland.
[5] Son of Calvin's secretary Nicolas des Gallars, and subsequently pastor in Orléans.
[6] Brother of Kaspar Olevianus.
[7] Later chancellor to the Elector Palatine, Frederick III. His brother Henry was the Elector's private physician.

Nicolas le More from Angers[8]
Stephano del Piano from Asti in Piedmont
Jean le Gaigneux from Tours
Emard Girouard from Loudun
Pierre Martel from Paris
Jean Malbois from Bourges
Hugues de Regnard from Auxonne
Jean Quenon from Hainault[9]
François Daniel from Orléans
Léon Colladon from Bourges
Jacques Perrin from Lorraine
Jean Patac from Digne (M)

Michel Varro from Geneva
Faustino Zenone from Venice
André Rupert from Fresinières
Bernard Sarrasier from Gascony
Germain Chauveton from La Châtre
Jean Mutonis from Grasse (M)
Gilles Solas from Montpellier
Jacques Symon from Tours
Jean de Cornère from Rouergne
Jean Allard from Mirepoix
Antoine Roman from Aix-en-Provence
Jean Antoine le Fort from Cuneo
François Térond from Sauve
Archambaud Colomiès from Sainte-Marie-d'Oléron
Antoine Durant from Cévennes
Nicolas Baudoin from Rouen
Pierre Regius from Lodève
Guillaume Serre from Condom
Jean de Cenesme from Paris

Michel Le Lièvre from Bayonne
Simon Gerard from Bourges[10]
Jean Antoine Sarrasin from Lyons
Théophile Sarrasin from Lyons
Simon Harson from Bayeux

[8] Later almoner to Henry of Navarre and a victim of the massacre of St Bartholomew.
[9] Later pastor of the Walloon church in Cologne.
[10] Also studied at Heidelberg; later professor of Greek at Lausanne.

Henry Withers from London
Jean de Serres from Villeneuve[11]
Goddred Gilby from Edenham[12]
Robert Nirmaud from Nîmes
Bersano Benesia from Caraglio
Charles Paschale from Coni
Etienne de Fos from Merry-la-Vallée
Claude Textor from Bresse[13]
Jean Pinault from Poitiers
Antoine Chauve from Saint-Saphorin[14]
Paul Dotaeus from Aigle
Hector de Corguilleray from Gâtinais
Florent Chrestien from Orléans[15]
Charles du Pont from Blois
Antoine Cathedrius from Laon
Johannes Nöth from Hammelburg in Franconia
Guillaume Pillot from Beaune
Nicolas de la Vefve from Châlons-sur-Marne
Jean Poterat from Troyes

Guillaume le Neveu from Orléans
Pierre Faber from Mauguio
Paul Baduel from Nîmes
Claude Dorsaune from Bourges
Jean de Lassus from Montauban
Jacques Saurin from Saint-André-de-Valborgne
Pierre Brichanteau from Hurepoix
Gaspard Desoubzmoullins from Aquitaine
Jean Marnix from Brussels
Philip Marnix from Brussels[16]
Aimé Brossard from Forez
Bertrand Brymerius from Bazas

[11] Later regent at Lausanne, and professor at Nîmes. A confidant of Henry IV, he fell into disfavour at Geneva as a result of his involvement in plans to reunite the confessions in France.

[12] Son of Anthony Gilby, minister of the English church in Geneva. On his return to London he published an English version of Calvin's *Admonition against Astrology*.

[13] Later a professor at Wittenberg.

[14] Later minister in Geneva and Rector of the Academy.

[15] Tutor to the young Henry of Navarre and subsequently his librarian.

[16] Leading figure in the noble opposition of 1566 and principal Calvinist spokesman of the Dutch Revolt. His brother Jean (above) was killed leading Calvinist forces at the battle of Oosterweel (1567).

Nicholas Chaillou from Saintes
Arnauld d'Andrein from Béarn
Grégoire Tregius from Tarbes
Pierre Melet from Rouergue
Arnold Westerwout from Groningen

Source: Stelling-Michaud, *Livre du Recteur* [G4], i. 81-3.

64 The Geneva Academy in difficulties

(i) Daniel De Dieu to Godfried Wingius,[1] 17 April 1579

Dear Lord and brother. In your letters you marvel that I have moved to another place so rapidly, and I asked for such a speedy answer to my request. But I have already written about these things in greater detail to Rotarius. No one should think that I despise the Genevan school or its teachers merely because I say that I myself was not able to profit there greatly. The fault lies with me as I was ill-equipped. Other scholars, who have already been to good schools, can be taught the deepest doctrine with greater ease. Thus it was my duty to choose where I could progress further, especially considering my advanced age and the few years that are granted to me. Such a place would be either one where the arts flourish with theology or where theology is expounded by a strict method. I already know that you have already realised what a good method can accomplish ... . Philosophy also is to be sought, or such is the advice of the most excellent theologians. These, as well as other sciences were previously taught most carefully at Heidelberg, when that Academy was flourishing during the lifetime of the Lord Prince Frederick. It was of such renown that even rich Genevans sent their sons there to study the arts and theology when they had finished school. Indeed, even Lord Beza caused his adopted son, David, to be enrolled in the *Collegium Sapientiae* so that he might learn privately from Ursinus, in addition to the public lectures. Many similar examples can be found, some of whom were also promoted in the ministry. At that time, therefore, it could have been said without condemning the Genevan school that the Heidelberg school was more famous for liberal arts than the one in Geneva, and also in theology. Nor do I despise it while saying that I could make better

---

[1] Godfried Wingius was minister of the Dutch church in London. De Dieu was one of the church's sponsored students, who had evidently moved away from Geneva without permission.

progress here than there. Not all places can be the same, nor do all doctors have the same gift of teaching. Rather there are diverse constitutions among the schools. But it is certainly most true that from the Genevan church and school, the most distinguished men have gone forth into every corner of the world where churches flourish to this day. But it is the unanimous admission of the Genevan ministers (which they often tell us) that the Genevan school was more fertile and productive in times past, than it is now. Nevertheless, it deserves to be called the most celebrated of all the churches in the whole world ... .

As for the school at Neustadt,[2] it grows daily from the influx of many students. Ursinus, one of the theologians, has nearly recovered, and will resume (God willing) his exposition of Isaiah and Aristotle's *Organon*. Doctor Zanchius continues in the epistle of the Ephesians as well as Aristotle's *Ethics*. Further, disputations have been instituted; private ones will also be instituted among us shortly. We have all the other things as I have indicated in my other letters. This month a synod is to be held of all the churches in Casimir's realm, at which, among other things, Zanchius's Latin confession is to be discussed. It was drafted a few months ago, and a copy was sent to the Zurich and Genevan ministers to get their opinion. Some copies may be printed and sent to all our churches to elicit their judgement before it is disseminated generally. It clearly refutes the heretics of our day, and especially the Ubiquitarians who have caused great trouble in the German Church, and whom no one but God alone can cure. The whole Latin version of Doctor Tremellius and Franciscus Junius appeared at this fair in five parts and is sold here for 5 florins each reckoned at 15 batzen. Would that our learned teachers would either correct our common version or make a new one altogether. I hope that you might wish to encourage this by your authority. Meanwhile I will endeavour to meet your expectations in my studies, in which I pray the Almighty God may pour out his Holy spirit upon me. Amen.

... You will always find me ready if I can do anything for you, especially in the matter of books, since Neustadt is only two days' journey from Frankfurt. Frankfurt, 17 April, in the year of the last days, 1579. Daniel De Dieu.

Source: Hessels, *Archivum* [D1], ii. 631-5 (no. 172).

[2] The school established on the lands of Duke Casimir when Ludwig VI introduced Lutheranism into the Palatinate, causing a major exodus of professors and students from Heidelberg.

(ii) Bèze negotiates to find teaching for the Academy, 1587

Upon being summoned before us MM. Bèze and Jacquemot proposed that, since they are anxious to re-establish the School,[1] in the first place M. Chevalier will lecture on Hebrew, once someone can be found to fill in for him in the parish of Celigny. As for Philosophy, M. Gaspard [Laurent] will acquit himself admirably. As far as the Greek chair is concerned they proposed that M. Rotan,[2] at the same time as fulfilling his duties as a minister, should also lecture on Greek. However the Italian Church, having no other way to provide for itself after the death of M. Balbani the Italian minister, has elected M. Rotan in his place, subject to the good-will of their Lordships. M. Rotan, while submitting himself to the will of that church and of their Lordships, has pointed out that he cannot remain a member of the Company of Pastors unless he holds some post in the Genevan Church. In the end, before departing, Bèze and Jacquemot suggested that in order to keep him as a member of their Company (as they wanted to do, since he is the most learned of men), he could be lent to the Italian Church for a limited period, and at the same time act as professor of theology. And by that means they would have three teachers of theology, as is the case in other famous cities, one to lecture on the Old Testament, one on the New Testament and the third to teach Commonplaces .... And to provide for the teaching of Greek, they advised the reinstatement of the chair which should then be given to Isaac Casaubon, who is, they say, very learned and renowned for the books he has published, and who is willing to take up the post.

When all this had been discussed, it was agreed that the said Rotan be retained as professor of theology, so that he can remain a member of the Company of Ministers, but that he be lent to the Italian Church for one year, at the end of which time they must provide themselves with another minister. The council would pay half his salary and the Italian Church the other half. Similarly, it was agreed that the said Casaubon be retained. It was also agreed to ask the Company whether they would agree to retrench by doing away with the sermons at

[1] A year earlier the City Council, in desperate financial straits and unable to raise the revenue to pay the professors, had dismissed them all and closed the Academy down, despite the protests and the fund-raising efforts of the Company of Pastors. Bèze was now doing everything in his power to re-establish the teaching.

[2] Jean-Baptiste Rotan, whose family came from the Paduan patriciate, had been brought up in Geneva as a member of the rich and flourishing Italian 'stranger' church; he had attended the Academy and between 1571 and 1574 pursued his studies further in Heidelberg under the celebrated Reformed professors Tremellius, Boquin and Zanchius.

Saint-Germain, since M. Rotan would no longer be able to furnish these, which would mean that hardly anyone would attend.

Source: Archives d'Etat Genève, Régistres du Conseil, 4 Sept. 1587: Charles Borgeaud, Histoire de l'Université de Genève (Geneva, 1900), i. 237-8.

65 The search for professors

(i) The Geneva Company,which has offered the chair of Hebrew to a young student whose studies were sponsored by the Church in Metz, seeks its agreement to postpone indefinitely his return

[*Théodore de Bèze and Jean Pinault, in the name of the Company, to the Church at Metz, Geneva, 18 July 1595*]

Sirs and most honoured brethren, although it is often the case that those who come begging for favours are not welcome, we have no fear that you will treat our request in this way. For we have weighed up in our consciences what we ourselves would do faced with a like request, and we know that in a similar case we would not be able to refuse you. Such is the friendship we believe you feel towards us, and such is the measure we have taken of you, knowing you to be engaged upon the advancement of God's Kingdom, using the means he has put at your disposal, that we are certain that you will do all you can, not only in your own Church but also in ours here, to be of service to all. We are also aware of the respect which all of you in general, and one of you in particular, have for this Church, a respect which we are sure you will not fail to show in this matter, where, as you will see, we seek only the greater good of the Church as a whole.

A year and a half ago, God took to himself our honoured brother M. Chevalier who was professor of Hebrew in the School. Since then we have tried without success to furnish ourselves with someone in his place. We have had some offers from Germany but things have not worked out. We have also had offers from the Swiss to send someone, but various considerations held us back, and we still are not provided.

In addition to the few lessons that our brother M. Casaubon has been giving on the Rabbis, we have asked M. D'Ivoy, who is, as we can see, one of our best students in Hebrew studies, to give in the School a course in Hebrew grammar so that we can establish a Hebrew text of the Psalms in accordance with the times. So, things have gone on more or less in this way, so that, with God's grace we have not been entirely deprived of Hebrew teaching. The talent which God has given M. D'Ivoy is lodged in a heart so humble and sincere that this has made him the better received, not only by those of his auditors whom he likes to call his 'fellow-learners' but also by us. We have come to hope that our Lord, who has given him the desire to excel, will bless him and make him, in due time, fully capable of carrying this responsibility. This arrangement, employing someone who is not too distant from our simple plain way of doing things, who knows us and whom we know, is more appropriate for us than tying ourselves up with someone else whom we know less well and who might not fit in so well with our customs. So the Company has gone so far as to decide to call him to this charge, and to establish him as a professor in our School, hoping that the City authorities will do likewise, provided, of course that it please God, through you, most honoured sirs and brethren, to give him to us. For he belongs to you and to your Church since you have for so long paid for his studies, in the hope that you have entertained that you would be able to make use of this. The Company agreed to make this request to you, as in all good will we now make it, requesting you to seek, and hoping that you will secure its acceptance at the hands of your Church.

In this matter, we had to start with M. D'Ivoy, upon whom the whole scheme is based, and without whose willing co-operation nothing could be done. It was here that we found the first difficulties, for he said that he did not feel he had it in him to fulfil the kind of duties we were expecting of him, that he in no way felt that he was superior to his fellow pupils, and that he would be much happier if he could just go on sitting beside them, a learner like themselves; added to which, as for himself, he felt entirely devoted to your Church, to which he felt himself obliged for so many benefits and so much support. He did not for a moment want this affair to be talked about, in case it occurred to someone to suspect him of being ungrateful towards you, or less attached to you than he ought to be, because that would be simply untrue, and very far from how he really felt.

When he had been reassured that this was an entirely dutiful response, and that we certainly did not want to turn him away from his duty, and that it was our intention to address ourselves to you only if God put it into your hearts to show such amity to this Church as to accede to our request, he was asked if he would then accept the call, which could be shown to be truly from God, confirmed by the testimony of this Church and of yours, and remain with us, he replied that he did not think this was very likely to happen because of his inadequacy for the post, but that if indeed God wanted him to do this, he knew that he would let himself be guided, and that he would take your advice about whether to accept, and that he would put himself in the frame of mind to accept whatever seemed to be right. That is what happened at this end, where as far as we can see, in the end there was no difficulty, nor with his father and mother either; we hope that they will find acceptable and good what has been proposed, and that they will be pleased that their son has been sought after for such a post, in which, living honoured and honourable, he has the means of being a credit to them and to their friends.

There remain, good sirs and honoured brethren, the difficulties which you on your side may feel. You have supported him, he belongs to you. You have maintained him with high hopes that if one day your Church had a yoke for him to bear he would carry it. Several of our brethren your pastors are broken-down and aged, and you are afraid that the Church would be incensed if you let this young man go. All this is readily apparent and we do not deny that it is unlikely that we will have an opportunity to make it up to you. The support you have given him will still have served for the glory of God and for the advancement of his Church, in the sense that if God in his Providence calls him here where he can start to serve immediately and more amply, we do not think that the intention of your Church will have been in any way betrayed. We are sure that your Church would be willing to dip into its funds and to supply this Church with an equivalent sum in an hour of need. And just think how much a man from your country and from your Church, whom we have set up here in a position like this, will be able in future years, to take special care of any young students you may want to send here to learn. And this Church would be under such an obligation to you, that there would be many other ways in which this could be useful to you, in an infinite number of different situations. We do not doubt for a moment that as a result of your approval of this suggestion your Church will accept it, and will rejoice that it has had the means and the opportunity to help this Church in its need.

We observe that given the numbers of pastors you have and the number of sermons you are able to provide, you are not, for the moment, too pressed. God, with the good courage he has given to our weaker brethren, will, if he wishes, redouble their strength, if they are ready to take on more in order to help their neighbours, while the more vigorous of our brethren will not spare themselves. One way and another, therefore, your Church remains very well supplied. Remember that if at any time in the future your Church needs help, and cannot get it elsewhere, this is what we have promised: we will help you by furnishing you with a man in recompense, if it is in our power to do so, so that your Church will not remain destitute. And if in the past you have had proof of our promptitude and of our good-will towards your Church, which we think of as our sister Church, offspring of the same father, how much may you hope for these in the future, when we are especially obliged to you, and when we have made you this promise.

We hope that by the grace of God the fruit which will result from your gesture to this Church, and consequently to others, will bring such satisfaction to you and to us, given that we have had regard in the matter for nothing except the glory of God and the edification of his Church, that God will show us that he has guided us throughout, and will give us every opportunity to bless and glorify him.

Good sirs and most honoured brethren, we await your favourable response, praying God that he will preserve your Church in all prosperity, and increase in it his grace and benediction, that he will fortify your pastors in their duties, and that you in your turn will benefit from this, to his great glory and to the edification of all.

Source: Registre de la Compagnie des Pasteurs [G2], vii. 219-22.

(ii) The Magistrates of Montpellier appeal to Geneva for pastors and professors

Sirs, the necessity in which we find ourselves in this town has driven us to have recourse to you, to whom all the churches of France are so much obliged, and who have worked so hard for the glory of God. Sirs, this Church [of Montpellier], although it is still large and impor-tant, is nevertheless badly supplied with pastors, having nowadays only two where it used to have four. On top of that there is here a large number of those who hold the contrary religion and who will stop at nothing to attract here preachers trained and fashioned in the Jesuits' way, to reduce the size of our flock, as far as they can. What is more, our condition in this province is so miserable that we have no means of increasing its size with incomers, however diligent we have been in trying to do so up to now. This is why we address ourselves to you today, entreating you with all the affection that we can, to send us Monsieur Goulart, so that our Church may be edified as much by his learning as by his pious life.

We make you the same prayer to send to our town the sieur de Casaubon, whom we would like to have here, to instruct our young people, whom we see crouching in the most hideous barbarity, and to drain custom away from the schools of the Jesuits which are to be found in our province and which nowadays enjoy such a vogue that even some of those of our religion send their children to them. We have already provided for the remuneration of M. Casaubon in the belief that you will not deny us this benefit, in according which to us, you would deepen the obligation we feel towards you.

We pray to God, sirs, that he will keep you in his holy care.

From Montpellier, 24 September 1595.

Your most humble and obedient servants, the Consuls, Council and Consistory of the town of Montpellier ... .

To *Messieurs* the ministers and professors of Geneva.

Source: Registre de la Compagnie des Pasteurs [G2], vii. 231.

(d) Politics in adversity. Calvinist solidarity in diplomacy and war

66 Three glimpses of the diplomatic calculations made in the circle of princes of the Rhineland Palatinate

(i) Draft of a Palatinate diplomatic instruction, October 1576

Our good Lord God, in order to help his Church, afflicted and oppressed by the tyranny of our day, has roused our lord the Prince-Elector Palatine to declare himself father and true sustainer of the Church, and our lord his son the duke John Casimir, twice to serve as another Joshua to those of the Reformed faith in France: their Excellencies, impelled by zeal and affection for the increase of God's glory and for the welfare, quiet and tranquillity of the Christian Commonwealth, hereby despatch N.N. to his lordship the prince of Orange and to the States of Holland and Zeeland.

Firstly, to rejoice with them that God has allowed them at this time to see and to taste the fruit of the constancy and labour which they have shown and endured during these civil troubles ... .

Secondly, so that N.N. may reliably learn in what precise state matters stand at present with the said lord Prince and States: this request is prompted not by curiosity but by paternal solicitude and by the desire to continue to help them faithfully, with all the good advice and counsel in their Excellencies' power.

If the situation is such that there is imminent prospect of a good peace N.N. shall exhort them not to refuse it, but rather to embrace it, showing in their actions the duty of true Christians, which is to seek peace.

... In the event that they shall enter into the negotiation of a peace, after settling that which regards the glory of God, and the public good and peace, N.N. shall remind them with what affection, piety and compassion our lord the Prince-Elector has aided them, without regard to his own disadvantage ... and that therefore reason, honesty and true gratitude ... should move them to repay their Excellencies faithfully, even before all other payments.

And because the sum involved is not small and its repayment may perhaps be too heavy a charge for Holland and Zeeland, who are known to be very short of resources as a result of the length of the war they have endured, ... N.N. shall make due and diligent demands and requests that the States of the Low Countries shall accept liability for the said sum and agree to pay it.

Furthermore, in the event that he sees that there is no means to do this promptly through lack of ready cash, N.N. shall request that the payment be made in salt or similar goods that can readily be sold for cash; or at least that the States shall promise with good and sufficient guarantees to pay at a set time, and as early as possible; and meanwhile for greater surety that they should assign to their Excellencies some ecclesiastical or seigneurial lands, from which little by little their Excellencies may reimburse themselves.

From the start N.N. shall observe carefully what form the public affairs of the Low Countries are likely to take in the case of peace. Since it seems likely that the people of the Low Countries will never again submit themselves to the absolute power of the King of Spain ... but that they will seek freedoms similar to those of the Swiss or the imperial cities in Germany, N.N. on his own initiative, using the prudence God has given him, may advise them on the best and surest course, which will contribute most to God's glory, which will offer best hope for the peace of the Christian Commonwealth, and which will ensure that the good right and title their Excellencies possess to certain places in that country shall be recognised and respected according to their merits.

On the other hand, in the event that N.N. shall learn that a good peace and public repose are not to be hoped for, but that war will continue for some time ... he shall point out to them that if they now fail in courage and in their will to persevere to the end, all that they have achieved and endured before will be in vain, and those who have been faithful in their support will lose heart ... . He shall exhort them to continue with manly courage ... to make free use of their remaining resources, so that they may purchase the true cap of liberty and escape from the intolerable servitude of conscience, internal and external, to which the Spanish tyrants seek shamefully to reduce them.

If N.N. finds them determined to continue the war ... and wishful that my lord the duke John Casimir should show towards them the faithfulness and assistance he has recently shown towards those of the Reformed faith in France, N.N. shall assure them on his Excellency's behalf of the promptness and good-will he will show towards them if he is required and duly invited to assist them. In consequence of which N.N. shall then enter into discussion with the said lord Prince and the States, to establish upon what footing and foundation, with what forces and where, they would like this help to come. Afterwards the said N.N. shall return and report to us with all speed, bringing with him some person of quality with whom one may for their part decide and conclude the said negotiations.

Finally N.N. shall point out to them in what ways it will be necessary, in the event of a continuation of the war, to establish understandings, correspondences and even leagues and confederations with certain princes, princesses, republics and cities, and that to this end embassies may be sent to England (where N.N. may expect to be sent and with whom he should maintain close contact), and similarly to Guelders, France, Poland, Denmark, Danzig and Constantinople.

(ii) Memorandum: Precautions to be taken by John Casimir in seeking financial aid for his army from the Queen of England, July 1577

Our first task is to persuade my lord the duke to accept the commitment by the Queen of England to provide at the next Frankfurt fair the recruiting costs of his army, in order to oblige Her Majesty actually to provide the sum she has promised. Those whom the ambassador sends back should bear the said acceptance, being fully assured by past experience that Her Majesty is less likely to fail in her promise to a prince of the Empire than to another, less when she is obliged to it than otherwise, and less when she shall hear that the funds she has promised have already been advanced by the said lord duke.

Nevertheless, to avoid any risk to the said duke, if he wishes he need not lay out the said funds in advance, but instead may negotiate with his colonels at Frankfurt on the basis of the jewelled rings he possesses, or by deducting that which relates to the promises of help contracted by the Queen of England. In this way he would have more money in hand, and will be able the better to persuade the colonels to advance the recruiting costs of their troops on the security of the said rings, helping them to meet their expenses by guaranteeing them interest on their advances either at the imperial rate or at the rate current in France at the end of the war.

The said lord duke should request Her Majesty ... to give her promise, before Christmas if possible, to hasten the despatch of the army. To extract further sums from Her Majesty secret negotiations should begin here with her ambassadors about what promises she may have of the use of the duke's army in her service, even for the recovery of Calais. The ambassador should be empowered to enter into a secret treaty with Her Majesty to this end, and by this means to persuade her to help with a larger sum. The ambassador should even be willing underhand and by connivance to allow some lords and gentlemen among her subjects to set out with a substantial detachment of infantry to make this easier to achieve ... .

(iii) Henry of Navarre to John Casimir, July 1585

My lord and cousin! I will say nothing of the present state of France because you know it. I will not represent to you the effects of the leagues and conspiracies made against the person of the King and his State; you will have heard of them from his own letters and from his ministers. Nor will I tell you of our own peacefulness, obedience and fidelity which now threatens to turn to our own ruin, since not only is the country handed over to the conspirators, but they meet also with honours and reward. All such conspiracies threaten ruin to the royal house of France, with which, as you will understand, my interest lies.

I have trusted you always as one of my best and principal friends, one of those most zealous for God's cause, which we all uphold. The time has come to put our shoulder to the wheel. The conspiracy is general, and of the greatest importance to Christendom, since our ruin will lead to the ruin of our neighbours. One of the first articles of their League is an oath not to lay down their arms until those who have separated from the Roman Church are entirely exterminated, as Beringham my valet-de-chambre, the bearer of this letter, will explain

[233]

to you orally and from the instructions I have given him. I beg you, my cousin, be good enough to read these, and to believe them as you would believe me. I beg you to show me in this emergency the benefit of that total friendship I expect from you, for in so just a cause, and one so important for all Christian princes, one should not be held back by the hesitations and difficulties which men usually bring forward. I have instructed the sieur de Ségur who has gone to England, to visit you as soon as he can. Meanwhile I have sent the said bearer to inform you of our situation and of our determination. I wait to hear from you by him, begging you, my cousin, very affectionately to regard as assured the continuation of my unchanging friendship ...

Henry.

Source: Von Bezold, *Briefe des Pfalzgrafen Johann Casimir* [Gy5], i. 209-12, 274-5, ii. 276-7.

67 England, Casimir and the Netherlands

Walsingham expresses his dislike of the unholy alliance between John Casimir and the Ghent radicals, in which he sees the hand of the zealot Beutterich

Francis Walsingham in Richmond to William Davison in Antwerp, 12 November 1578:

Sir,... touching the letters you thought meet to be sent unto Casimir and the Gantois, I forbore to move Her Majesty therein, for that I fear she would have caused them to be written in so hard and sharp terms as would rather breed contempt than redress.

I hope the good counsel both he and they shall receive from you in Her Majesty's name will take good effect, which you may deliver either in sharp or sweet terms as to you shall seem meet.

Beutterich would be roundly dealt withal, who will be the ruin of that gentleman his master, that otherwise might prove a good instrument in God's Church. By the said Beutterich's lewd advice there is a practice entertained with Châtillon in Languedoc to divide the churches in that province from the rest of the churches in France and to draw them to yield themselves under Duke Casimir's protection, persuading them from depending on the King of Navarre, as a man light and unconstant. This good fellow with these villainous practices will prove a very firebrand of contention ... .

If you find not Duke Casimir conformable to do that which may be for the common good, and so consequently to Her Majesty's satisfaction, you shall not need then to press the States to pay unto him the 60,000 guilders. For I assure you, seeing the course he taketh, Her Majesty is sorry that she ever brought him into the country.

To remove the opinion that Her Majesty should be a faulter of his disordered proceedings, you may give copies out of such speeches as you deliver unto him and to the Gantois in Her Majesty's name, which you may cause to be translated into Flemish, that they may be dispersed among the vulgar people, in which you shall do well to lay the fault on Beutterich and excuse the Duke; and touching the Gantois, to charge the heads and excuse the people.

Source: J.M.B.C. Kervyn de Lettenhove, *Relations politiques des Pays Bas et de l'Angleterre sous le règne de Philippe II* (Brussels, 1888-1900), xi. 128-9.

68 Preserving the Protestant inheritance: the last Testament of the Duke of Bouillon

Testament of Guillaume Robert de la Marck, Duc de Bouillon, Prince Souverain de Sedan, Geneva, 29 October 1587[1]

First, we ... recommend our soul to God the Creator, praying him to pardon the faults and offences we have committed against His Majesty and to take and accept in recompense for these the merit of the death and passion of his son Jesus Christ, our saviour, and that when it pleases him to separate our soul from its body that he will set it and commune with it in his holy Paradise, there to remain perpetually glorious with the rest of his elect.

And disposing of our goods, we bequeath in the first place to the hospital of this town of Geneva 100 écus; to the College of the said

[1] The premature and unexpected death of the young Guillaume Robert de la Marck was a great blow to those of his party. By making this will Bouillon intended to frustrate the hopes of his Catholic heir-presumptive the Count of Maulévrier and to preserve the Protestant character of his independent Principality of Sedan, strategically placed in relation to France, the Low Countries, and the western provinces of the Empire, and the seat of a Reformed Academy. His intentions succeeded; a marriage was arranged between Charlotte and the militant Calvinist nobleman Henri de la Tour d'Auvergne, who was allowed, after some dispute, to assume on her death in 1594 the title Duc de Bouillon in his own right. He then married a daughter of William of Orange. As Bouillon he became celebrated, or notorious, as an active proponent of diplomatic and military initiatives in defence of the godly cause.

place 200 écus, to the fund for the poor French people in the city 200 écus, and to the fund for the Italians 100 écus.

Item, to the College at Sedan 600 écus; to the poor of Sedan 500 écus ... [then follow bequests of money and of the Duke's horses to individual retainers and servants]

We settle the remainder of our property not disposed of above ... and especially our lands and sovereign territory of Sedan, Jametz and Raucourt, upon our dearly beloved sister Charlotte de la Marck, our sole and universal heiress, to whom by right of nature our said property should belong, being desirous that after our death, if we die without legitimate children, our sister shall take possession of all our said properties and enjoy full ownership of them.

And we make this bequest charged with the condition that our said sister and her successors and all those who administer the said sovereignties for her shall not innovate or alter anything in the settlement of the Reformed religion, and that her successors also shall see to it that the said religion is well and truly maintained and exercised in the said places of Sedan, Jametz and Raucourt and in all their dependencies just as it has been maintained there since the time of our late and honoured lord and father, and as it is still practised there under our authority; it is our will that when our sister's hand is sought in marriage that she marries in accordance with the wishes, advice and consent of the King of Navarre and of their Lordships the Princes of Condé and the Duke of Montpensier, to whom she has the honour to be related; and we entreat them most humbly to give her a husband worthy of her birth and one who practises the Reformed religion ... .

On account of the friendship he has always shown us we beg and require Monsieur de la Noüe to do us the service of moving to Sedan and of living there until such time as our sister is married or of competent age, in order to oversee and direct the safe preservation of our place at Jametz and all the other dependencies of our sovereign territories, which we wish to remain under the protection of and in the service of the Crown of France. It is our will that all our governors, captains and officers ... shall continue in their posts, obeying and respecting the said Sieur de la Noüe, under the authority of my sister, as they have done and do for ourselves in person.

Source: Eugènie Droz, 'Jean Hellin, Pasteur à Sedan', *Chemins de l'Hérésie. Textes et Documents* (Geneva, 1976), iv. 208-14.

69 Fund-raising for Geneva, 1594. Report to the Geneva Council of its envoy in Holland, 1594

Monday 15 April 1594: Noble Jacques Anjorrant, having returned from the Low Countries, has made his report as follows:

My charge and commission was principally to obtain from Messieurs the States of the United Provinces a grant of money for this State, and letters of approval for its doctors.

In pursuit of the first aim I sought letters of authorisation which would prove effective, the sovereign State of the United Provinces consisting of the States-General (which is an assembly of deputies from all the United Provinces) not in permanent session, but meeting in response to the pressure of the business it receives, and of the States of each of the separate provinces, that is to say deputies of the nobility and of the towns, which also are not convened except when there are many matters to resolve ... . It was necessary for me to address myself to these colleges, for on my arrival the States-General and the States of Holland had not yet assembled in The Hague, which is where they meet. I also made a rapid visit to Zeeland, presenting myself to the Councillor-Deputies, so that the magistrates of the towns would be informed of my main demand. I established this by my presence, or, as far as the other provinces were concerned, by letter.

A little time after my return to The Hague, the States of the province of Holland and West Friesland having assembled, I read my proposition, having handed over my letters of authorisation. Following my instructions I made them understand as well as I could, just how important was the cause, using the most appropriate and suitable arguments to lead them and to coax them all towards a good resolution. In the event the resolution could not be taken because of the foot-dragging of a mere three out of the eighteen towns which make up their States. For it is a maxim of state with them that votes concerning the raising of money or the allocation of privileges must be unanimous and with no abstentions. In the end, the three towns concerned did acquiesce in the decision of the majority to allocate a sum of 24,000 florins.

However, because of the difficulties in which their State finds itself, and the infinite number of extraordinary expenses which arise from these, and because of the costs incurred during the siege of Geertruidenberg, our friends, to whom it fell to propose the grant, judged that it would be impossible to come to a final resolution unless the States could see the prospect of some sort of a profitable return on the money they were laying out, in addition to that part of it set aside for the support of their students. They advised that the States would want documents to be drawn up in which the assets of this republic would be a surety to the States on their outlay. Since on the terms of my letters of accreditation I had no power to give any such undertaking, and since I judged that it was not open to me in ancient law or right to do so without prior authorisation, and as my accreditation was in the first place to the States-General, I presented myself in their assembly and made the representations I had been instructed to make on your behalf. However, since not all the members of the assembly were present, the best they could do was to pass a resolution authorising me to approach the provinces individually, and to furnish me with letters of recommendation.

Given the unity of purpose which exists between the States and His Excellency [Count Maurice] of Nassau it seemed to me advisable, for the better advancement of our scheme, to have letters from him. Accordingly I went to see his Excellency to obtain letters like those I had already presented to the States-General to give to the States of each of the provinces.

Having obtained these I made my way promptly to Friesland where I found the Governor, Monsieur the Count William [William-Louis of Nassau] to be quite well-disposed towards this State, together with other leading persons, whom I found to be very zealous, staunch and whole-hearted. After I had been heard on two separate occasions in Leeuwarden, the capital city, it was agreed to offer the sum of 5,000 florins in the form of a loan to support this State and to be paid within a few months; and during my time in the said place I negotiated by letter with Emden, from which 900 francs should have been received.

That being done, I returned via Utrecht, in which place I made my proposal before the Sstates, and returned to The Hague to receive that part of the money promised by Holland, but because the letters of giving me authorisation had not arrived, I could at first touch only half of it, that is to say 1,200 livres. Having put this sum into exchange in Amsterdam I went directly to Utrecht, where I received the sum of 1,000 livres in the form of a gift.

A few days before the September fair, the letters of authorisation having at last arrived, I obtained the other part of the Holland loan, also amounting to 1,200 livres, having exchanged what facilitating documents I was empowered to exchange. Promptly I despatched as much as I could find of this money in the form of bills of exchange by express courier to Cologne.

Because it was needful for me to stay in Amsterdam at that juncture, when the summons came from Friesland to go there to pick up the sum promised, I sent Abraham Quait in my stead, with secure credentials, to receive the said sum of 5,000 livres; once this was received we despatched it in safe hands just at the time of the exchange.

Next, having sent a copy of my proposal to the two remaining provinces, I made my way to Zeeland with my letters. Here I found public life in such a state of confusion that an infinite number of difficulties arose. In order to get over these I found it expedient to approach one by one the six towns which form the body of the States; I had to present myself four times before them, so divided was the State. In the end I obtained the sum of 4,000 florins in the form of a loan, plus 300 florins as a recompense for the delay. For all of which I left a simple receipt with no conditions about how the money was to be spent or how it was to be paid back.

My intention was to make a tour of those towns in Brabant in which there is sympathy for the cause of the United Provinces, having been told that this would be agreeable to some of them. I wanted to tell them about the condition of our State, and to point out to them how celebrated they would become and how highly they would be honoured if they would persist in maintaining their solidarity with the States. I began by travelling towards Bergen-op-Zoom, where I was well received, but since it is a garrison town and all in ruins I secured no more than 50 livres for the trouble of my journey. It was not possible to go to the other towns, the times did not permit it. After that I made a trip to Arnhem, a town in the area called Veluwe in Guelders, where, on the strength of my letters of authorisation, a resolution was passed to donate 1,000 livres for the support of the poor, which sum I received. I found more people well-disposed towards this State there than in any other place.

There remains Overijssel, the last and the poorest of the provinces. I was advised that it would be a waste of time to go there, and I was content to accept its letters of excuse, once I had been assured that the letters concerning approval of the doctors would be sent there.

Now, to come to this second point, namely the letters of approval of the doctors: considerable difficulty has been experienced in trying to get full and authentic letters on this matter, because they are afraid of prejudicing the interests of their universities, and needed to be assured that the subvention was in no way to be at the expense of these, there being no more troublesome business in the world than finding money for these and for what depends upon them. In order to obtain these letters I had to take the time to talk to all the provinces to

[239]

make sure that the resolution on this issue was not taken before the vote on the subvention, for that would have prejudiced my main negotiation. I argued that the enemy was not only plotting the total subversion of the State [of Geneva] but above all the ruin of the School, in which hope he was receiving an annual subvention from the Popes, and that it was necessary to foil his efforts by upholding the good name of the School. I got them to acquiesce in my demand.

Passing through Germany and negotiating in the Low Countries in the name of your Lordships, I realised that Geneva still has a great reputation and I noticed that the principal renown of the city comes from the fact that God has granted it such grace that for sixty-two years the purity of religion has been preached there unspotted by any sect or heresy, and from the School which has flourished through the renown and esteem afforded to the distinguished persons who have taught there and who have been and continue to be celebrated all over the world in theology, in jurisprudence, in the Hebrew language, in Greek and in humane letters, so much so that a man is taken for learned if he has merely had the good fortune to hear them teach.

And, since this would have been worth little if it had not all been regulated with good discipline, Geneva has no less renown for the good order and discipline which prevail there. They have such a high opinion of the young men who have studied in Geneva, that they are regarded as very well trained, and for that reason are early given responsibility. In consequence it is the good discipline which prompts fathers and parents to send their children here, many in the Low Countries, I know, wanting to withdraw them from France, Germany and England to put them to school here, believing the good opinion they have heard about it, opinion which I took care to confirm.

On this point, I beg you in the name of God and on behalf of Messieurs of the States of the United Provinces and especially of those of the duchy of Guelders and of Zutphen, to oblige them by guarding and keeping an eye on their young men for fear that they become debauched.

And since the reputation of a town depends also on the printing trade, an infinite number of people who love our State, beg you to ensure that order is maintained with regard to the quality of the paper and the correctness of the books, because if this is not done all kinds of damage can result. This must be put right without delay, especially nowadays when new printing centres are being established all over the place. Also because there is hardly a prince or a state which is not setting up a university, we must take care to keep our School well supplied with learned and famous men. Also it is necessary with all possible diligence to keep in touch by letter with all those who are affectionately disposed towards this State, because a falling-off in such correspondence alienates sympathy and kills off good-will, as people round here will testify; conversely, through letters we can bind them more and more closely to this State, which is what they desire, and which will make it very much easier to get gifts instead of loans.

Since those of the town of Emden (a maritime city in East Friesland, and the earliest town in Germany to receive the purity of religion) have contributed, as far as their means will allow, to the relief of your poor with the sum of 900 francs, it would be proper to write to them to thank them, to pay them some attention and to console them in their present afflictions.

Since the 1,000 livres from Arnhem, already received, were also dedicated to the relief of the poor, it would be very good to give them satisfaction. And because it would be damaging to this State if the ministers were seen to have some justified discontentment or complaint, it is expedient for the good of the State that the ministers and the Seigneurie are at one. The name of Monsieur de Bèze is revered above all, and he has very great renown, letters from him carrying more weight than the letters of anyone else, the King [of France] excepted ... .

Those who have witnessed to me the honour and affection in which they hold your State include, apart from Messieurs of the States, both collectively and individually, Monsieur the Prince of Orange, who, when bidding me farewell, charged me to assure you of his whole-hearted friendship; Madame the Princess [Louise de Coligny] who has shown me her full backing and support, and who charged her son, the young prince [Frederick Henry], to assure me, on my departure, of his friendliness and of the great feelings of obligation which she said she felt towards this State; the young prince promised in return to dedicate himself to the good and service of this State.

Having left the Provinces I came to Heidelberg, where I put in a plea with His Highness (the prince of Anhalt being present at the time) that he would continue to show good-will towards this State; he replied that he wanted nothing better than to show his affection. I paid a separate call upon Madame the Elector's wife [Louise Juliana de Nassau] and told her all about the present state of things in this republic, begging her to remonstrate with Monsieur the Prince Palatine, and to point out to him how much damage he would do to his reputation if he compelled Messieurs of Geneva to the payment of their debt, given the poverty in which they find themselves, and that the other princes had come to recognise that at the least difficulty he encountered he began to chase up the most trivial and recent of debts. I said the same thing to the Count of Wittgenstein, who made excuses for having pursued your Lordships in this manner. I spoke in the same tenor to the leading councillors, and they promised me that they would raise the matter in the council, assuring me that if they made no headway, a simple letter from your Lordships, setting out the charges on your revenue,and showing how little your tax-yield provided in the way of help, that these letters, if they were addressed to the prince's council, would serve to delay the need to repay ... .

[Anjorrant's report ends here.]

The said Sieur Anjorrant brought back letters from Monsieur the Count Maurice of Nassau, Messieurs the States-General of the United Provinces of the Low Countries, and Madame the Princess of Orange; also letters from the States of Holland and West Friesland, from Guelders, duchy of Zutphen, from Messieurs Buzanval, Oldenbarnevelt ... , etc.

Alongside these the Council inspected the letters of approval for doctors of theology, law, medicine, and of all other liberal arts and sciences, which the said Seigneur de Sully [Anjorrant] had obtained and brought back from the States of the Low Countries, that is to say, Holland, Zeeland, Friesland, Utrecht, the Duchy of Guelders, and the county of Zutphen, which declare in five separate letters patent that they consent that the doctors who have completed their studies in the said sciences here [in Geneva] shall be received and approved by their States, exactly as they if they had been received, passed and approved in the other universities of Italy, Germany, France, Flanders and other parts of Europe, and what is more that not only those who are promoted here to the degrees of master, licentiate and doctor shall be reputed and held in the same honour, place and degree as is merited by those graduating elsewhere, but also that they shall enjoy greater privileges, favours, prerogatives and pre-eminence, because the city and republic of Geneva is seen by all Christians to stand above the others, as the most celebrated in the sciences and the most constant and persevering in the faith; this final clause about preference being found in the letters patent of the States of Zeeland, of Guelders and of Zutphen ... .

Source: H. de Vries de Heekelingen, *Genève, pépinière du calvinisme hollandais* (2 vols., The Hague, 1916-24), ii.372-81 (no. 179).

INDEX

INDEX

11; assassination of, 111-2

collections, 214-5

colloquy, in France, 72, 76, 88, 211; French churches in England, 213; Geneva, 218 *see also classis,* company of pastors

communion, *see* Lord's Supper

communion tokens, 47

company of pastors (company of ministers, congregation of ministers), Geneva, 26-7, 50n, 113, 117-8, 207, 208, 214, 218; Heidelberg, 207; Holland, 176; London, 214

Condé, Henri de Bourbon, prince de, 99, 100, 112, 113, 236; suspended from Lord's Supper 115-6

Condé, Louis de Bourbon, prince de, 80, 89, 91, 92, 212

conferences, Reformed and Catholics, 89, 119; and Lutherans, 210

confession(s) of faith, personal, at Antwerp, 133; authorised version, 99; mutual recognition of,158, 209; presented, 77; profession of, before Lord's Supper, 163, 167, 168, 173, 177, 182-3; subscription to, 73, 93, 99, 158, 172, 182, 219-20

congregations, organisation of, 67-70, 133-4, 162-3, 163-4, 166-7, 170-1, 182 *see also* conventicles

consistory, at Bourges, 69, at Dordrecht, 163-6; at Geneva, 22, 27-8, 29, 38, 46-8, 50; at Paris, 68; at Tours, 70; authority of upheld, 94, 96-7, 98; elections for, 96, 13-4, 192; formation of, 76, 158, 159, 163, 170-1; function of 48, 50, 72, 74, 75, 182; in noble households, 93; grant to secure 'liberties' of, sought, 119 *see also* dancing, deacons, discipline, elders, Morély

conventicles, heretical, 63-4; secret assemblies, 86 *see also* preaching

dancing, opposed, 29, 76, 188

deacons, duties of, 74, 174-5; elections of, 159, 164, 167; in rural parishes, 170-1; responsibility to, 172 *see also* consistory, elders, poor relief

Dieu, Daniel de, minister, 189-90, 223-4

discipline, ecclesiastical, at Dordrecht, 164-6; Geneva, 22, 27-8, 29-30, 42; La Rochelle, 115-6; Strasburg, 20; Tours, 70; in rural parishes, 194; controversy about, 103-4; guidance on, 96; in matrimonial affairs, 164-5; synods on, Emden (1571), 160-1, Dordrecht (1578), 183 *see also* consistory, Lord's Supper

doctor, office of, 177

doctrine, of Church, 210-1; disputes about, 137-8; divisions concerning, 207, 210-1; Anabaptist, 134-5; Lutheran, 135, 210;

Reformed, summary of, 133; *see also* catechism, confessions of faith, perfectionism, predestination, scripture

Dordrecht, Reformation at, 161-6; *classis* of, 170-1; synods of (1574), 171-4 (1578), 182-4

dress and fashion, modesty advised, 94, 115

ecclesiastical and civil powers, relations between, at Geneva, 28, 41-5, 46-8; in Netherlands, 171-89; matters reserved to civil powers, matrimonial, 173; dress, 94; separation of, 107-11 *see also* magistrates

edicts, of religion, Fontainebleau (1547), 61; Châteaubriand (1551), 60-6; Amboise (1563), 91-3; (1585), 116-8; Nantes (1598), 120-4, 126-8

education, Protestant, academies in France, 125-6; Geneva, Academy at, 235-6; first professors, 45-6; syllabus of, 218-9; first students, 219-23; in decline, 223-4; difficulty in attracting teachers, 225-9; good name of, 240-1, 242; Heidelberg, university (*Collegium Sapientiae*) of, 223; Leiden, university of, 177, 182, 195-6; Montauban, academy at, 126; Montpellier, academy at, 126, 229-30; Neustadt, school (*Casimiranum*) at, 224; Nîmes, academy at, 126; Saumur, academy at, 126; Sedan, academy at, 236; disputations, academic, 219, 224 *see also* Jesuits, Paris, schools

elders, 50, 88; duties of, 74, 177, 178, 181; (s)election of, 47-8, 159, 178; subscribe to confession, 182 *see also* consistory

Elizabeth I, Queen of England, 207, 232-3, 234-5

Emden, 133-6, 138, 159, 169, 211, 238, 241; synod of, 158-61

excommunication, *see* suspension and excommunication

exiles, *see* Geneva, Palatinate

Farel, Guillaume, 19, 20, 21, 83

fast-days, 75, 115, 163, 164, 188, 206, 211-3

festivals, Catholic, observance of by Reformed, 121, 123

Frederick III, elector palatine, 223, 230, 231

freedom of religion, for nobility, 91, 120-1; for Reformed, 120-4, 125

Gallican Church, union with condemned, 119-20

games, permitted and forbidden, 105, 106-7

Geneva, 29, 66, 68, 70, 100, 102, 210, 217, 223-4; and conspiracy of Amboise, 78-80; and Calvin, 19-20, 21-2, 26, 27-8, 41-5; attraction of, 36-8; and Reformed churches in France, 71-2, 96, 99; hospital at, 235;

[244]